MAX **BEMIS** MICHAEL **DIALYNAS**

LUCY DREAMING™

BOOM! STUDIOS

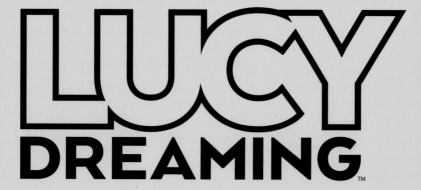

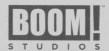

Ross Richie CEO & Founder
Joy Huffman CFO
Matt Gagnon Editor-in-Chief
Filip Sablik President, Publishing & Marketing
Stephen Christy President, Development
Lance Kreiter Vice President, Licensing & Merchandising
Phil Barbaro Vice President, Finance & Human Resources
Arune Singh Vice President, Marketing
Bryce Carlson Vice President, Editorial & Creative Strategy
Scott Newman Manager, Production Design
Kate Henning Manager, Operations
Spencer Simpson Manager, Sales
Sierra Hahn Executive Editor
Jeanine Schaefer Executive Editor
Dafna Pleban Senior Editor
Shannon Watters Senior Editor
Eric Harburn Senior Editor
Whitney Leopard Editor
Cameron Chittock Editor
Chris Rosa Editor
Matthew Levine Editor
Sophie Philips-Roberts Assistant Editor
Gavin Gronenthal Assistant Editor
Michael Moccio Assistant Editor
Amanda LaFranco Executive Assistant
Jillian Crab Design Coordinator
Michelle Ankley Design Coordinator
Kara Leopard Production Designer
Marie Krupina Production Designer
Grace Park Production Design Assistant
Chelsea Roberts Production Design Assistant
Elizabeth Loughridge Accounting Coordinator
Stephanie Hocutt Social Media Coordinator
José Meza Event Coordinator
Holly Aitchison Operations Coordinator
Megan Christopher Operations Assistant
Rodrigo Hernandez Mailroom Assistant
Morgan Perry Direct Market Representative
Cat O'Grady Marketing Assistant
Breanna Sarpy Executive Assistant

LUCY DREAMING, January 2019. Published by BOOM!
Studios, a division of Boom Entertainment, Inc. Lucy
Dreaming is ™ & © 2019 Max Bemis & Michael Dialynas.
Originally published in single magazine form as LUCY
DREAMING No. 1-5. ™ & © 2018 Max Bemis & Michael Dialynas.
All rights reserved. BOOM! Studios™ and the BOOM! Studios
logo are trademarks of Boom Entertainment, Inc., registered
in various countries and categories. All characters, events,
and institutions depicted herein are fictional. Any similarity
between any of the names, characters, persons, events,
and/or institutions in this publication to actual names,
characters, and persons, whether living or dead, events, and/
or institutions is unintended and purely coincidental. BOOM!
Studios does not read or accept unsolicited submissions of
ideas, stories, or artwork.

BOOM! Studios, 5670 Wilshire Boulevard, Suite 400,
Los Angeles, CA, 90036-5679. Printed in China. First Printing.

ISBN: 978-1-68415-301-5, eISBN: 978-1-64144-154-4

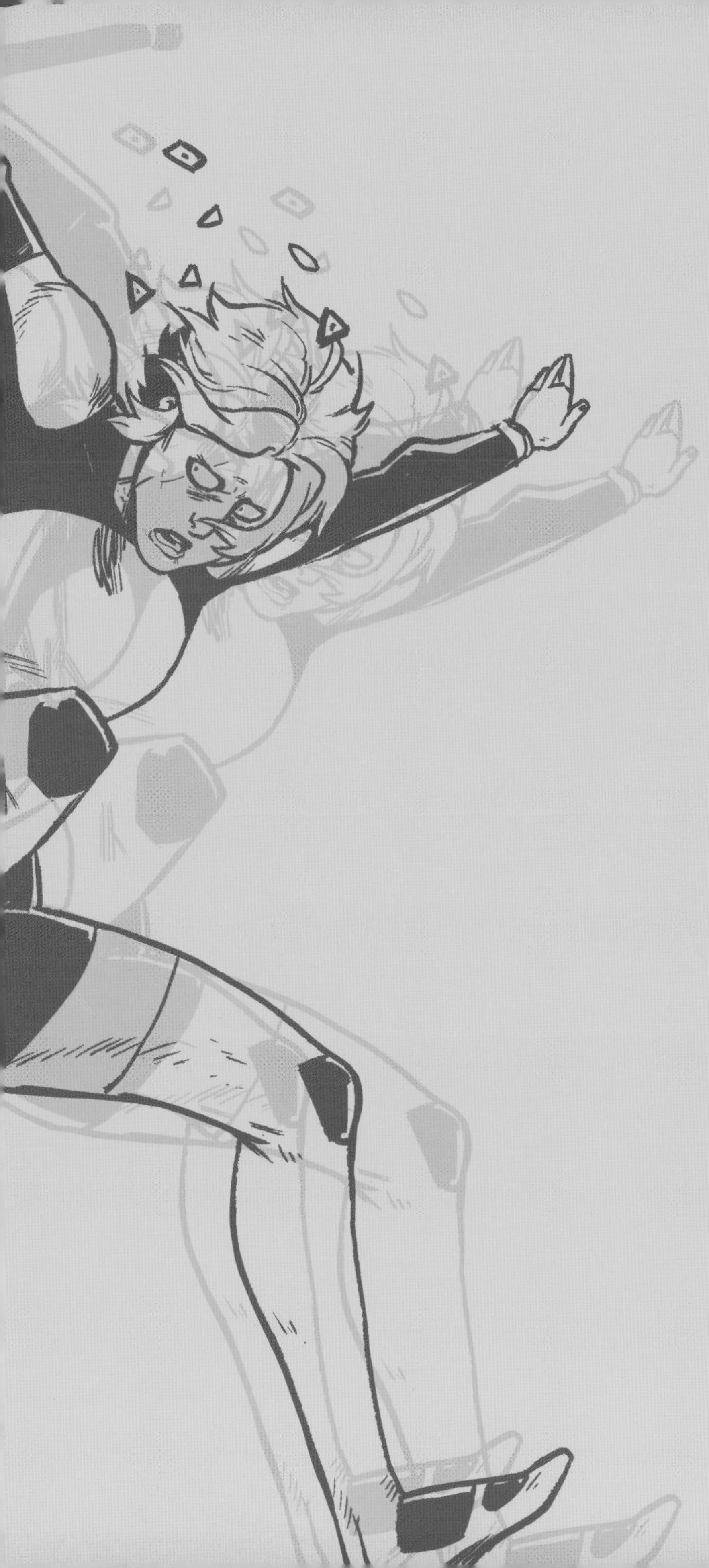

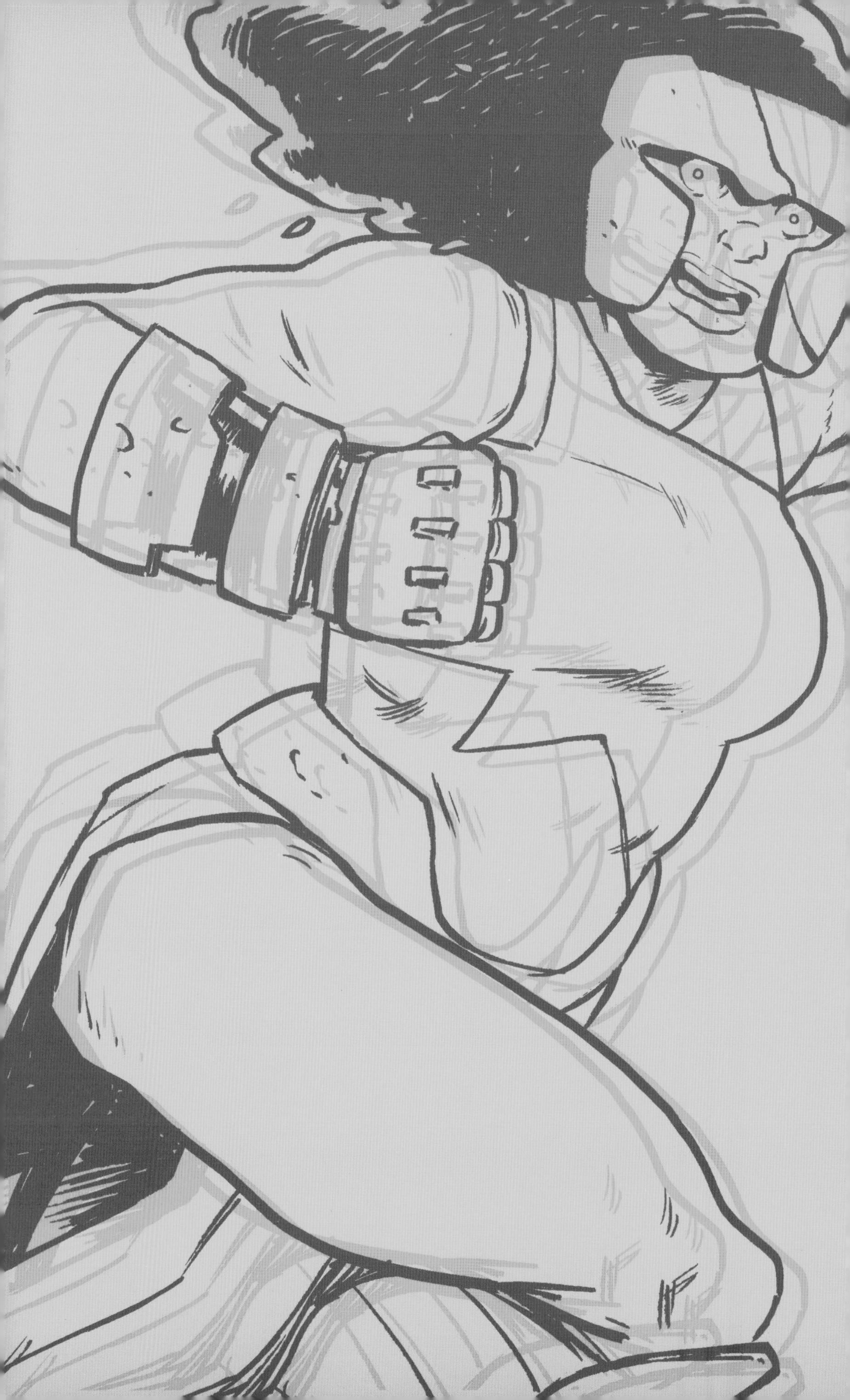

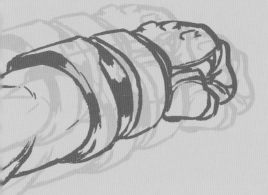

WRITTEN BY
MAX BEMIS

ILLUSTRATED BY
MICHAEL DIALYNAS

LETTERED BY
**COLIN BELL &
ED DUKESHIRE**

COVER BY
MICHAEL DIALYNAS

DESIGNER
SCOTT NEWMAN

EDITOR
ERIC HARBURN

LUCY
DREAMING ™

CREATED BY **MAX BEMIS** & **MICHAEL DIALYNAS**

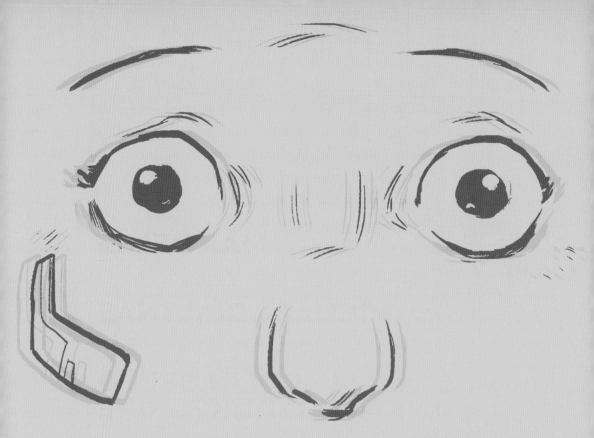

CHAPTER
ONE

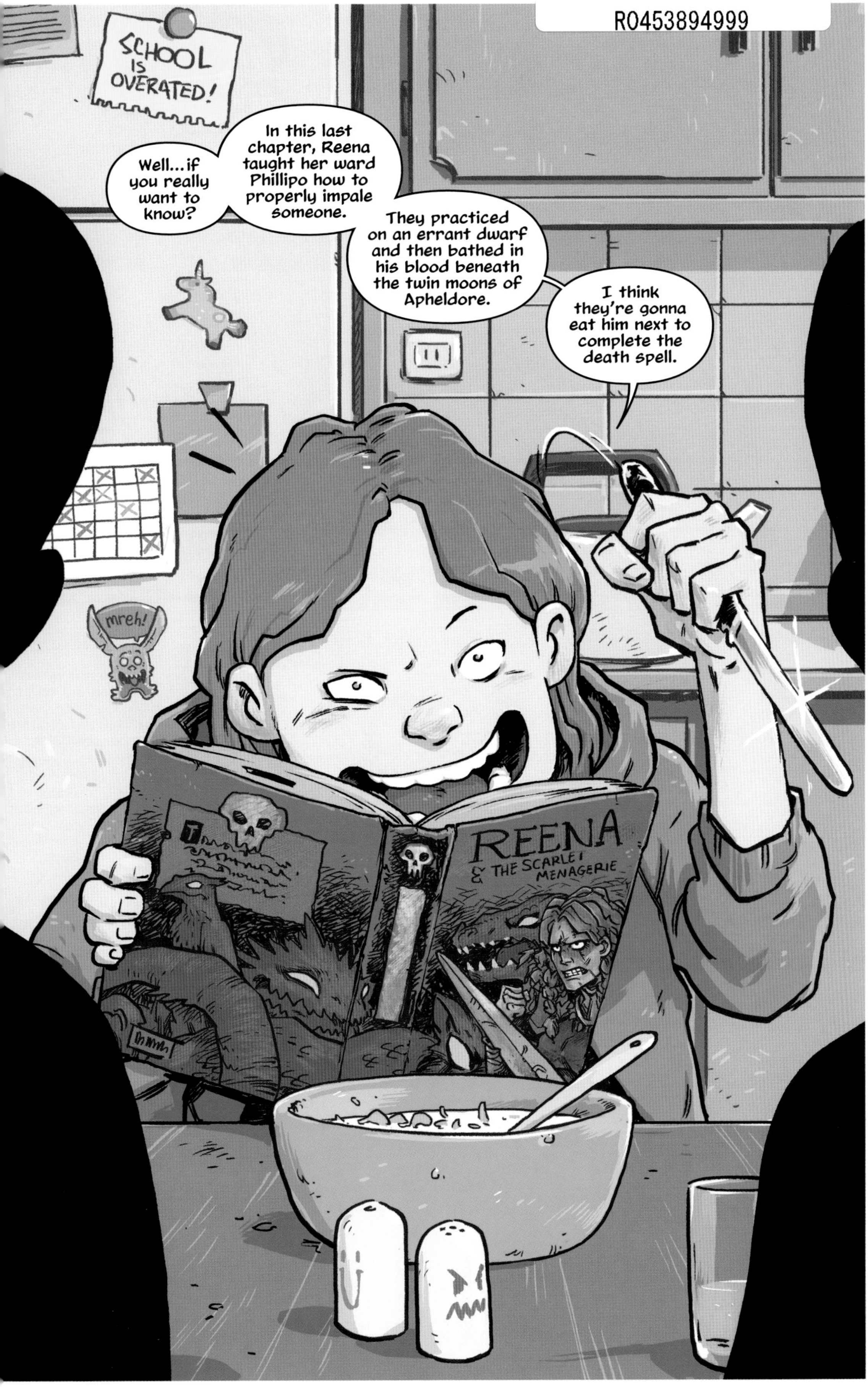
SCHOOL IS OVERATED!
Well...if you really want to know?
In this last chapter, Reena taught her ward Phillipo how to properly impale someone.
They practiced on an errant dwarf and then bathed in his blood beneath the twin moons of Apheldore.
I think they're gonna eat him next to complete the death spell.
mreh!
REENA & THE SCARLET MENAGERIE

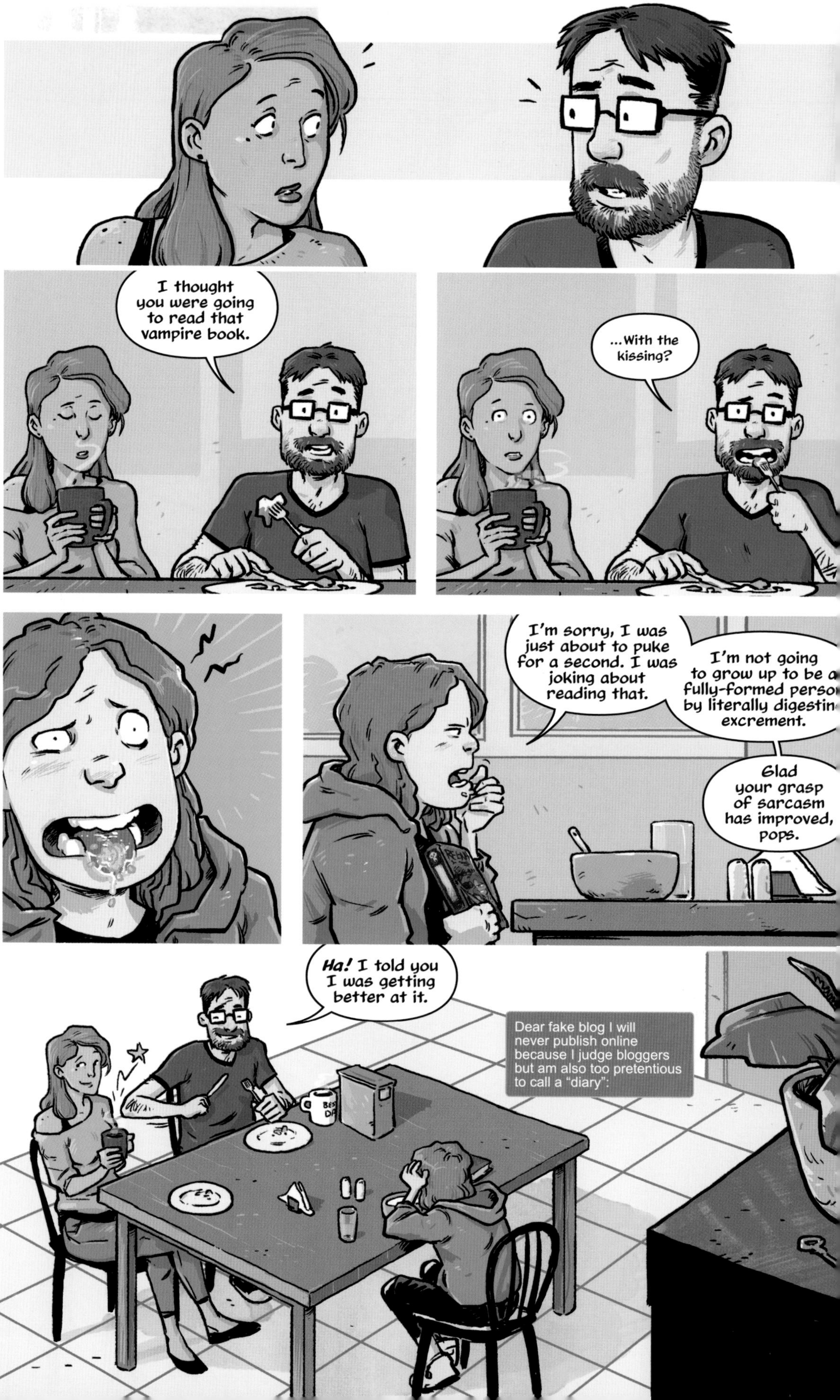
I thought you were going to read that vampire book.
...With the kissing?
I'm sorry, I was just about to puke for a second. I was joking about reading that.
I'm not going to grow up to be a fully-formed perso by literally digestin excrement.
Glad your grasp of sarcasm has improved, pops.
Ha! I told you I was getting better at it.
Dear fake blog I will never publish online because I judge bloggers but am also too pretentious to call a "diary":

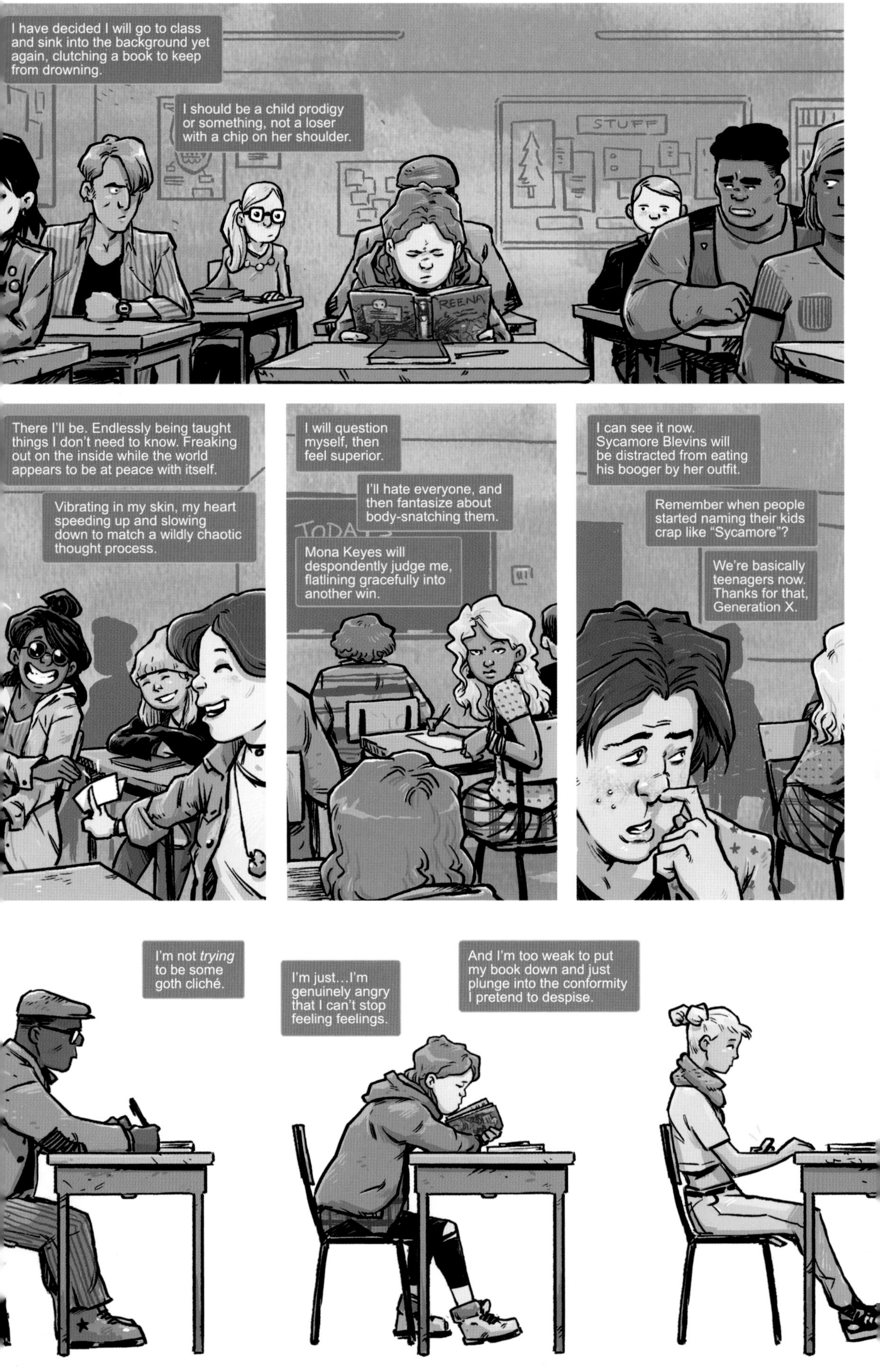
I have decided I will go to class and sink into the background yet again, clutching a book to keep from drowning.
I should be a child prodigy or something, not a loser with a chip on her shoulder.
STUFF
REENA
There I'll be. Endlessly being taught things I don't need to know. Freaking out on the inside while the world appears to be at peace with itself.
Vibrating in my skin, my heart speeding up and slowing down to match a wildly chaotic thought process.
I will question myself, then feel superior.
I'll hate everyone, and then fantasize about body-snatching them.
Mona Keyes will despondently judge me, flatlining gracefully into another win.
I can see it now. Sycamore Blevins will be distracted from eating his booger by her outfit.
Remember when people started naming their kids crap like "Sycamore"?
We're basically teenagers now. Thanks for that, Generation X.
I'm not *trying* to be some goth cliché.
I'm just…I'm genuinely angry that I can't stop feeling feelings.
And I'm too weak to put my book down and just plunge into the conformity I pretend to despise.

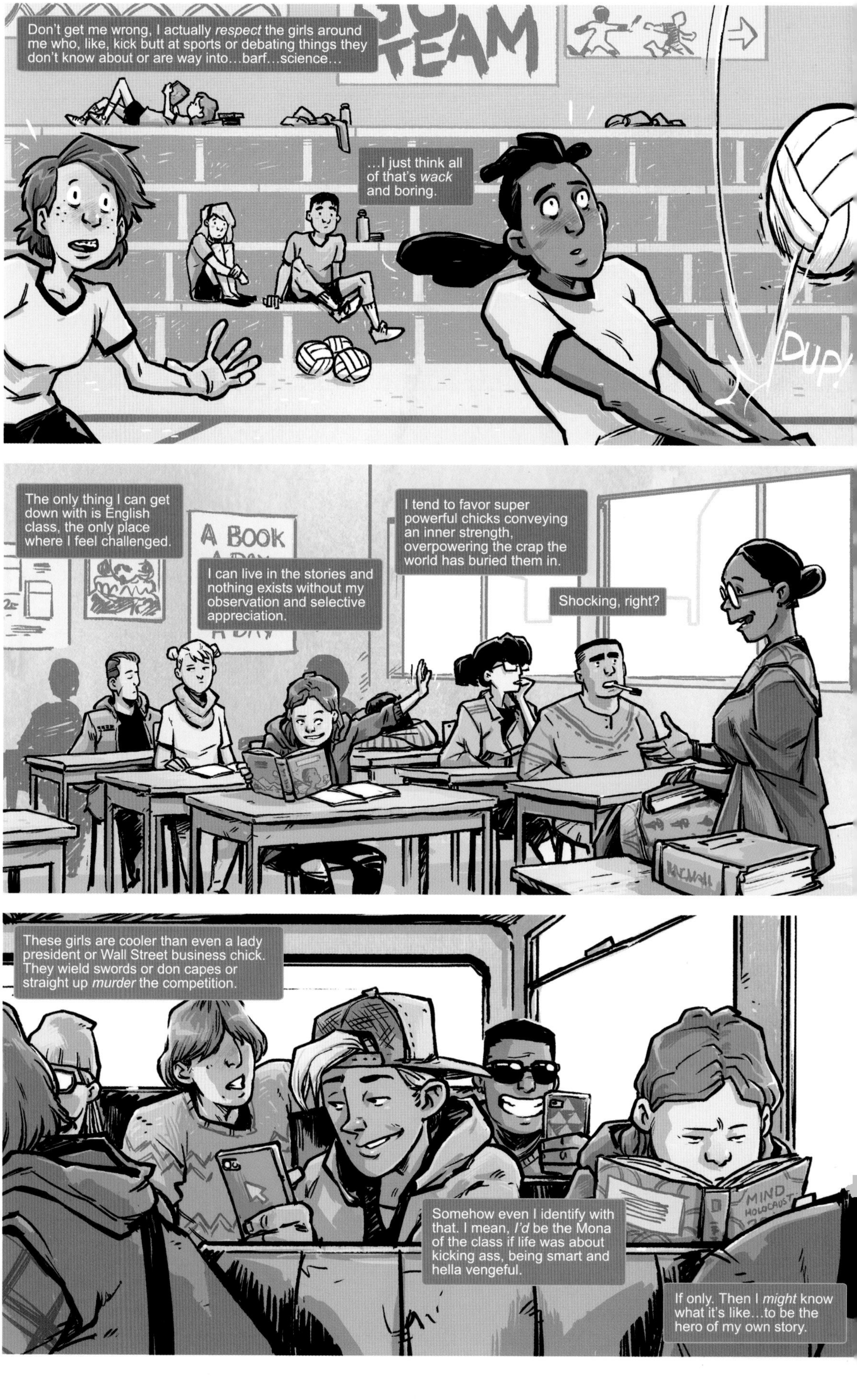

TEAM
Don't get me wrong, I actually *respect* the girls around me who, like, kick butt at sports or debating things they don't know about or are way into…barf…science…
…I just think all of that's *wack* and boring.
DUP!
The only thing I can get down with is English class, the only place where I feel challenged.
A BOOK
I can live in the stories and nothing exists without my observation and selective appreciation.
I tend to favor super powerful chicks conveying an inner strength, overpowering the crap the world has buried them in.
Shocking, right?
These girls are cooler than even a lady president or Wall Street business chick. They wield swords or don capes or straight up *murder* the competition.
Somehow even I identify with that. I mean, *I'd* be the Mona of the class if life was about kicking ass, being smart and hella vengeful.
MIND
If only. Then I *might* know what it's like…to be the hero of my own story.

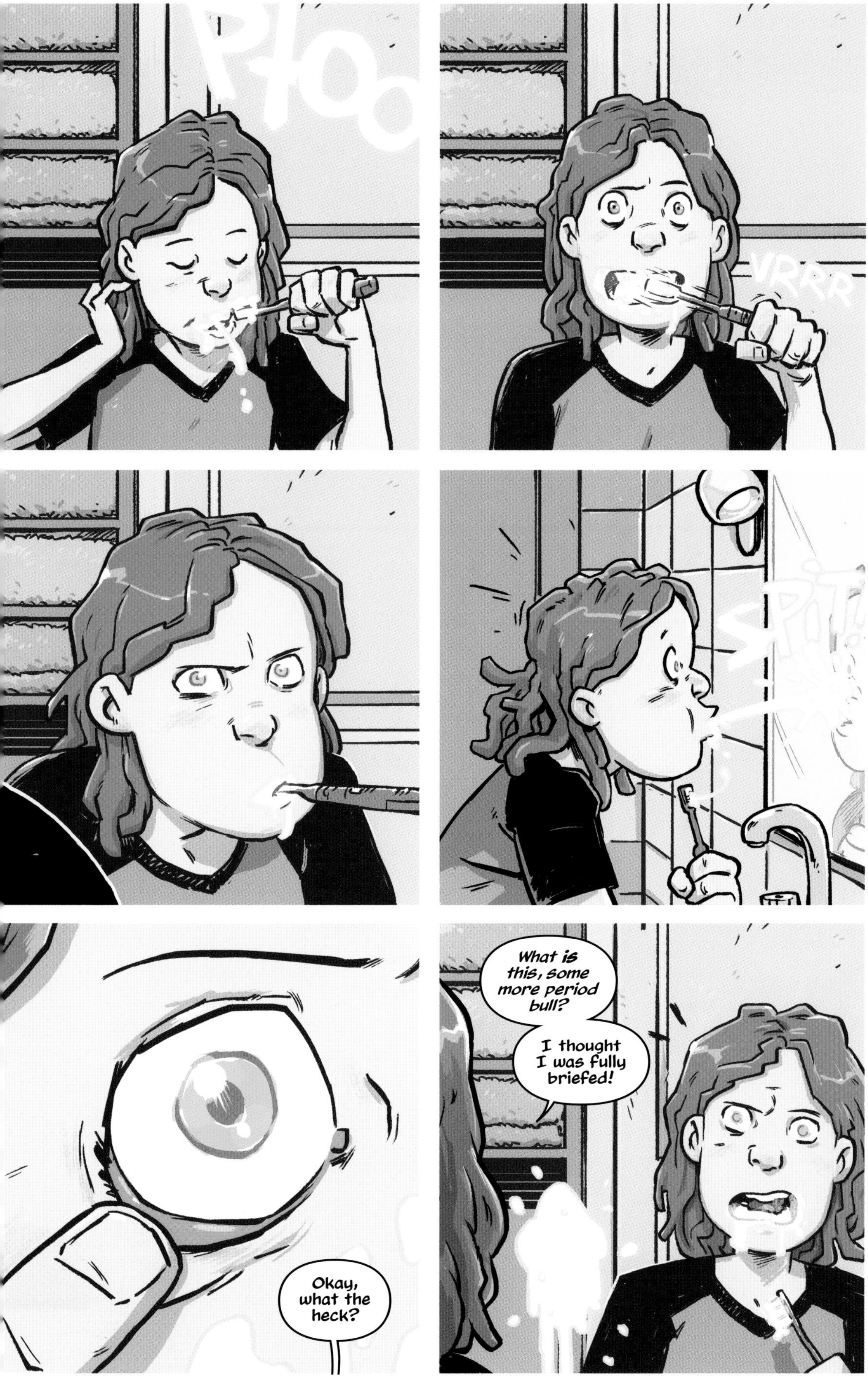
PTOO
VRRR
SPIT!
Okay, what the heck?
What is this, some more period bull?
I thought I was fully briefed!

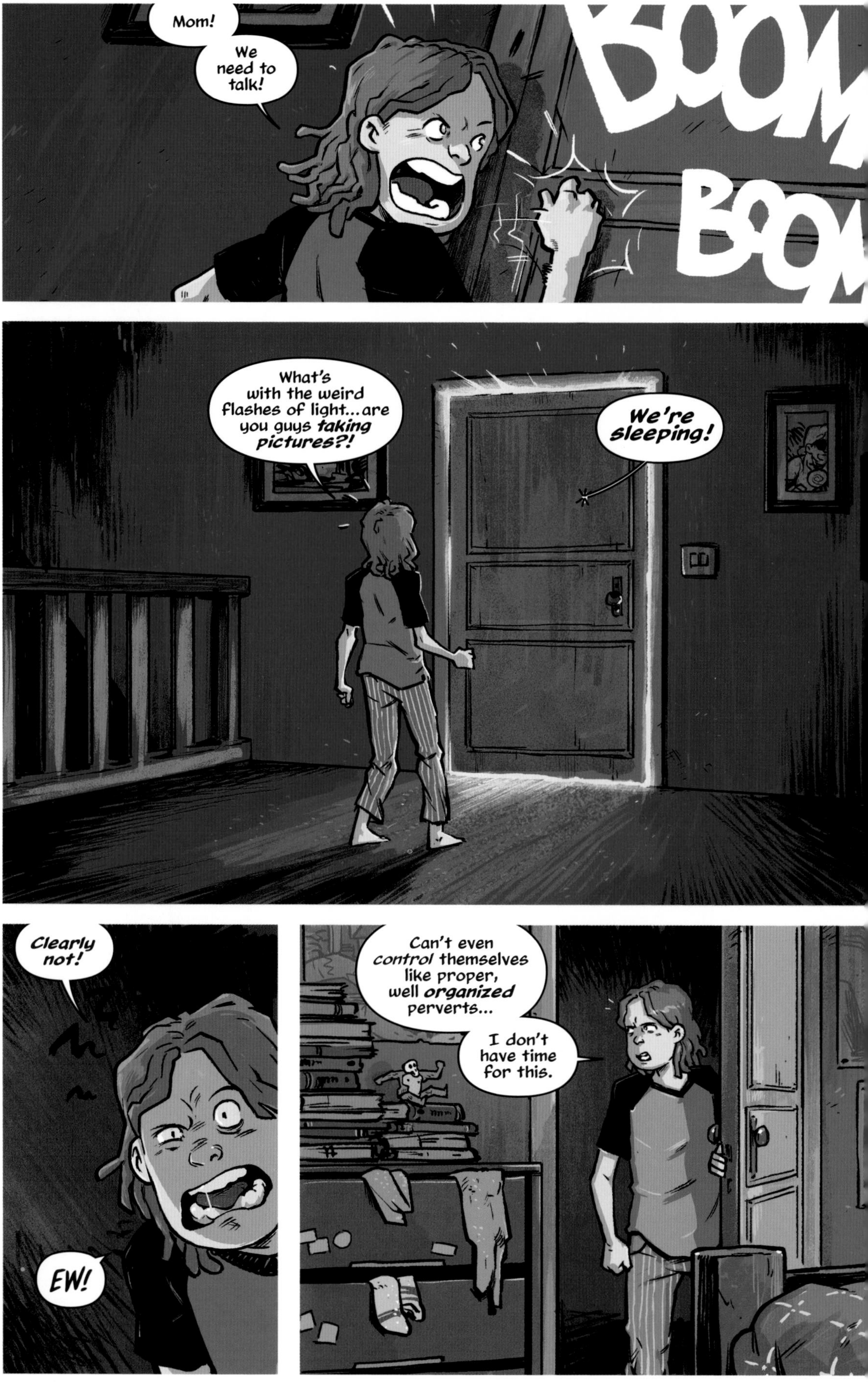

Mom!
We need to talk!
BOOM
BOOM
What's with the weird flashes of light...are you guys *taking pictures?!*
We're sleeping!
Clearly not!
EW!
Can't even *control* themselves like proper, well *organized* perverts...
I don't have time for this.

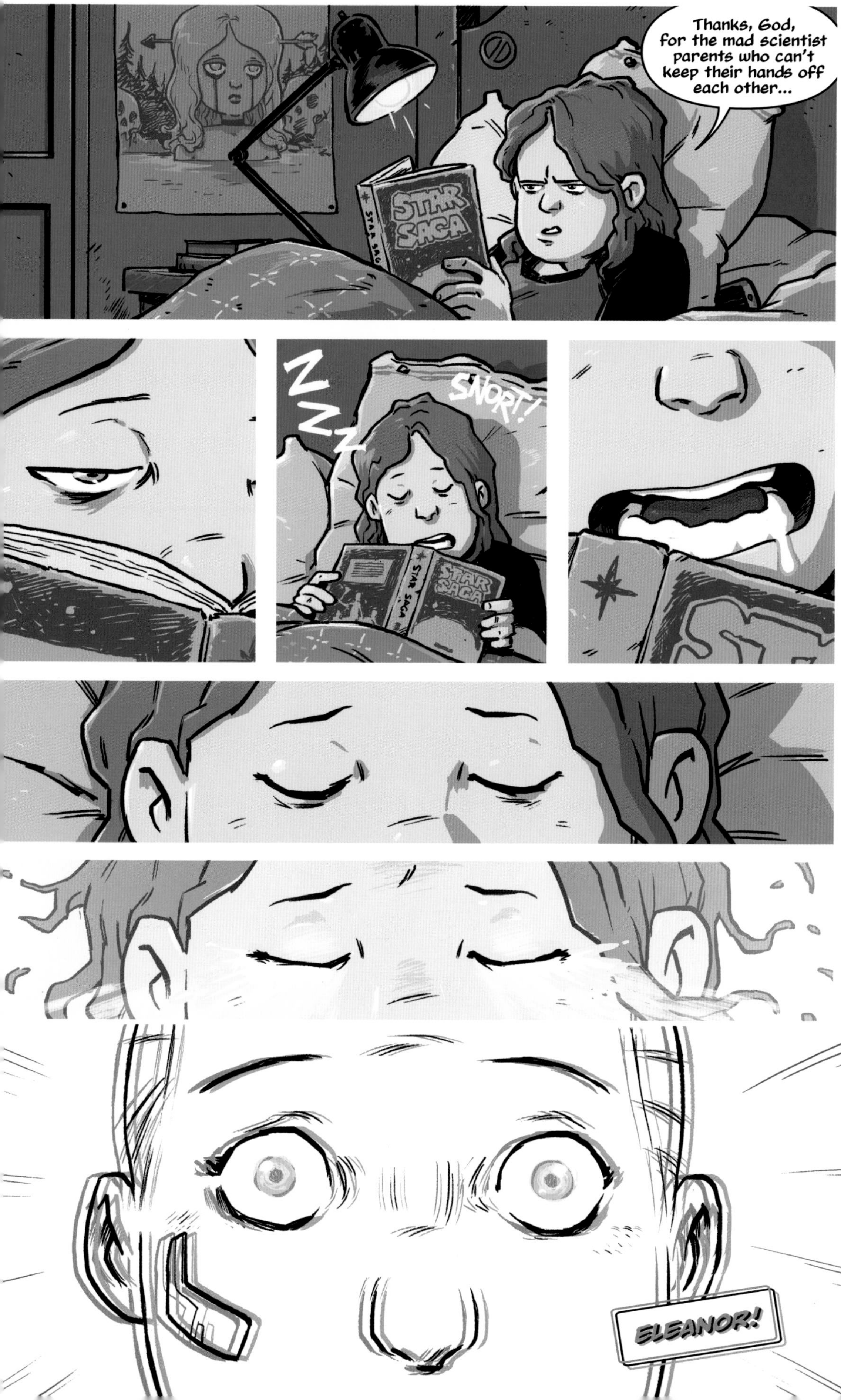

Thanks, God, for the mad scientist parents who can't keep their hands off each other...
STAR SAGA
Z Z Z
SNORT!
STAR SAGA
ELEANOR!

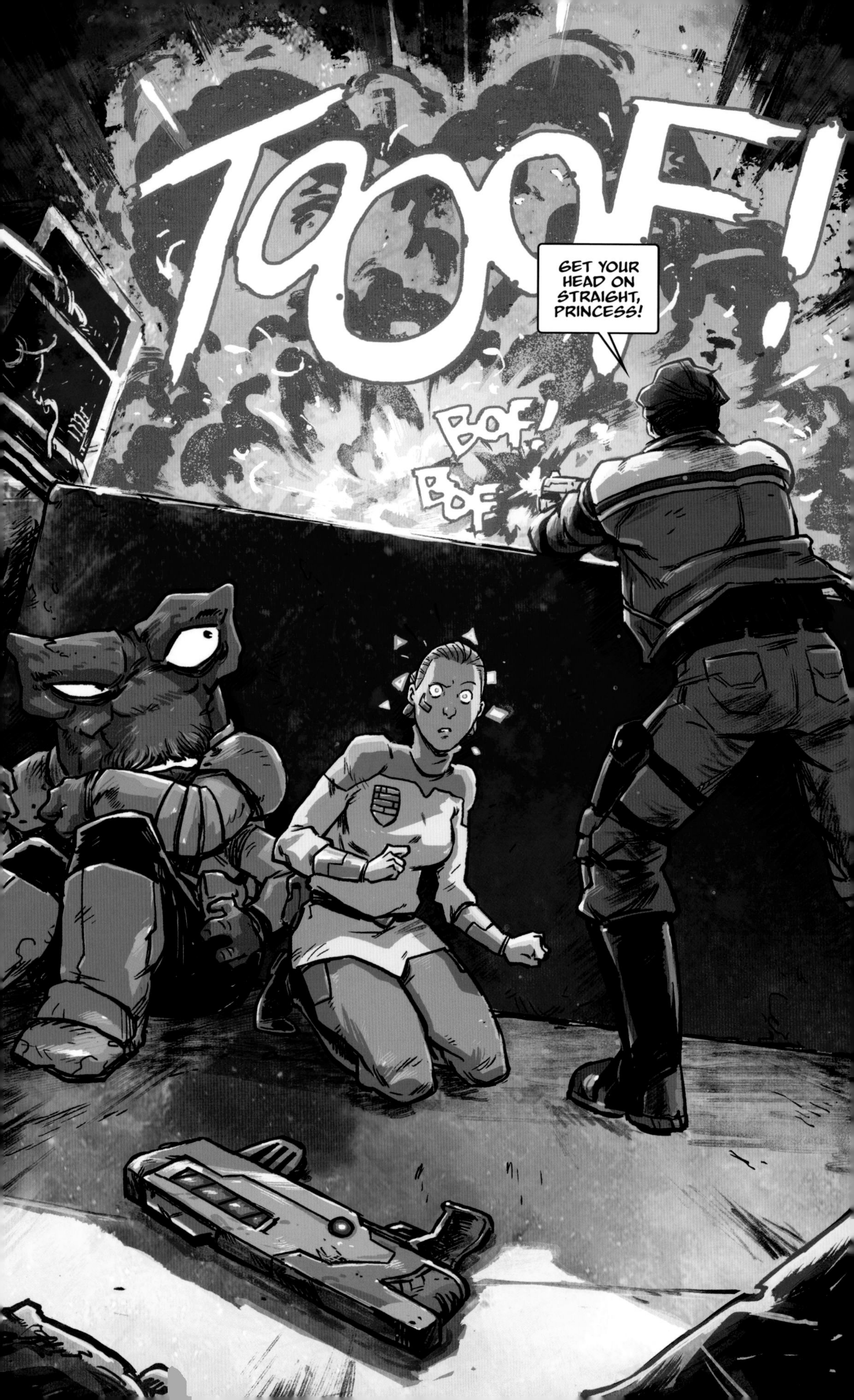
TOOOF!
GET YOUR HEAD ON STRAIGHT, PRINCESS!
BOF!
BOF

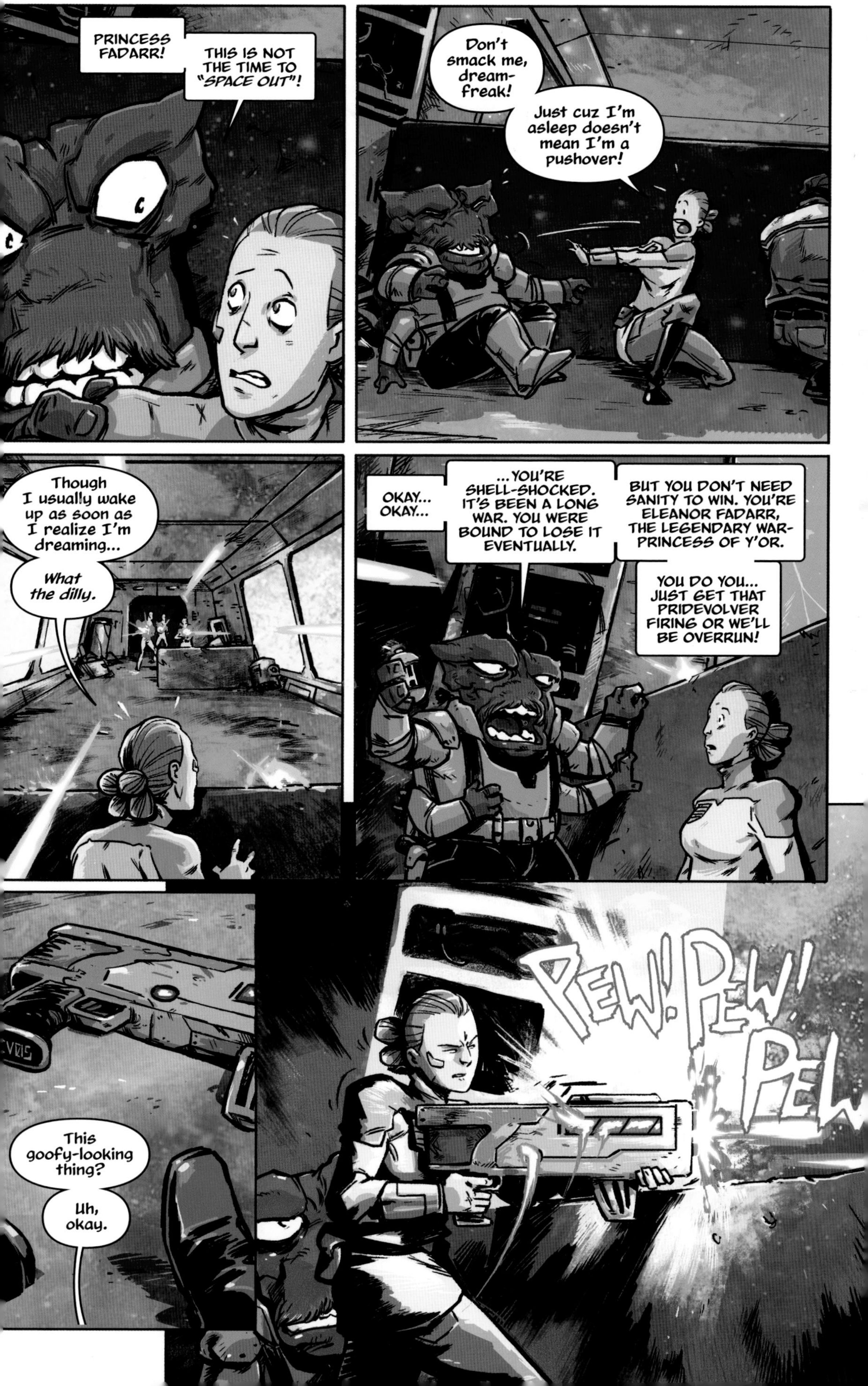
PRINCESS FADARR!
THIS IS NOT THE TIME TO "SPACE OUT"!
Don't smack me, dream-freak!
Just cuz I'm asleep doesn't mean I'm a pushover!
Though I usually wake up as soon as I realize I'm dreaming...
What the dilly.
OKAY... OKAY...
...YOU'RE SHELL-SHOCKED. IT'S BEEN A LONG WAR. YOU WERE BOUND TO LOSE IT EVENTUALLY.
BUT YOU DON'T NEED SANITY TO WIN. YOU'RE ELEANOR FADARR, THE LEGENDARY WAR-PRINCESS OF Y'OR.
YOU DO YOU... JUST GET THAT PRIDEVOLVER FIRING OR WE'LL BE OVERRUN!
This goofy-looking thing?
Uh, okay.
PEW! PEW! PEW

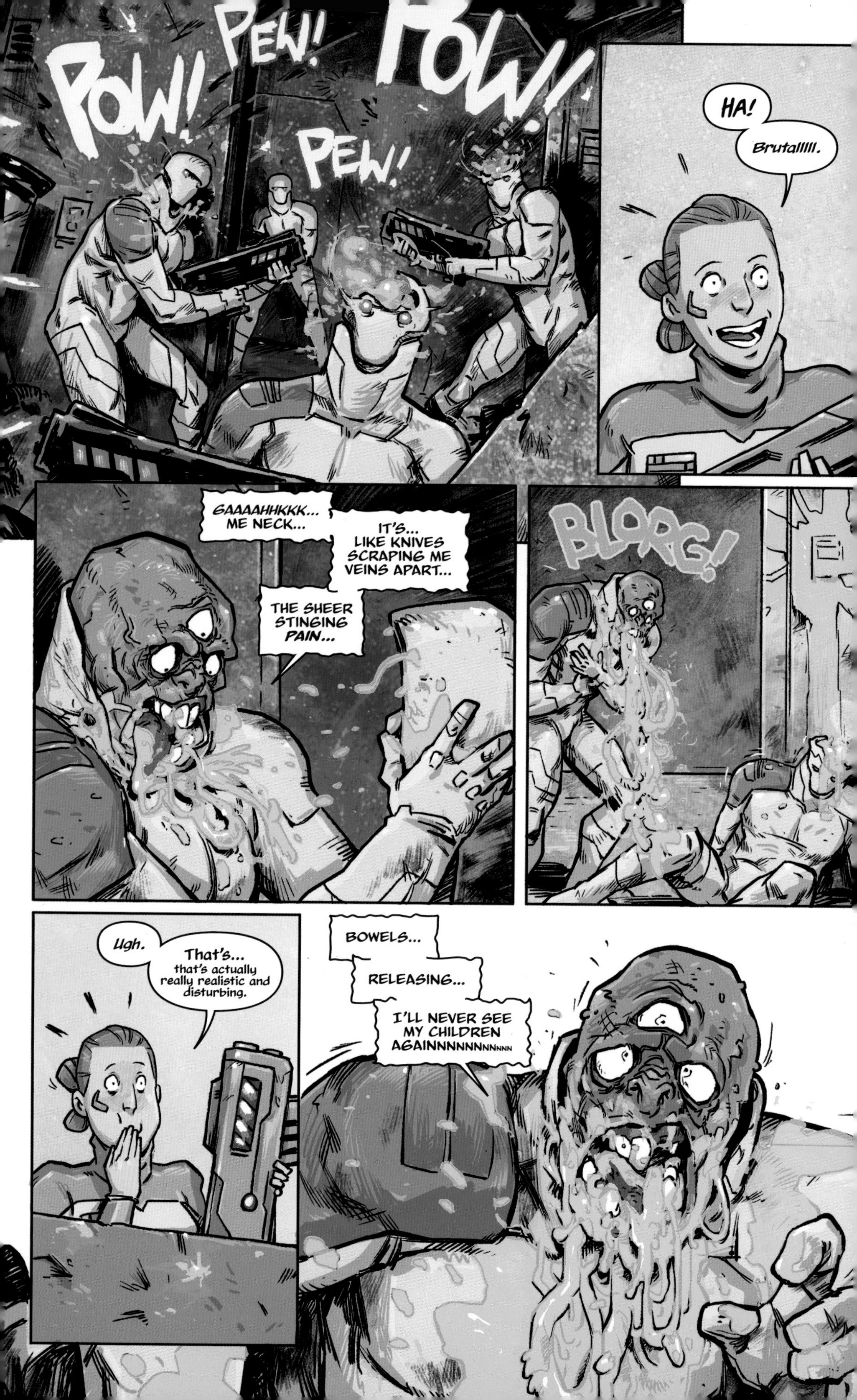
POW! PEW! POW!
PEW!
HA!
Brutallll.
GAAAAHHKKK... ME NECK...
IT'S... LIKE KNIVES SCRAPING ME VEINS APART...
THE SHEER STINGING PAIN...
BLORG!
Ugh.
That's... that's actually really realistic and disturbing.
BOWELS...
RELEASING...
I'LL NEVER SEE MY CHILDREN AGAINNNNNNNNNNN

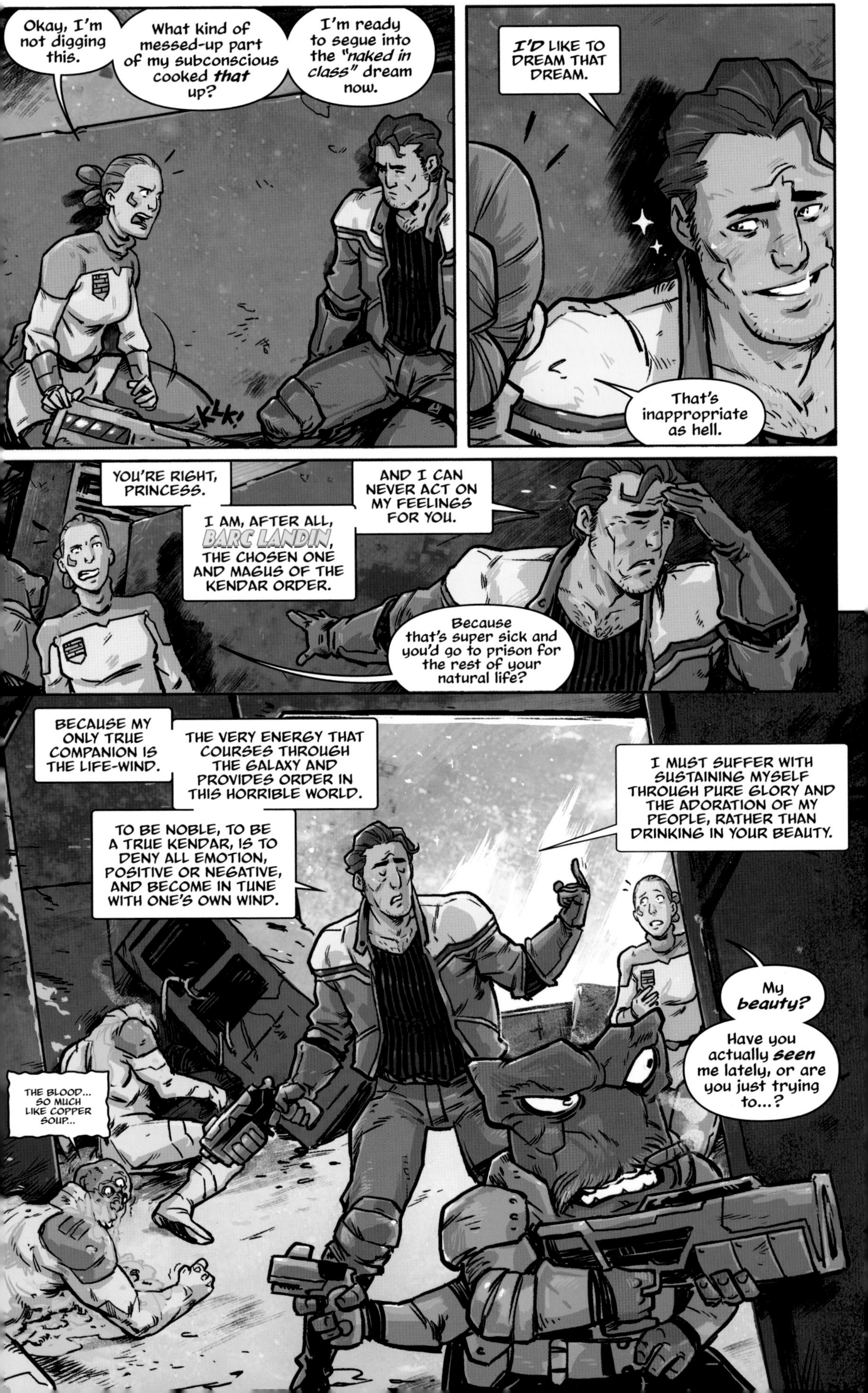
Okay, I'm not digging this.
What kind of messed-up part of my subconscious cooked *that* up?
I'm ready to segue into the *"naked in class"* dream now.
KLIK!
I'D LIKE TO DREAM THAT DREAM.
That's inappropriate as hell.
YOU'RE RIGHT, PRINCESS.
AND I CAN NEVER ACT ON MY FEELINGS FOR YOU.
I AM, AFTER ALL, BARC LANDIN, THE CHOSEN ONE AND MAGUS OF THE KENDAR ORDER.
Because that's super sick and you'd go to prison for the rest of your natural life?
BECAUSE MY ONLY TRUE COMPANION IS THE LIFE-WIND.
THE VERY ENERGY THAT COURSES THROUGH THE GALAXY AND PROVIDES ORDER IN THIS HORRIBLE WORLD.
TO BE NOBLE, TO BE A TRUE KENDAR, IS TO DENY ALL EMOTION, POSITIVE OR NEGATIVE, AND BECOME IN TUNE WITH ONE'S OWN WIND.
I MUST SUFFER WITH SUSTAINING MYSELF THROUGH PURE GLORY AND THE ADORATION OF MY PEOPLE, RATHER THAN DRINKING IN YOUR BEAUTY.
My *beauty?*
Have you actually *seen* me lately, or are you just trying to...?
THE BLOOD... SO MUCH LIKE COPPER SOUP...

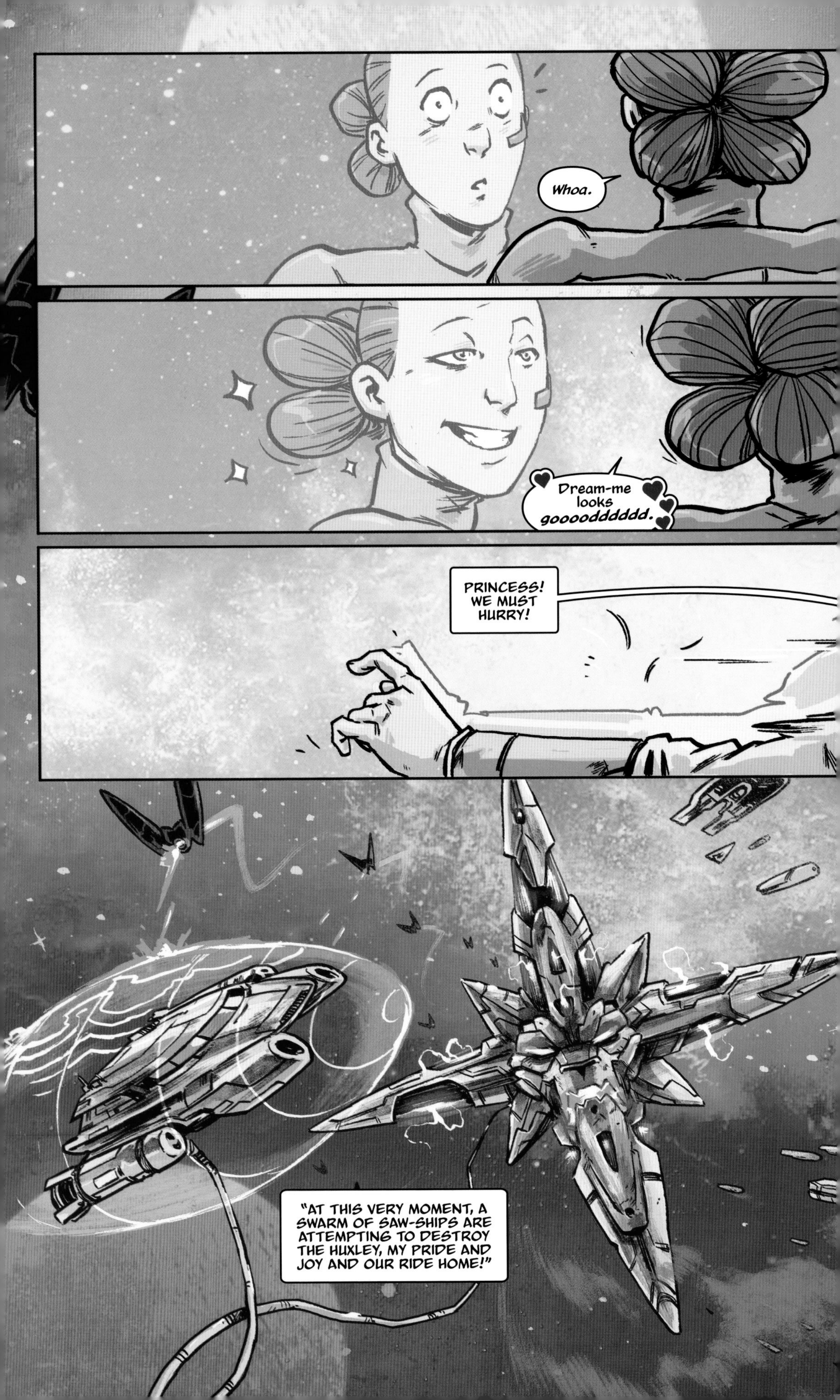
Whoa.
Dream-me looks gooooddddd.
PRINCESS! WE MUST HURRY!
"AT THIS VERY MOMENT, A SWARM OF SAW-SHIPS ARE ATTEMPTING TO DESTROY THE HUXLEY, MY PRIDE AND JOY AND OUR RIDE HOME!"

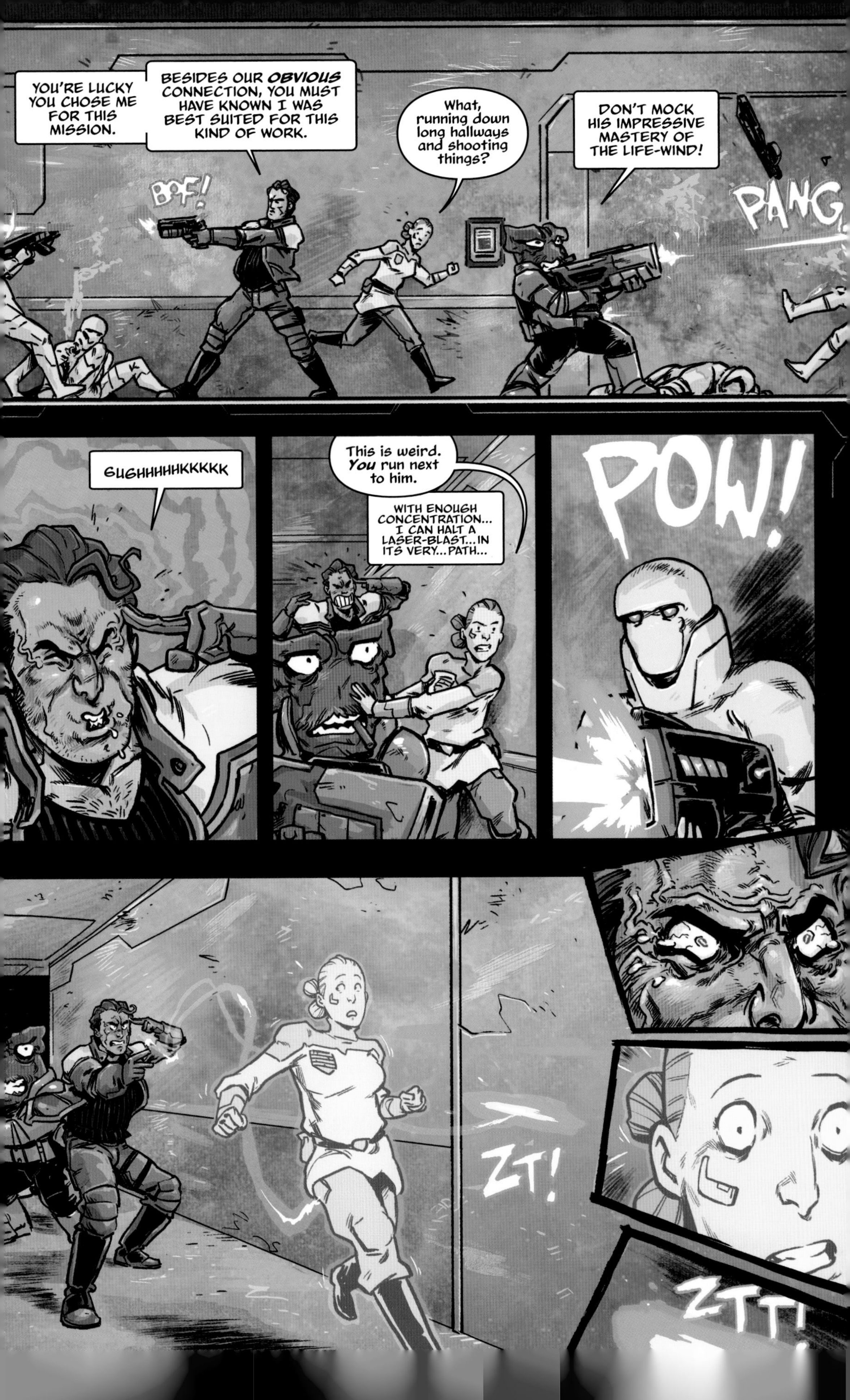
YOU'RE LUCKY YOU CHOSE ME FOR THIS MISSION.
BESIDES OUR OBVIOUS CONNECTION, YOU MUST HAVE KNOWN I WAS BEST SUITED FOR THIS KIND OF WORK.
BOF!
What, running down long hallways and shooting things?
DON'T MOCK HIS IMPRESSIVE MASTERY OF THE LIFE-WIND!
PANG
GUGHHHHHKKKKK
This is weird. You run next to him.
WITH ENOUGH CONCENTRATION... I CAN HALT A LASER-BLAST...IN ITS VERY...PATH...
POW!
ZT!
ZTT!

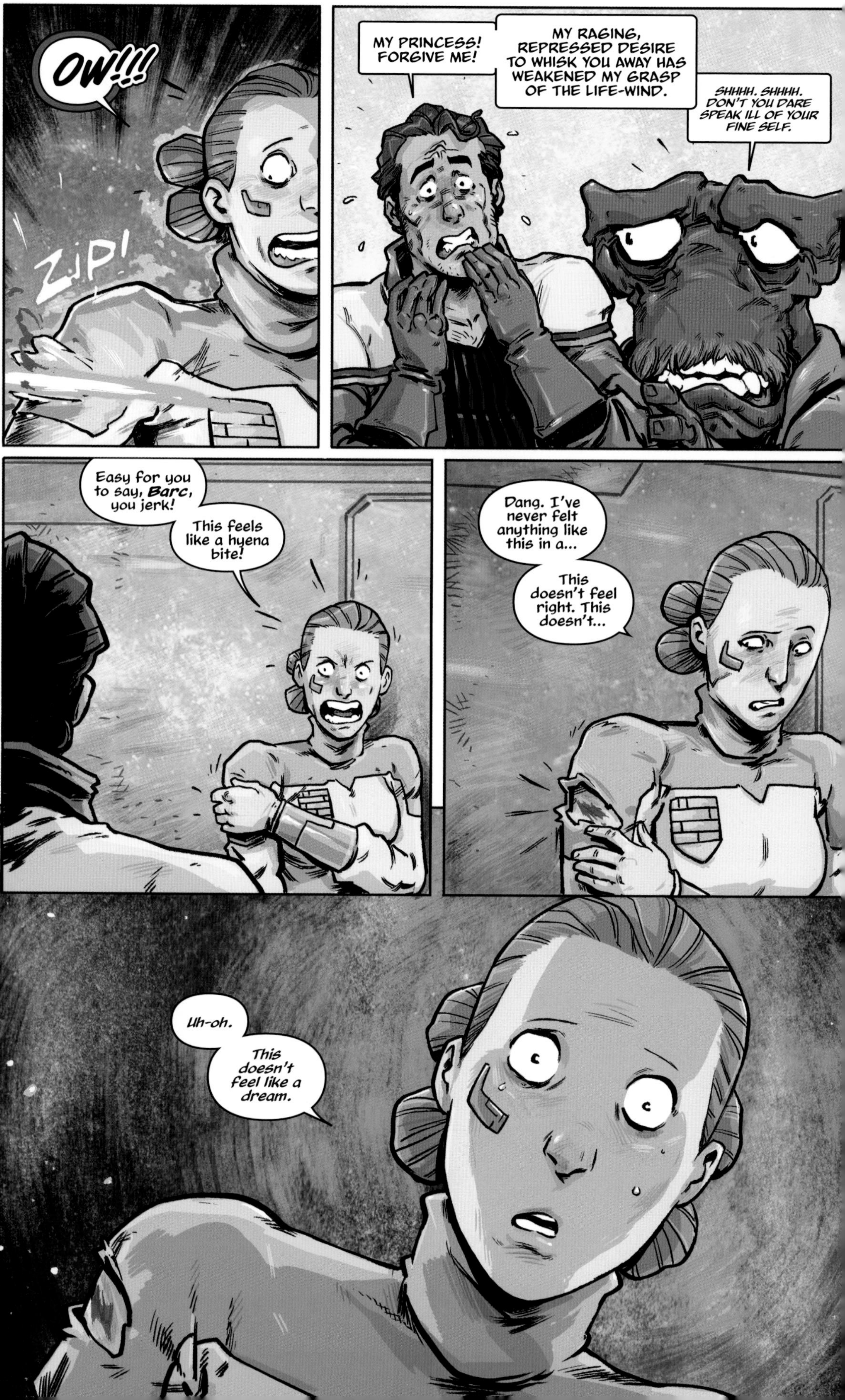
OW!!!
ZIP!
MY PRINCESS! FORGIVE ME!
MY RAGING, REPRESSED DESIRE TO WHISK YOU AWAY HAS WEAKENED MY GRASP OF THE LIFE-WIND.
SHHHH. SHHHH. DON'T YOU DARE SPEAK ILL OF YOUR FINE SELF.
Easy for you to say, Barc, you jerk!
This feels like a hyena bite!
Dang. I've never felt anything like this in a...
This doesn't feel right. This doesn't...
Uh-oh.
This doesn't feel like a dream.

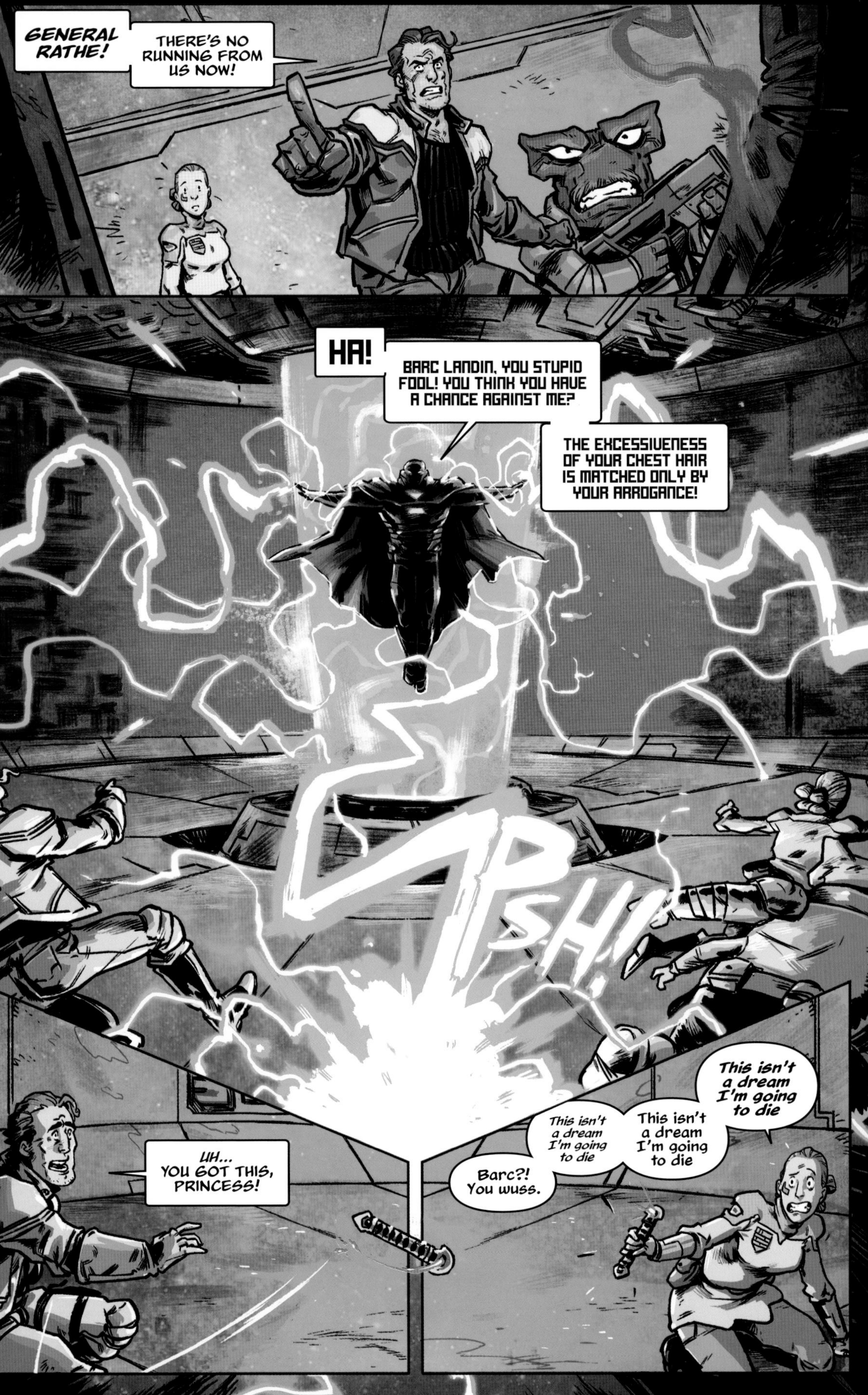
GENERAL RATHE!
THERE'S NO RUNNING FROM US NOW!
HA!
BARC LANDIN, YOU STUPID FOOL! YOU THINK YOU HAVE A CHANCE AGAINST ME?
THE EXCESSIVENESS OF YOUR CHEST HAIR IS MATCHED ONLY BY YOUR ARROGANCE!
ZPSH!
UH... YOU GOT THIS, PRINCESS!
Barc?! You wuss.
This isn't a dream I'm going to die
This isn't a dream I'm going to die
This isn't a dream I'm going to die

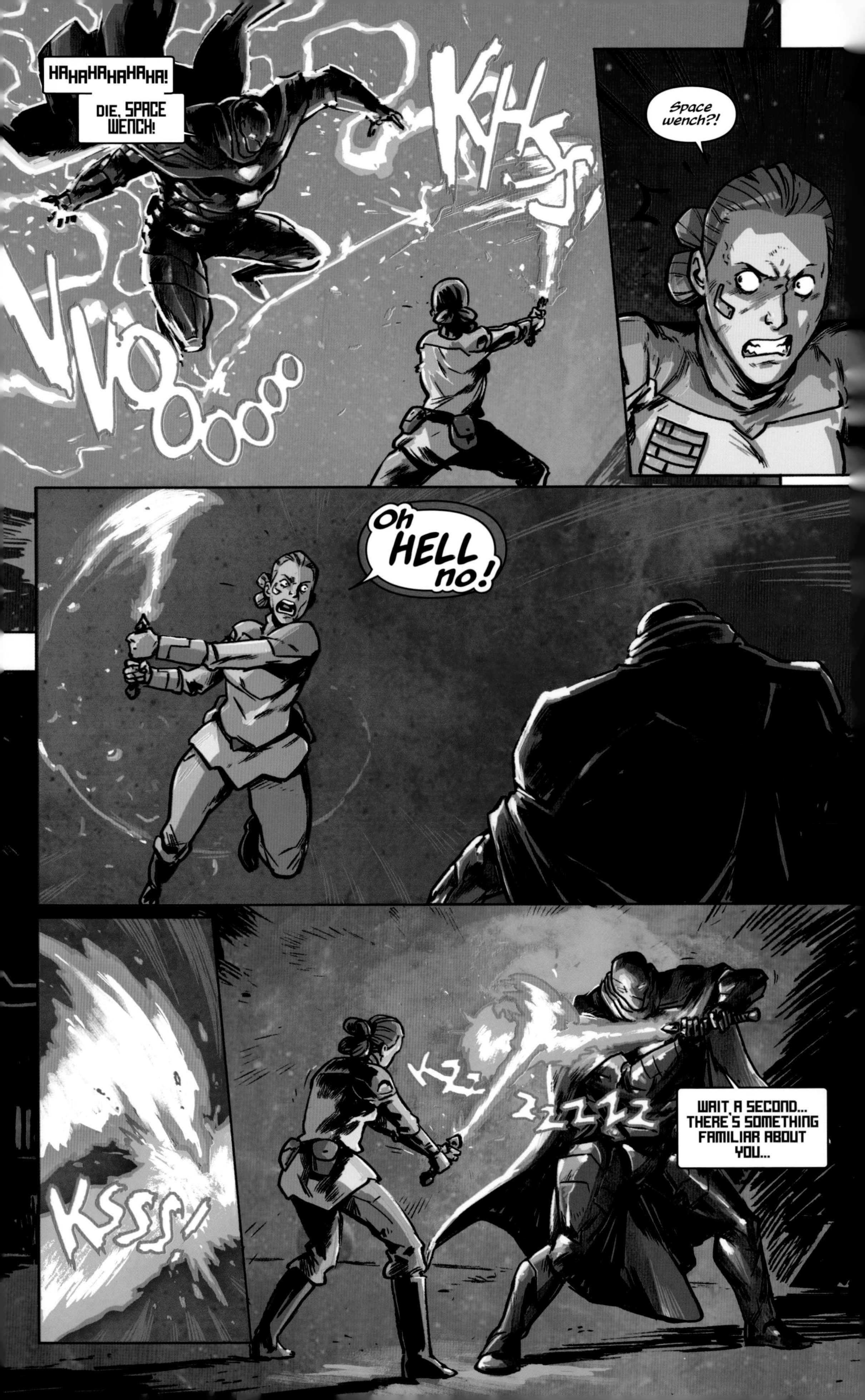
HAHAHAHAHAHA!
DIE, SPACE WENCH!
KHSSS
VVOOOOOO
Space wench?!
Oh HELL no!
KZZ
ZZZZZZ
KSSS!
WAIT A SECOND... THERE'S SOMETHING FAMILIAR ABOUT YOU...

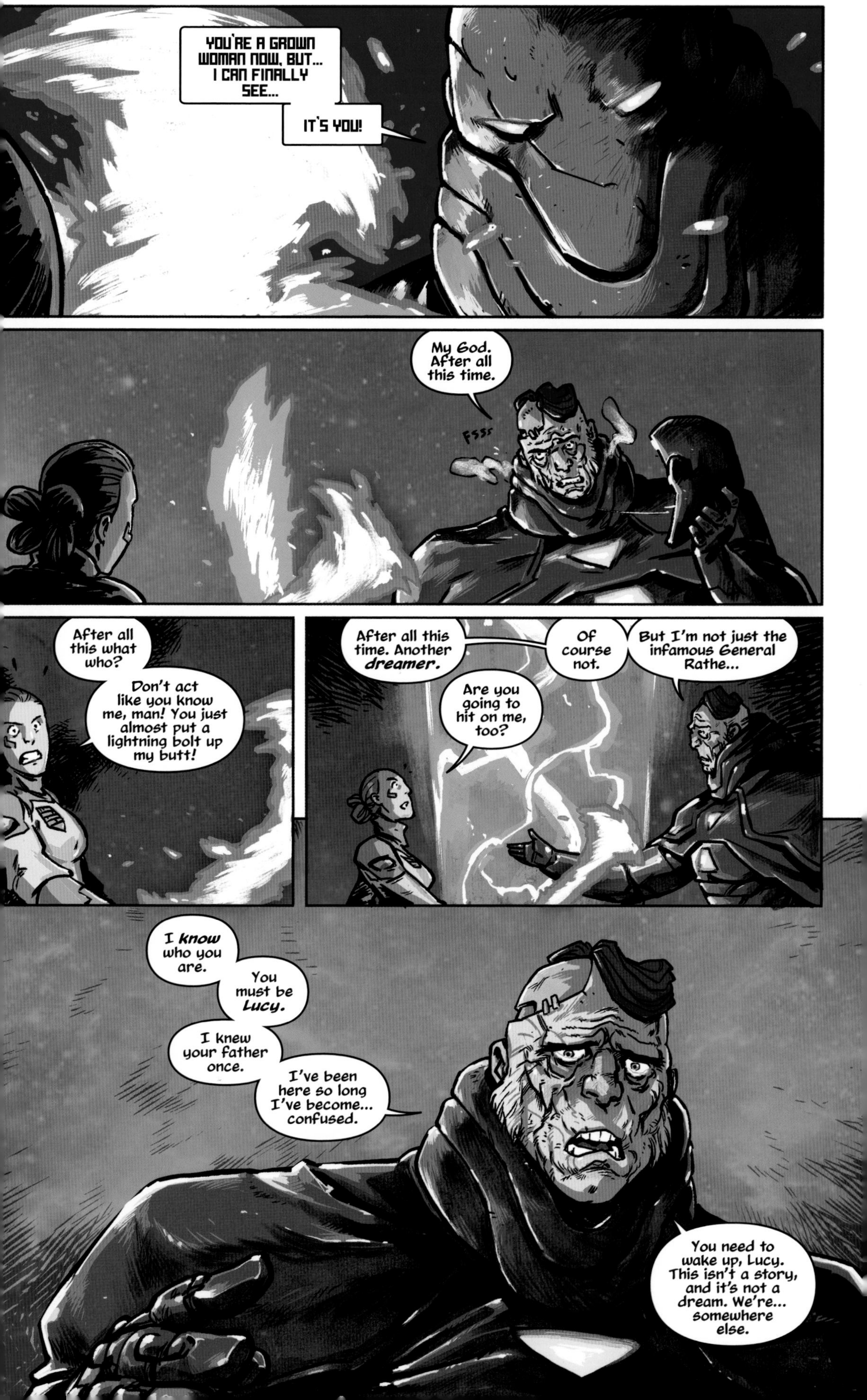
YOU'RE A GROWN WOMAN NOW, BUT... I CAN FINALLY SEE...
IT'S YOU!
My God. After all this time.
FSSS
After all this what who?
Don't act like you know me, man! You just almost put a lightning bolt up my butt!
After all this time. Another *dreamer.*
Are you going to hit on me, too?
Of course not.
But I'm not just the infamous General Rathe...
I *know* who you are.
You must be *Lucy.*
I knew your father once.
I've been here so long I've become... confused.
You need to wake up, Lucy. This isn't a story, and it's not a dream. We're... somewhere else.

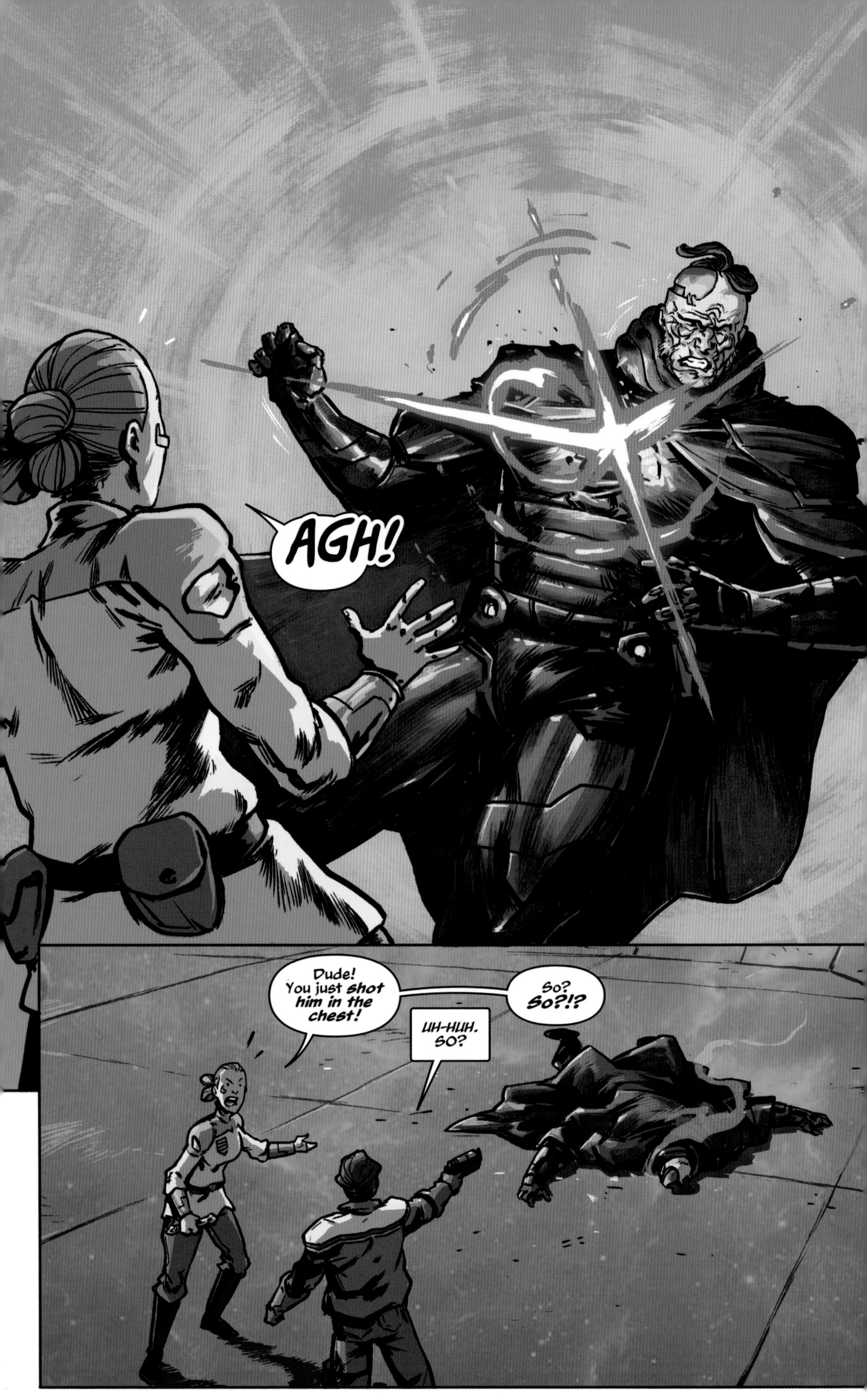
AGH!
Dude! You just shot him in the chest!
UH-HUH. SO?
So? So?!?

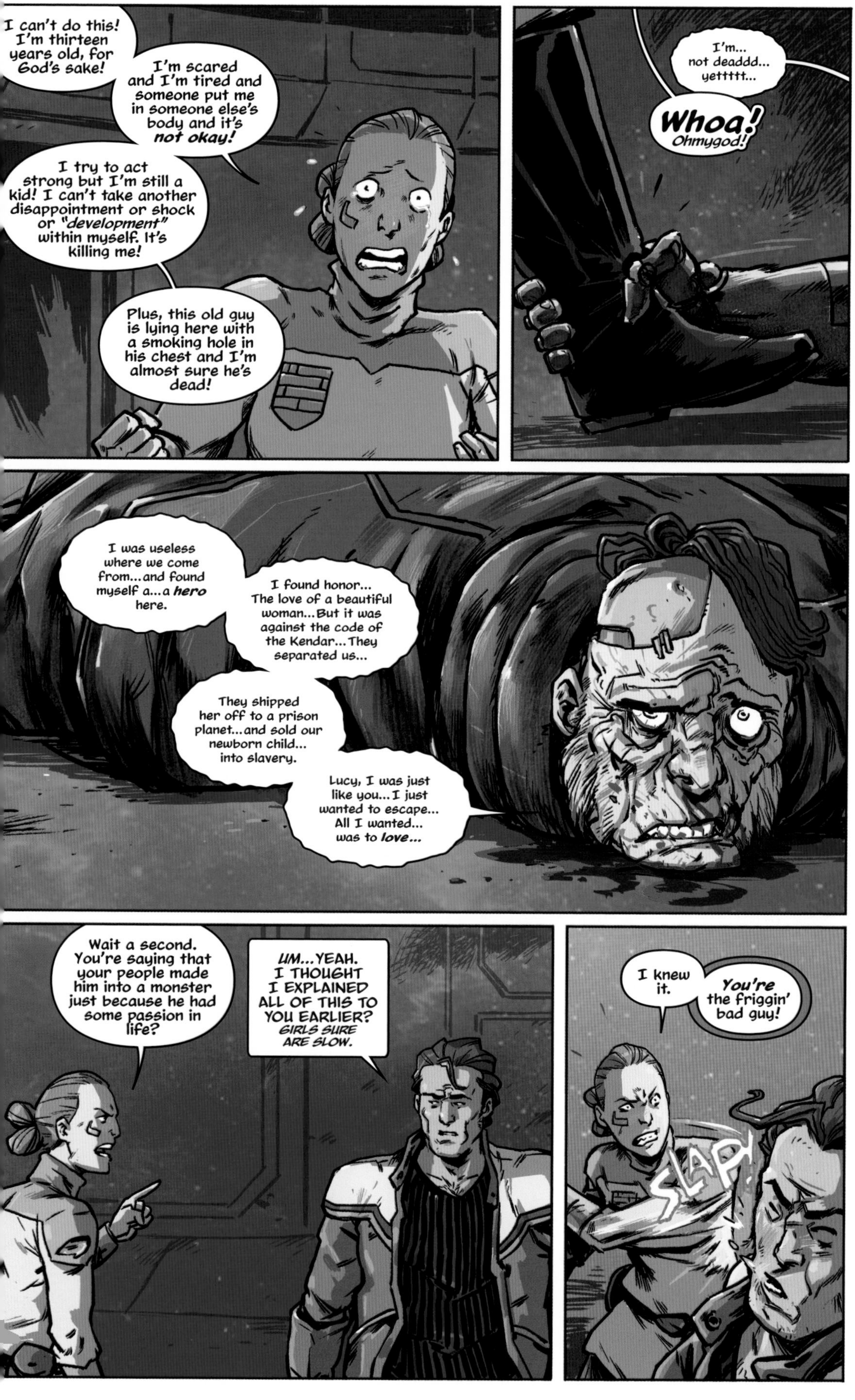
I can't do this! I'm thirteen years old, for God's sake!
I'm scared and I'm tired and someone put me in someone else's body and it's *not okay!*
I try to act strong but I'm still a kid! I can't take another disappointment or shock or *"development"* within myself. It's killing me!
Plus, this old guy is lying here with a smoking hole in his chest and I'm almost sure he's dead!
I'm... not deaddd... yetttttt...
Whoa! Ohmygod!
I was useless where we come from...and found myself a...a *hero* here.
I found honor... The love of a beautiful woman... But it was against the code of the Kendar... They separated us...
They shipped her off to a prison planet...and sold our newborn child... into slavery.
Lucy, I was just like you... I just wanted to escape... All I wanted... was to *love...*
Wait a second. You're saying that your people made him into a monster just because he had some passion in life?
UM...YEAH. I THOUGHT I EXPLAINED ALL OF THIS TO YOU EARLIER? *GIRLS SURE ARE SLOW.*
I knew it.
You're the friggin' bad guy!
SLAP!

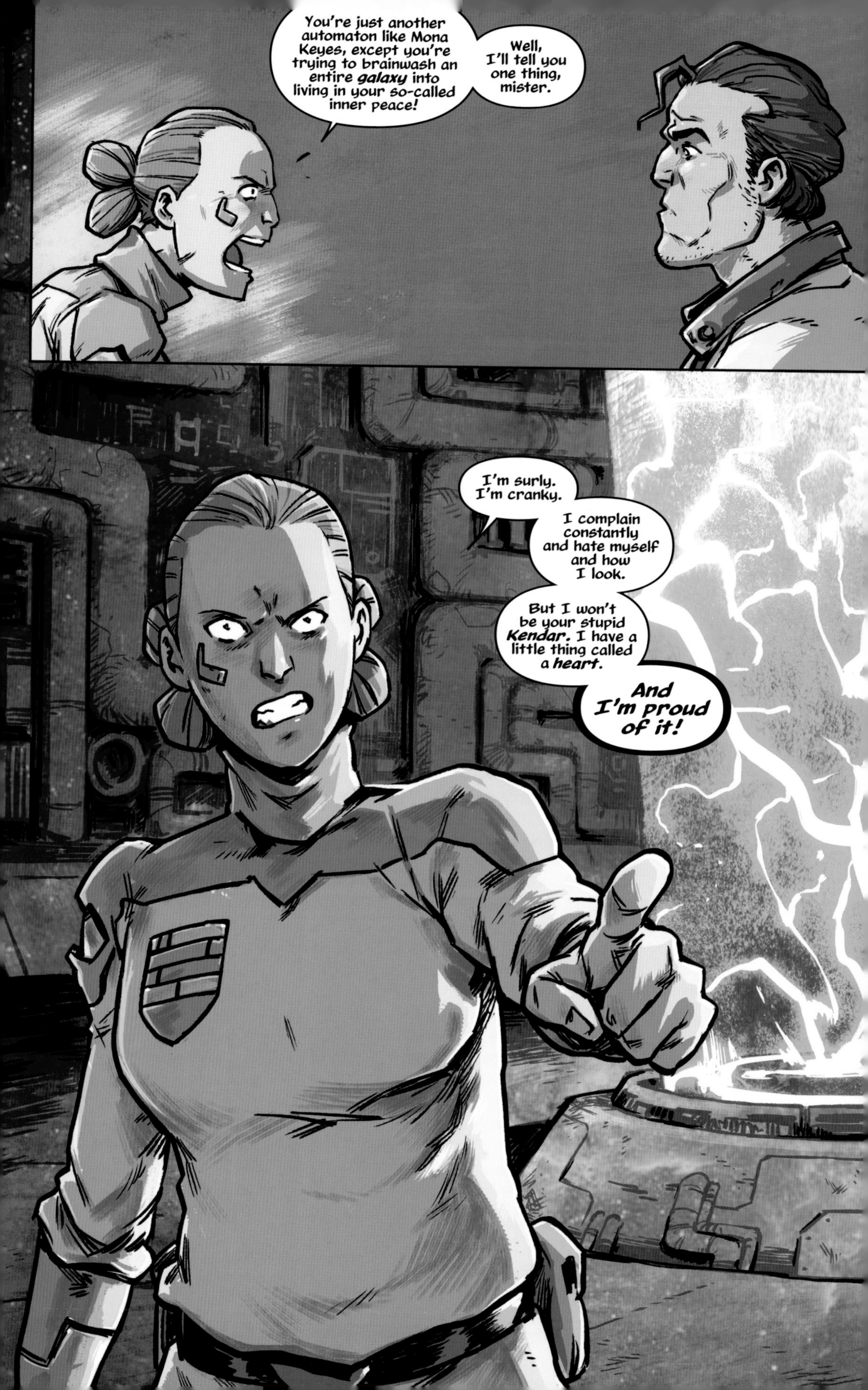

You're just another automaton like Mona Keyes, except you're trying to brainwash an entire *galaxy* into living in your so-called inner peace!
Well, I'll tell you one thing, mister.
I'm surly. I'm cranky.
I complain constantly and hate myself and how I look.
But I won't be your stupid *Kendar*. I have a little thing called a *heart*.
And I'm proud of it!

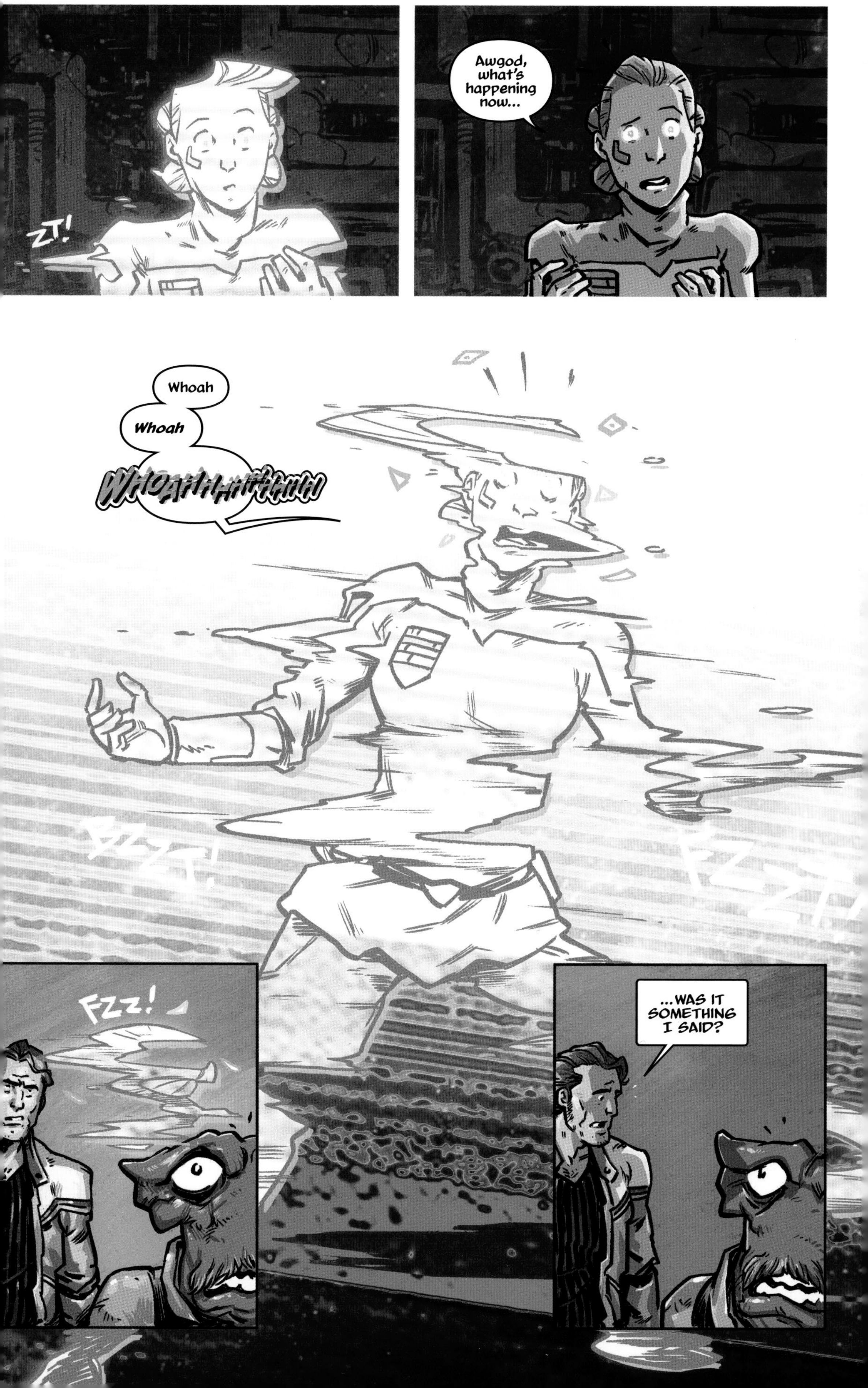
ZT!
Awgod, what's happening now...
Whoah
Whoah
WHOAHHHHHHHHHHH
BZZT!
FZZZT!
FZZ!
...WAS IT SOMETHING I SAID?

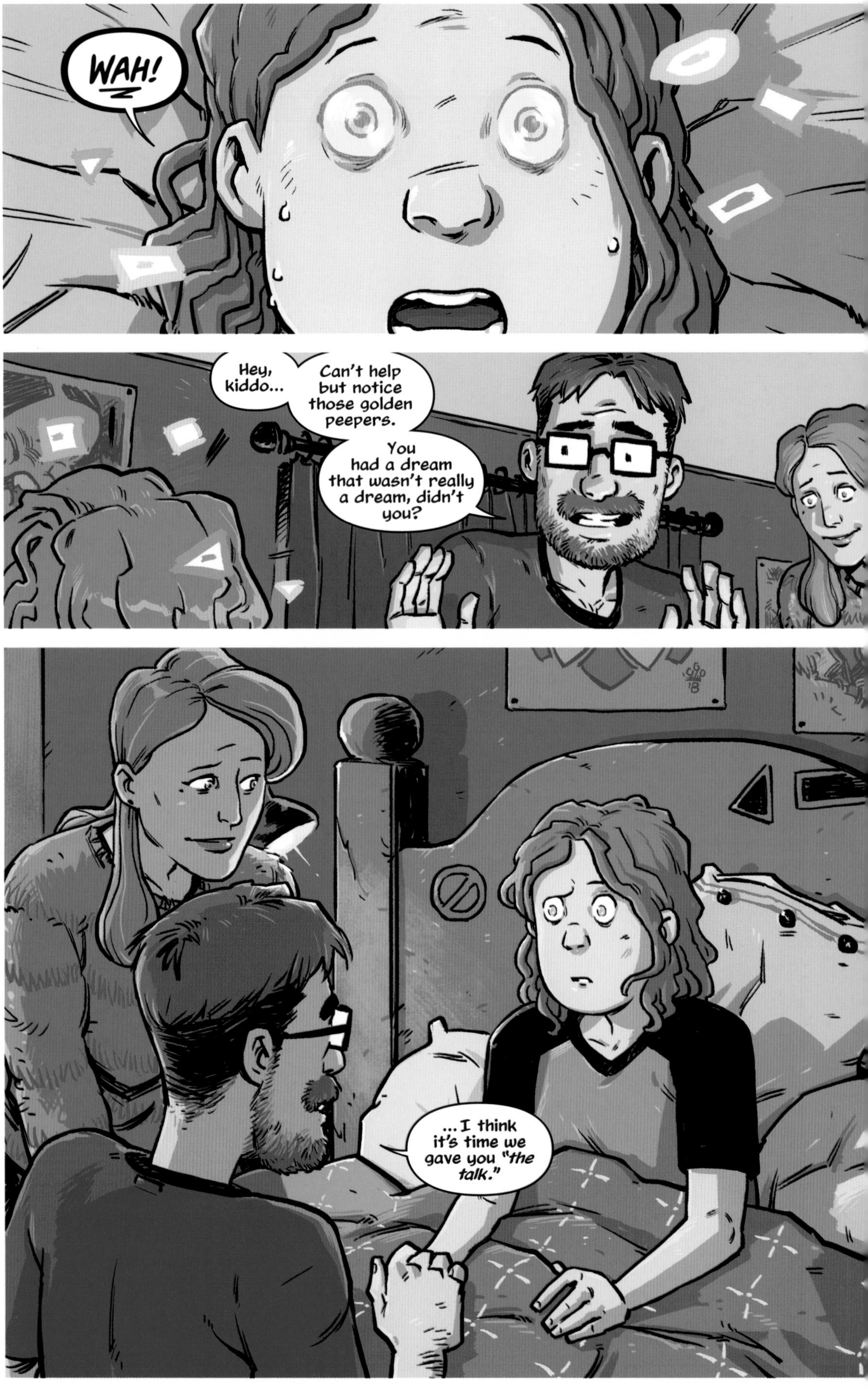
WAH!
Hey, kiddo...
Can't help but notice those golden peepers.
You had a dream that wasn't really a dream, didn't you?
...I think it's time we gave you *"the talk."*

ISSUE ONE COVER BY
MICHAEL DIALYNAS

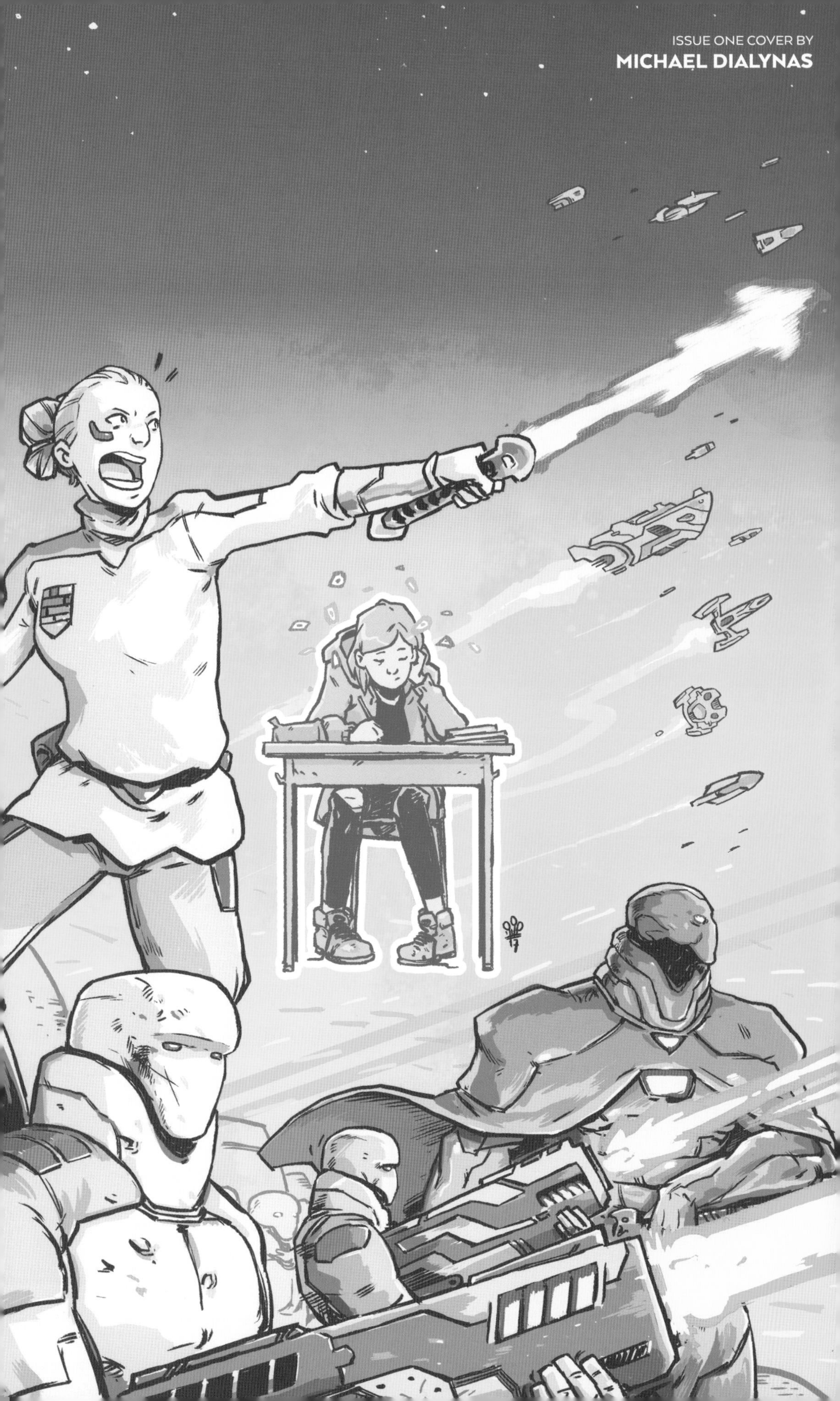

CHAPTER
TWO

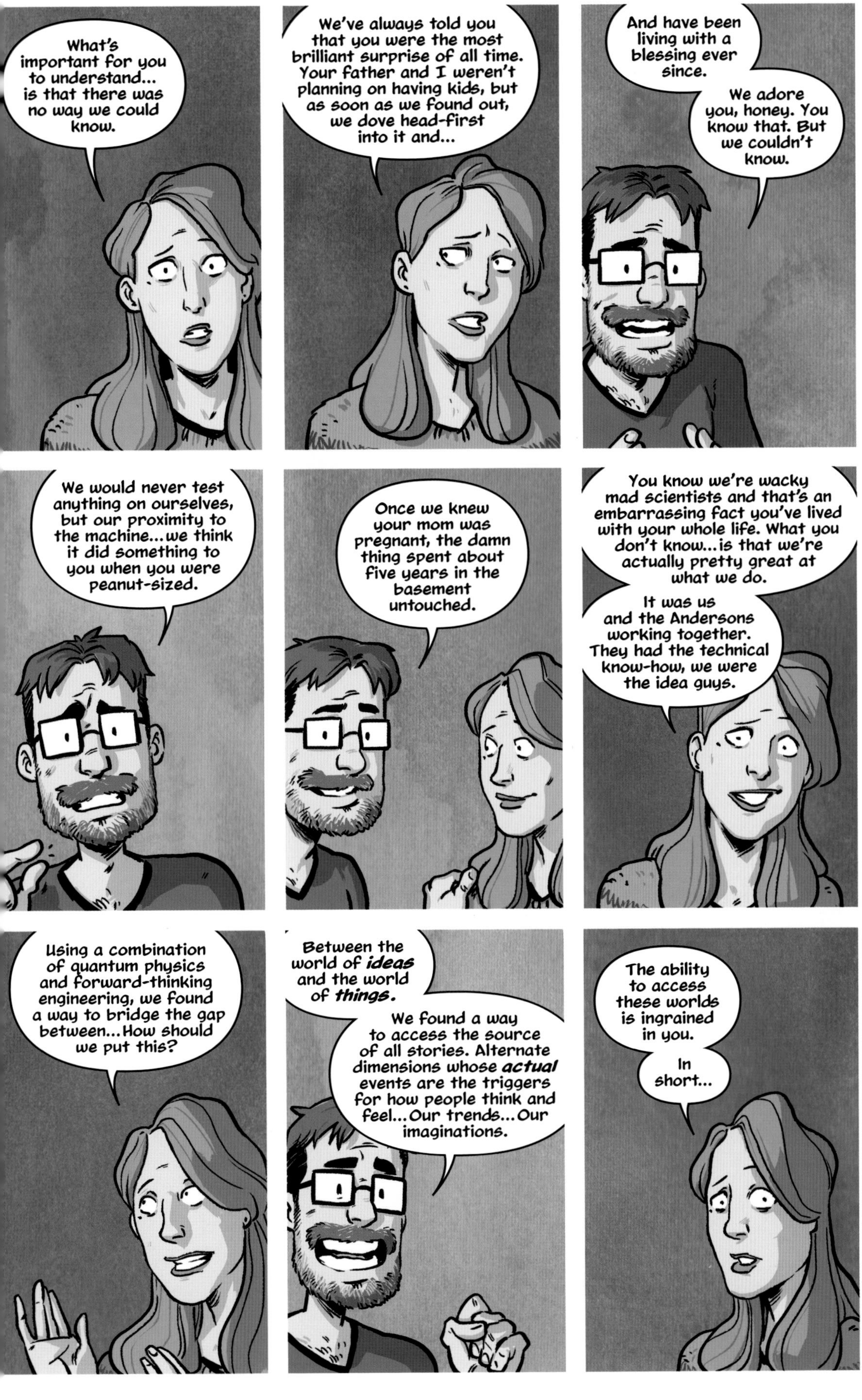
What's important for you to understand... is that there was no way we could know.
We've always told you that you were the most brilliant surprise of all time. Your father and I weren't planning on having kids, but as soon as we found out, we dove head-first into it and...
And have been living with a blessing ever since.
We adore you, honey. You know that. But we couldn't know.
We would never test anything on ourselves, but our proximity to the machine...we think it did something to you when you were peanut-sized.
Once we knew your mom was pregnant, the damn thing spent about five years in the basement untouched.
You know we're wacky mad scientists and that's an embarrassing fact you've lived with your whole life. What you don't know...is that we're actually pretty great at what we do.
It was us and the Andersons working together. They had the technical know-how, we were the idea guys.
Using a combination of quantum physics and forward-thinking engineering, we found a way to bridge the gap between...How should we put this?
Between the world of *ideas* and the world of *things.*
We found a way to access the source of all stories. Alternate dimensions whose *actual* events are the triggers for how people think and feel...Our trends...Our imaginations.
The ability to access these worlds is ingrained in you.
In short...

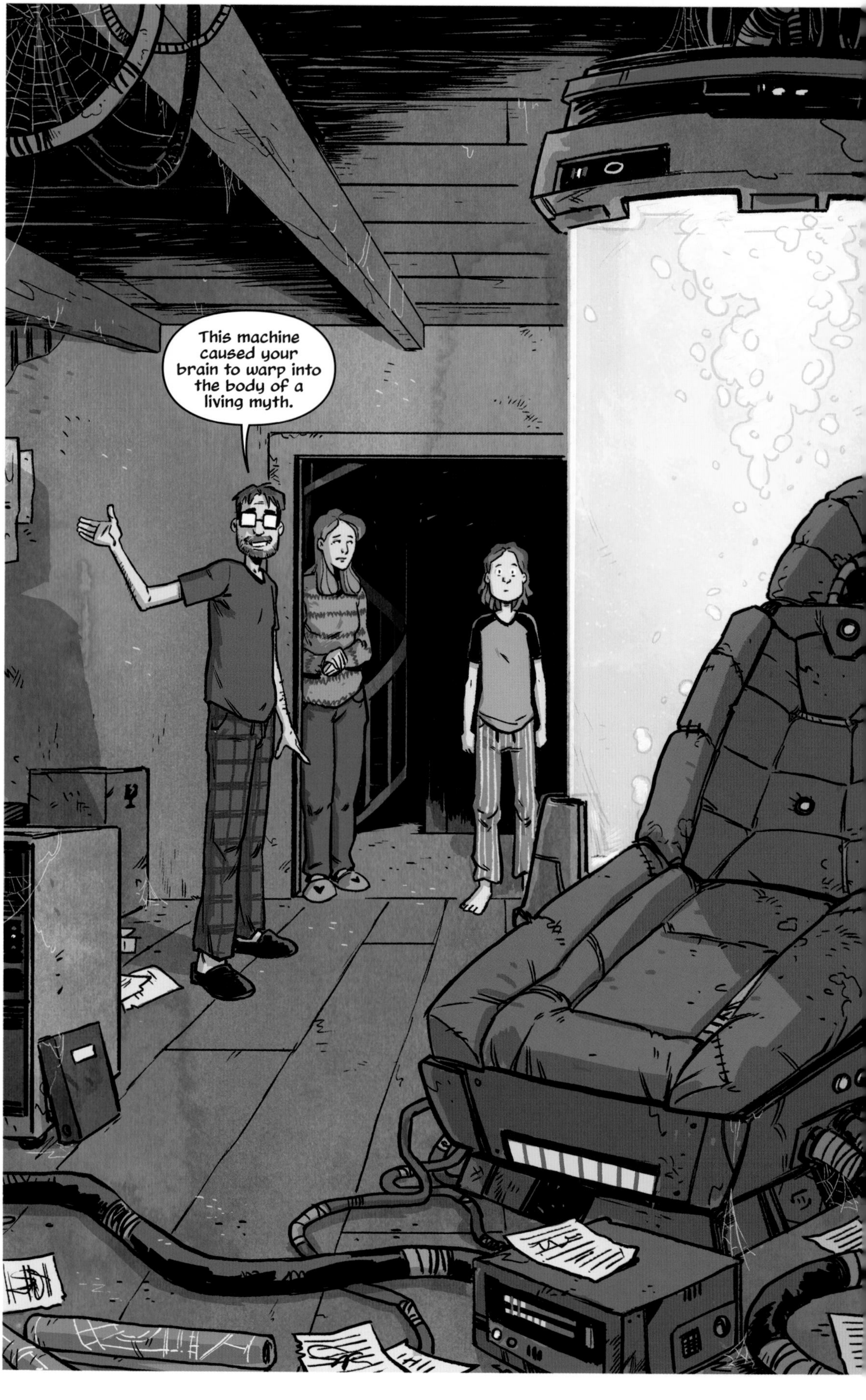
This machine caused your brain to warp into the body of a living myth.

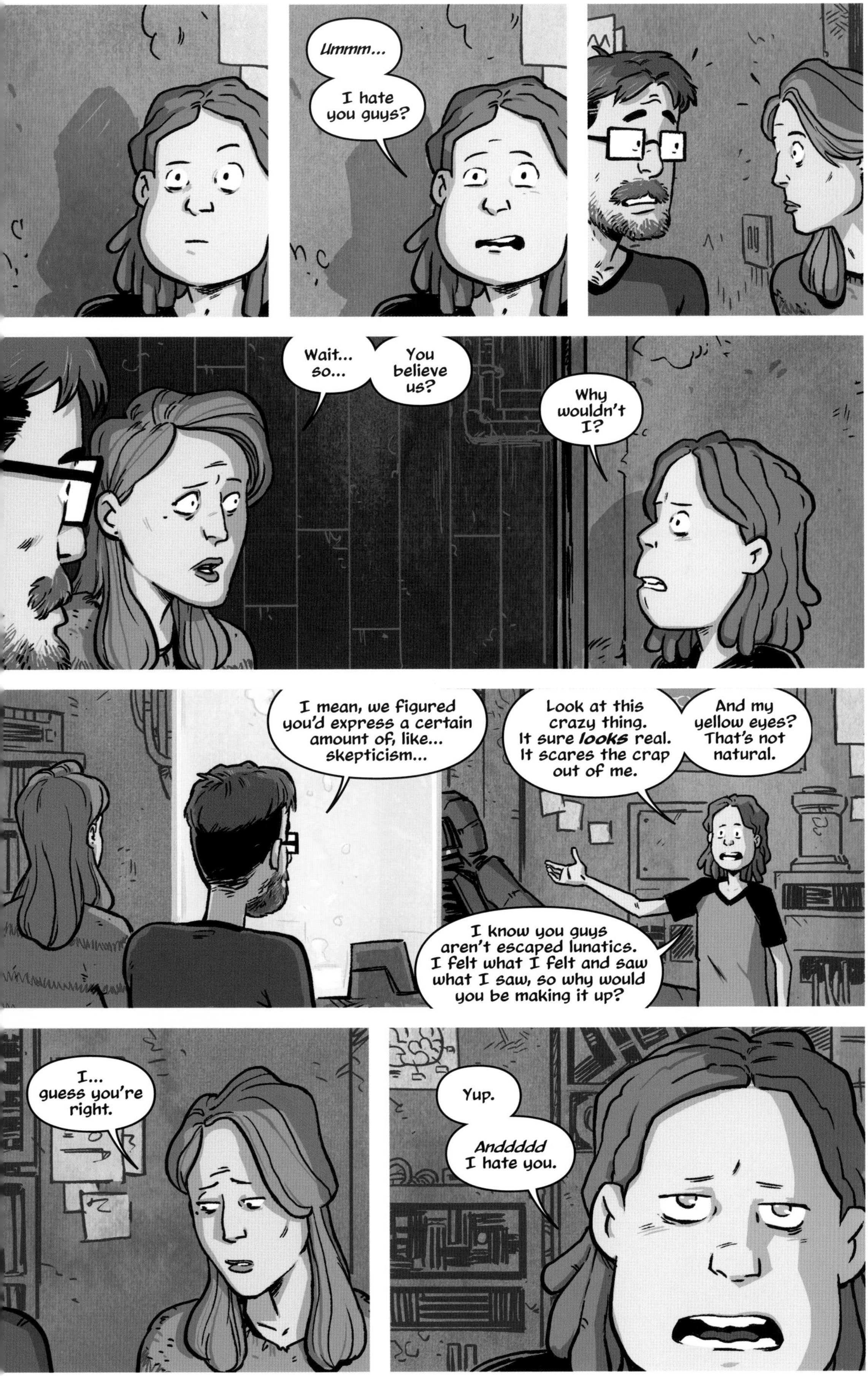
Ummm...
I hate you guys?
Wait... so...
You believe us?
Why wouldn't I?
I mean, we figured you'd express a certain amount of, like... skepticism...
Look at this crazy thing. It sure *looks* real. It scares the crap out of me.
And my yellow eyes? That's not natural.
I know you guys aren't escaped lunatics. I felt what I felt and saw what I saw, so why would you be making it up?
I... guess you're right.
Yup.
Andddddd I hate you.

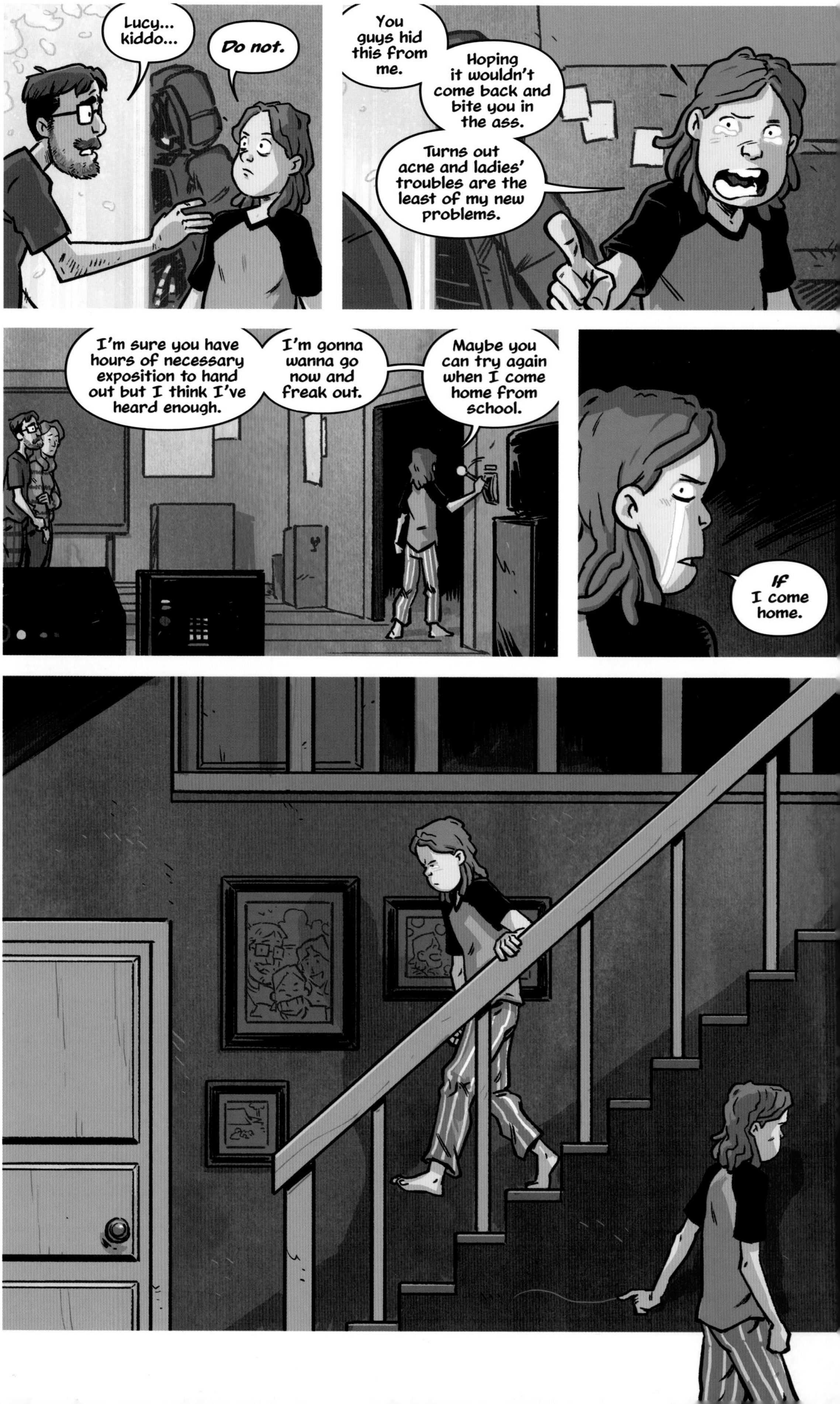
Lucy... kiddo...
Do not.
You guys hid this from me.
Hoping it wouldn't come back and bite you in the ass.
Turns out acne and ladies' troubles are the least of my new problems.
I'm sure you have hours of necessary exposition to hand out but I think I've heard enough.
I'm gonna wanna go now and freak out.
Maybe you can try again when I come home from school.
If I come home.

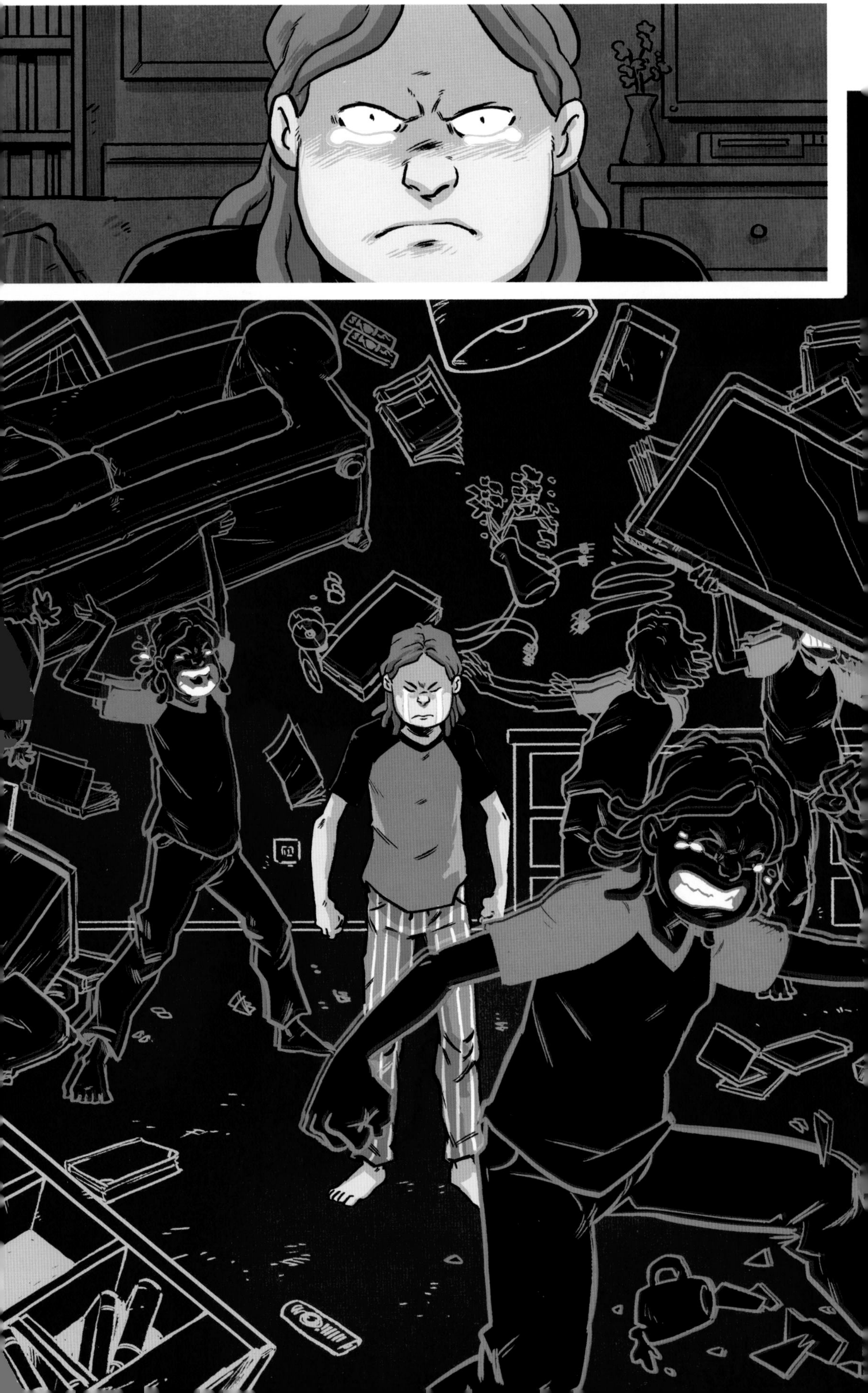

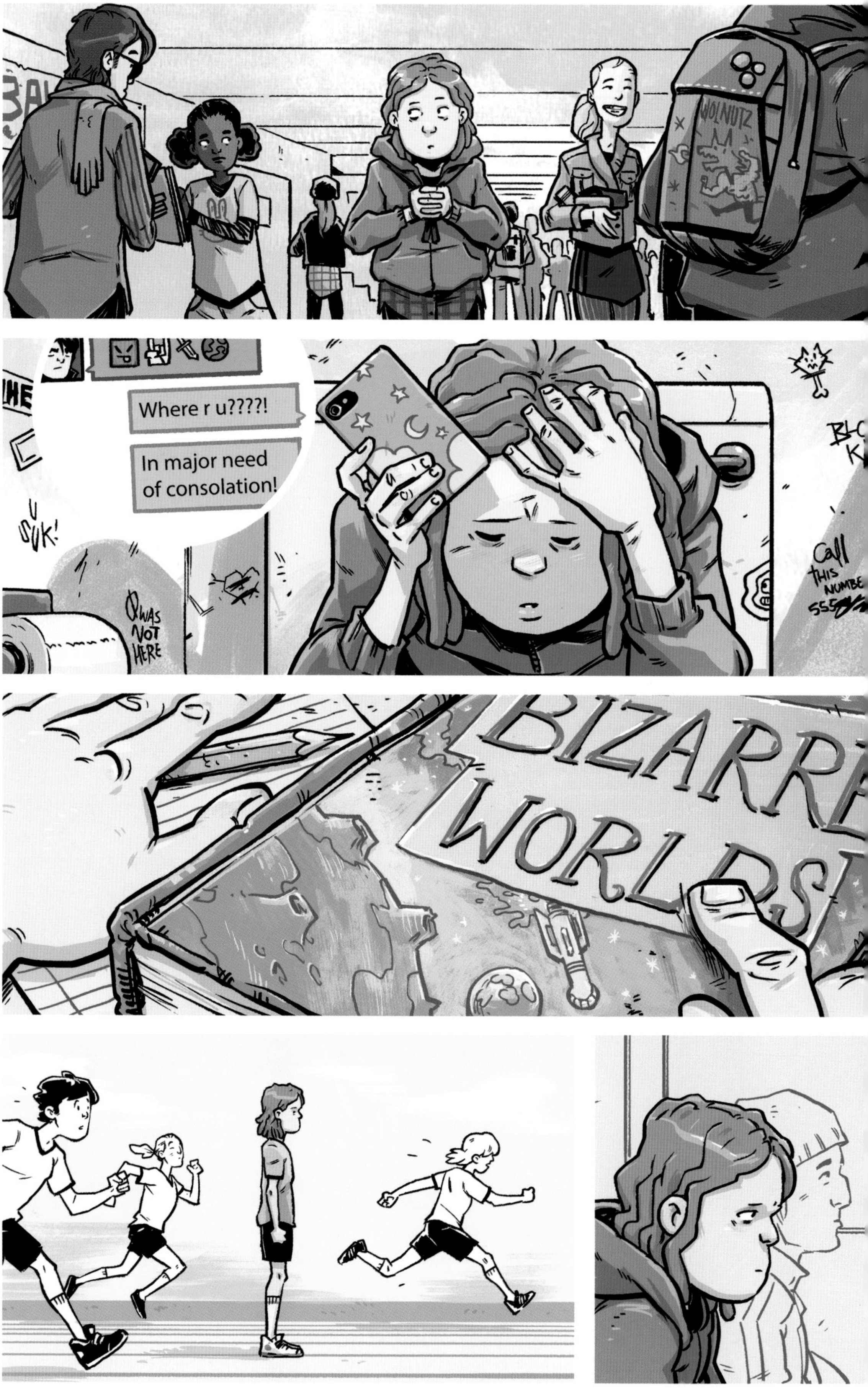
WOLNUTZ
Where r u????!
In major need of consolation!
U SUK!
WAS NOT HERE
Call THIS NUMBE
WORLDS

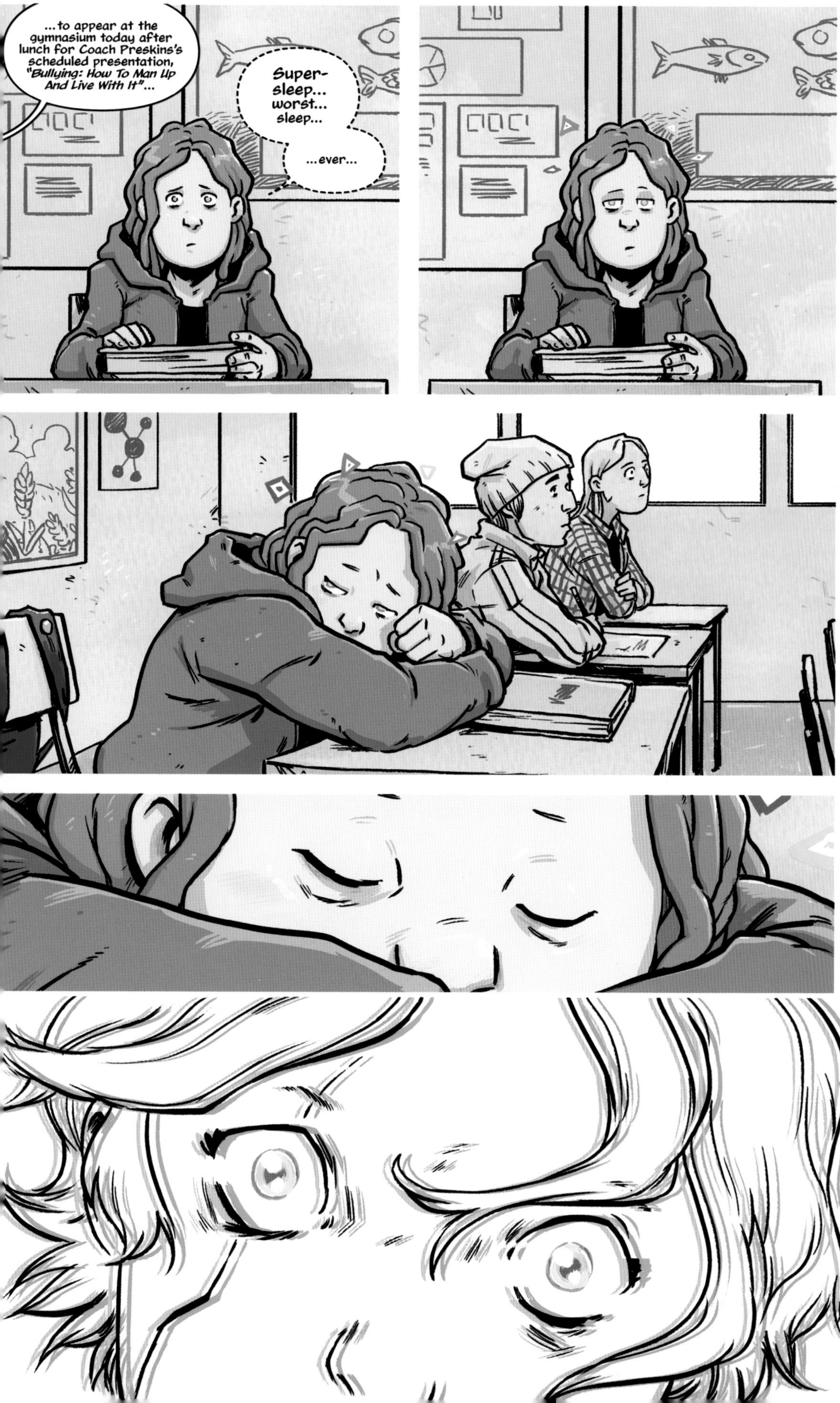
...to appear at the gymnasium today after lunch for Coach Preskins's scheduled presentation, *"Bullying: How To Man Up And Live With It"*...
Super-sleep... worst... sleep...
...ever...

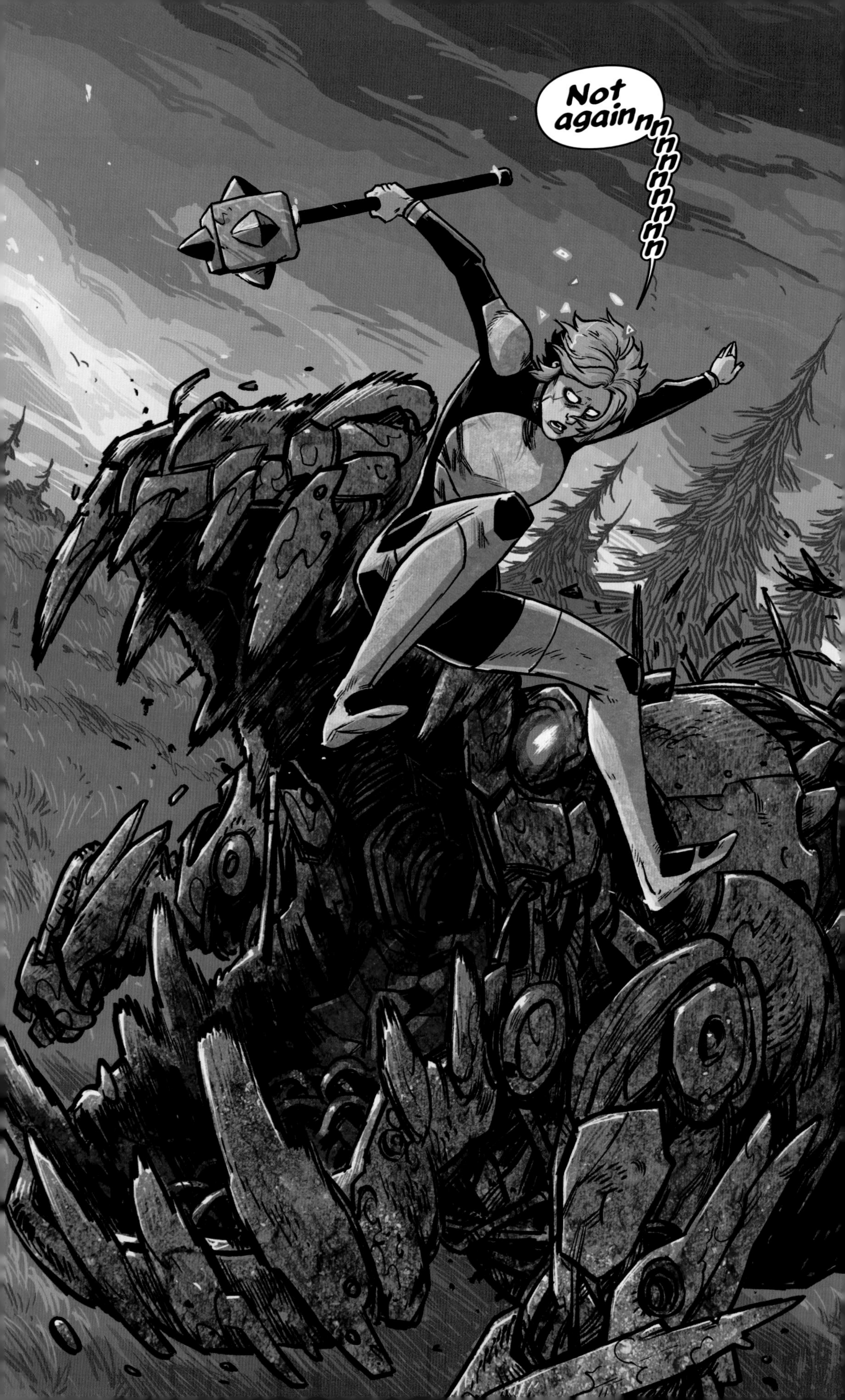
Not againnnnnnnnnn

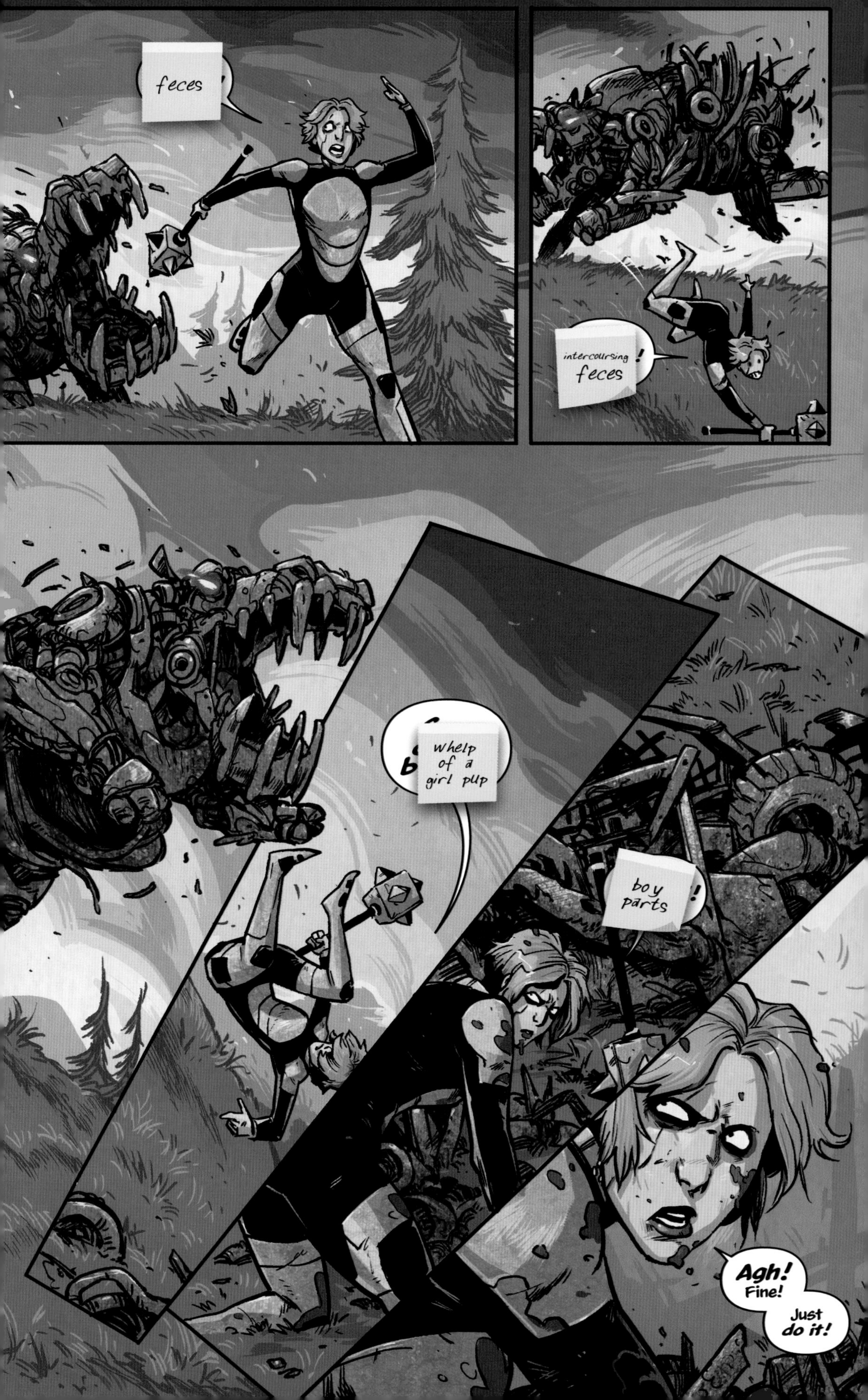

feces
intercoursing feces!
whelp of a girl pup
boy parts!
Agh! Fine!
Just do it!

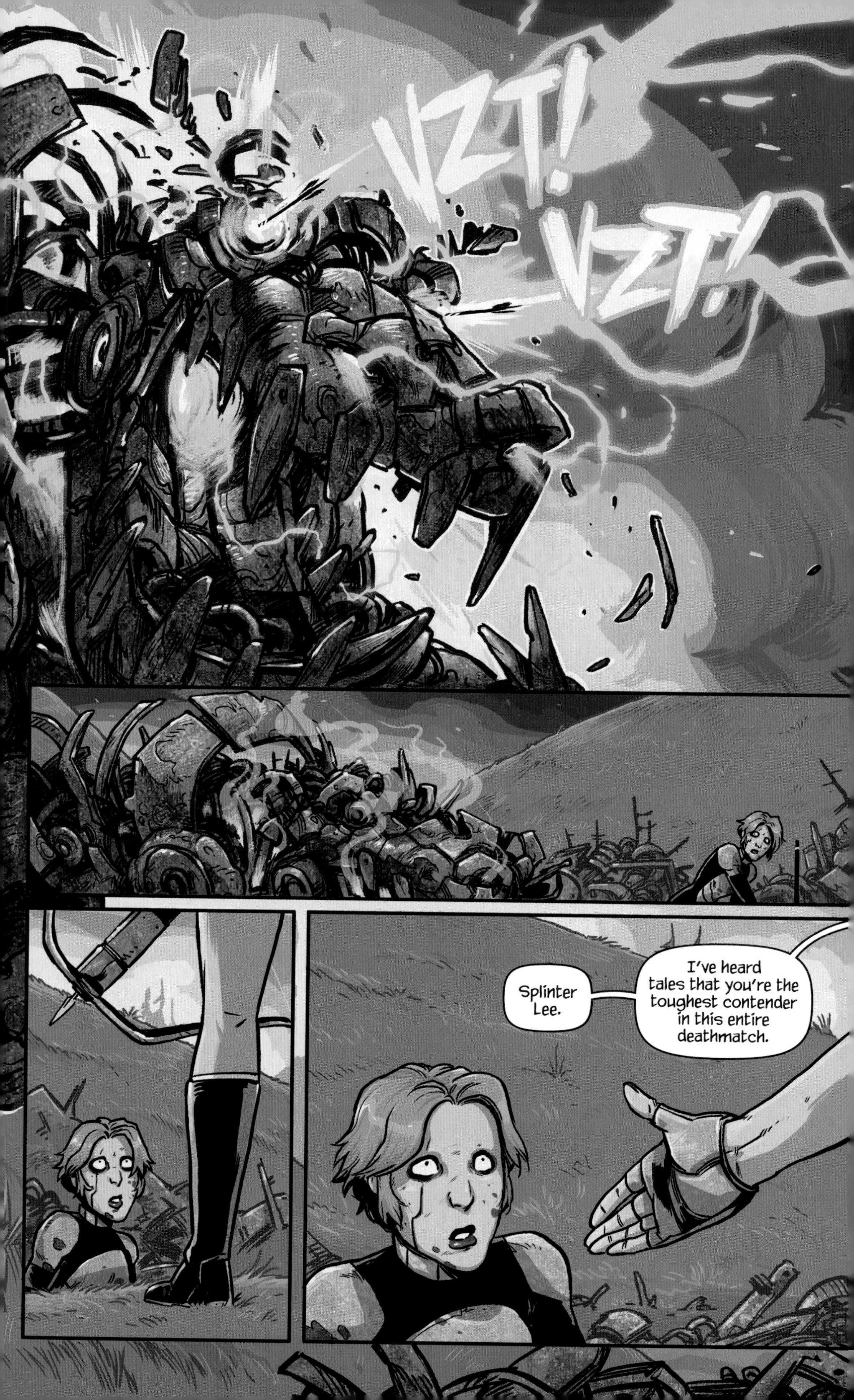
VZT!
VZT!
Splinter Lee.
I've heard tales that you're the toughest contender in this entire deathmatch.

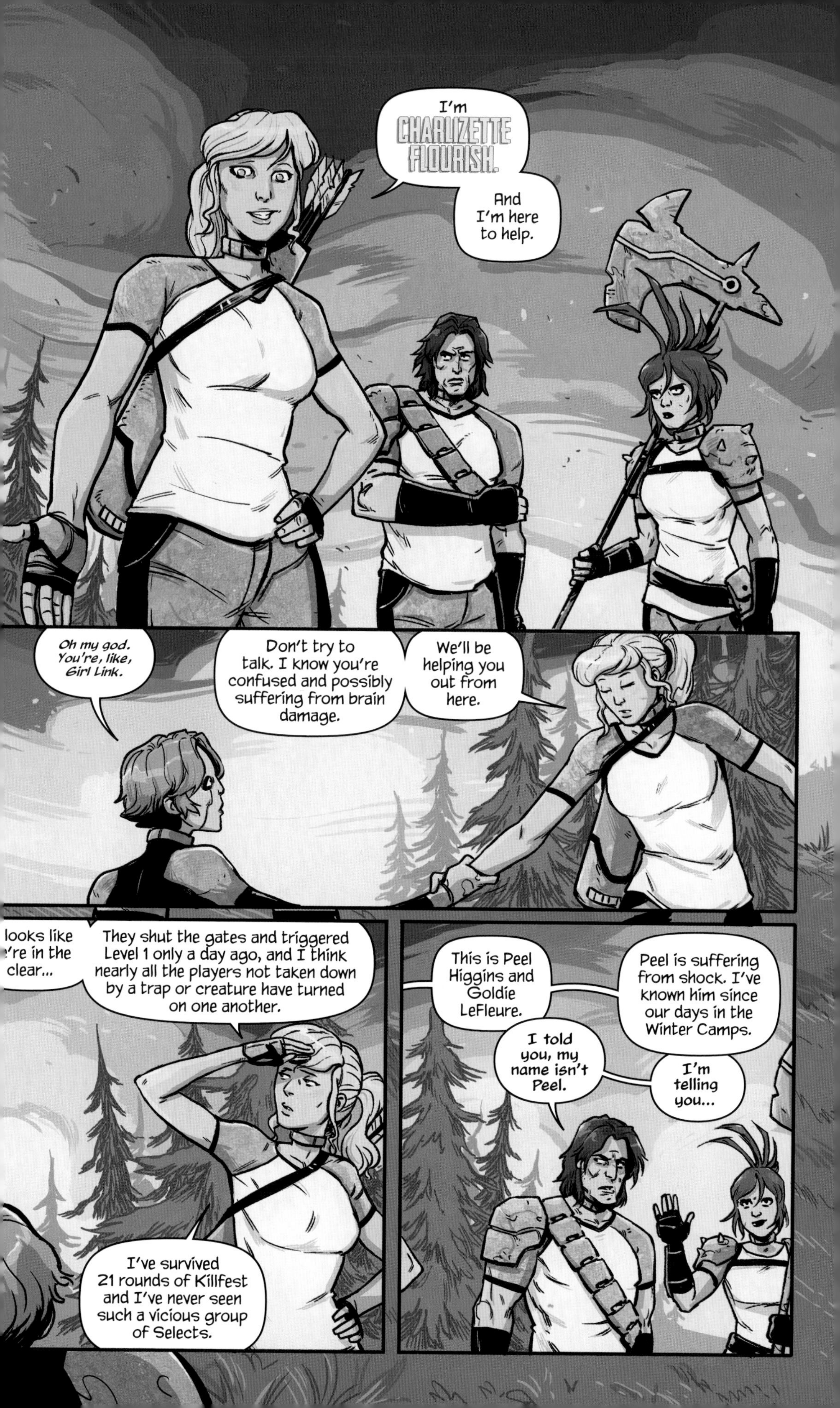
I'm CHARLIZETTE FLOURISH.
And I'm here to help.
Oh my god. You're, like, Girl Link.
Don't try to talk. I know you're confused and possibly suffering from brain damage.
We'll be helping you out from here.
looks like 're in the clear...
They shut the gates and triggered Level 1 only a day ago, and I think nearly all the players not taken down by a trap or creature have turned on one another.
I've survived 21 rounds of Killfest and I've never seen such a vicious group of Selects.
This is Peel Higgins and Goldie LeFleure.
Peel is suffering from shock. I've known him since our days in the Winter Camps.
I told you, my name isn't Peel.
I'm telling you...

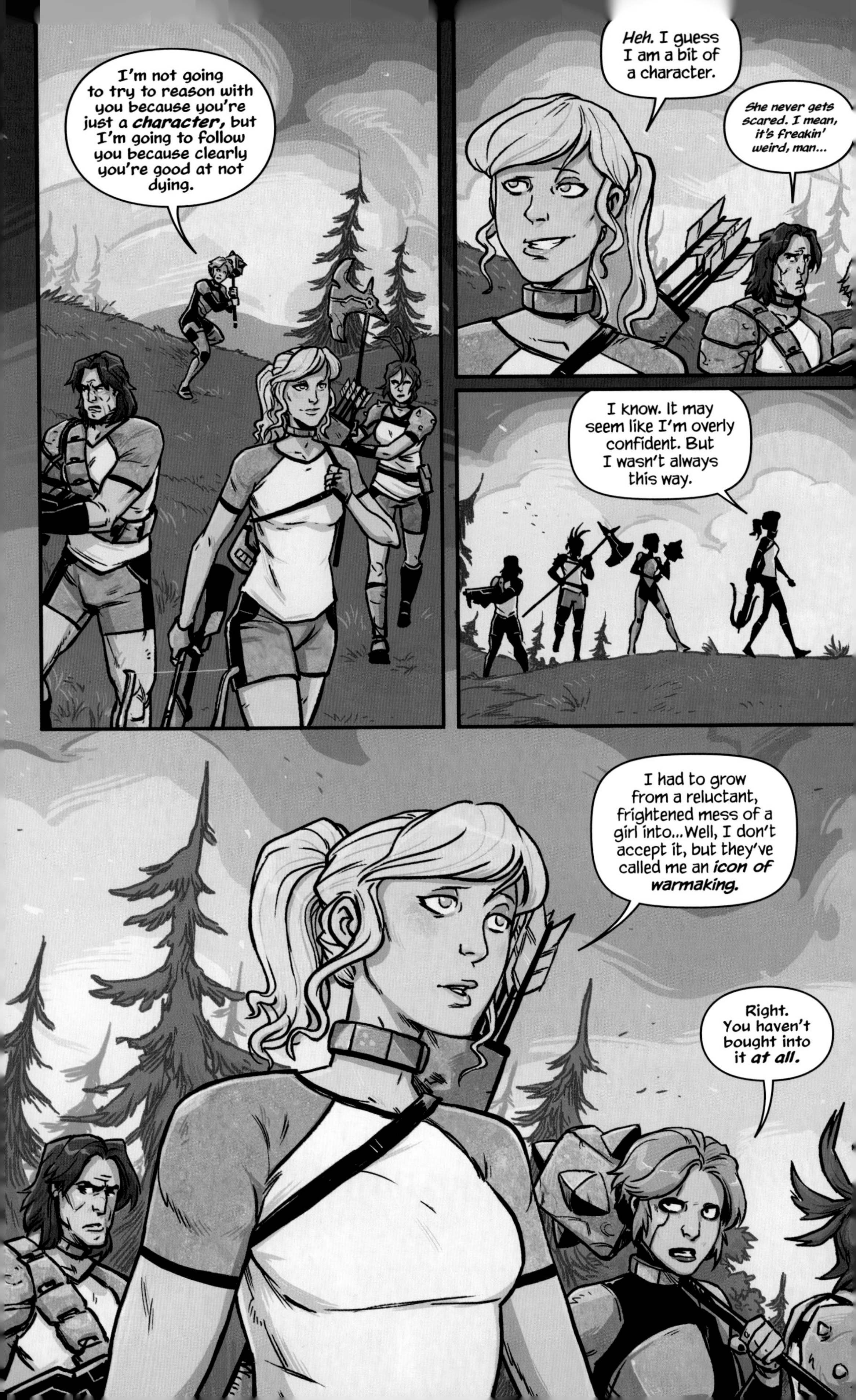
I'm not going to try to reason with you because you're just a *character,* but I'm going to follow you because clearly you're good at not dying.
Heh. I guess I am a bit of a character.
She never gets scared. I mean, it's freakin' weird, man...
I know. It may seem like I'm overly confident. But I wasn't always this way.
I had to grow from a reluctant, frightened mess of a girl into...Well, I don't accept it, but they've called me an *icon of warmaking.*
Right. You haven't bought into it *at all.*

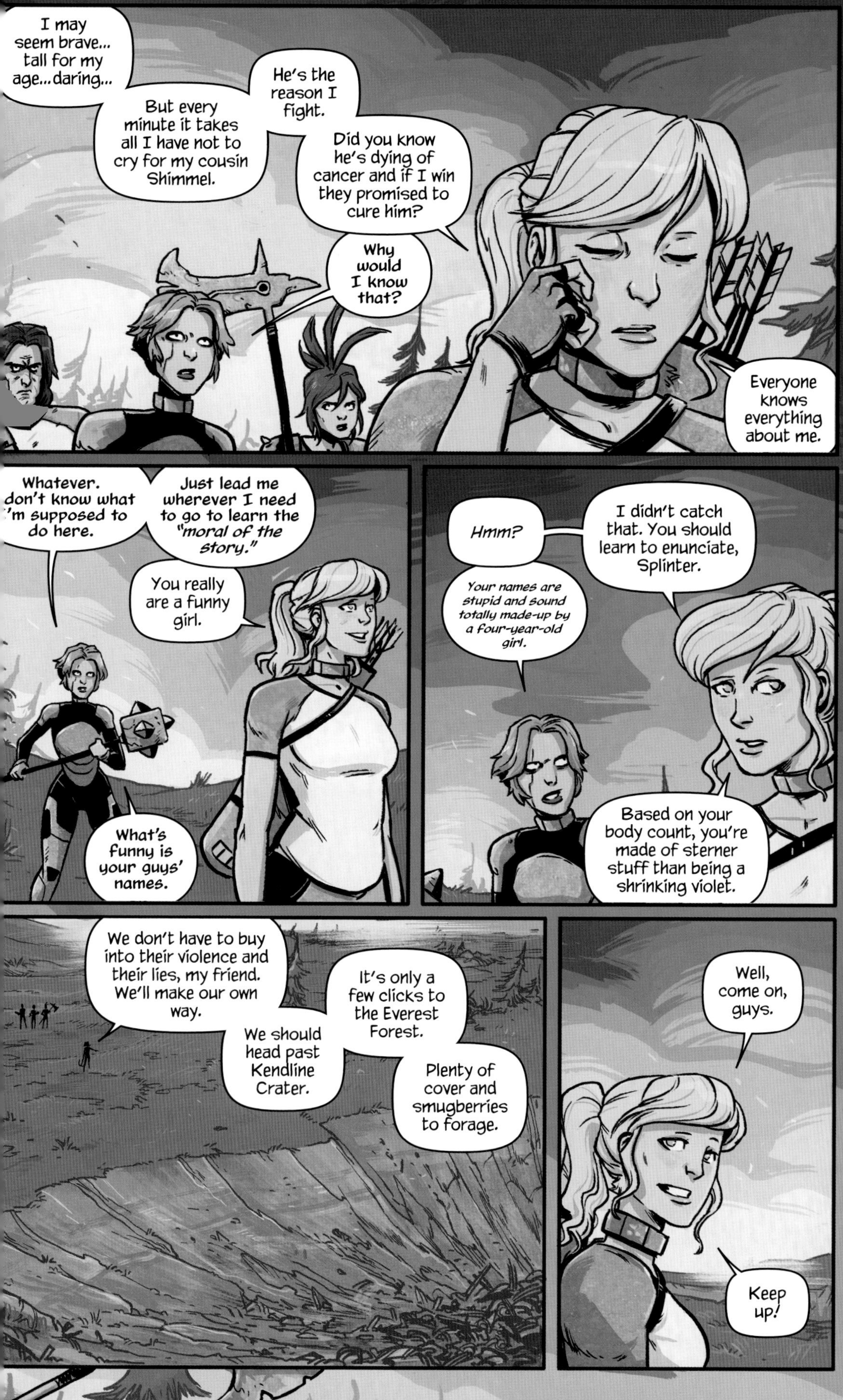

I may seem brave... tall for my age...daring...
But every minute it takes all I have not to cry for my cousin Shimmel.
He's the reason I fight.
Did you know he's dying of cancer and if I win they promised to cure him?
Why would I know that?
Everyone knows everything about me.
Whatever. don't know what 'm supposed to do here.
Just lead me wherever I need to go to learn the "moral of the story."
You really are a funny girl.
What's funny is your guys' names.
Hmm?
I didn't catch that. You should learn to enunciate, Splinter.
Your names are stupid and sound totally made-up by a four-year-old girl.
Based on your body count, you're made of sterner stuff than being a shrinking violet.
We don't have to buy into their violence and their lies, my friend. We'll make our own way.
It's only a few clicks to the Everest Forest.
We should head past Kendline Crater.
Plenty of cover and smugberries to forage.
Well, come on, guys.
Keep up!

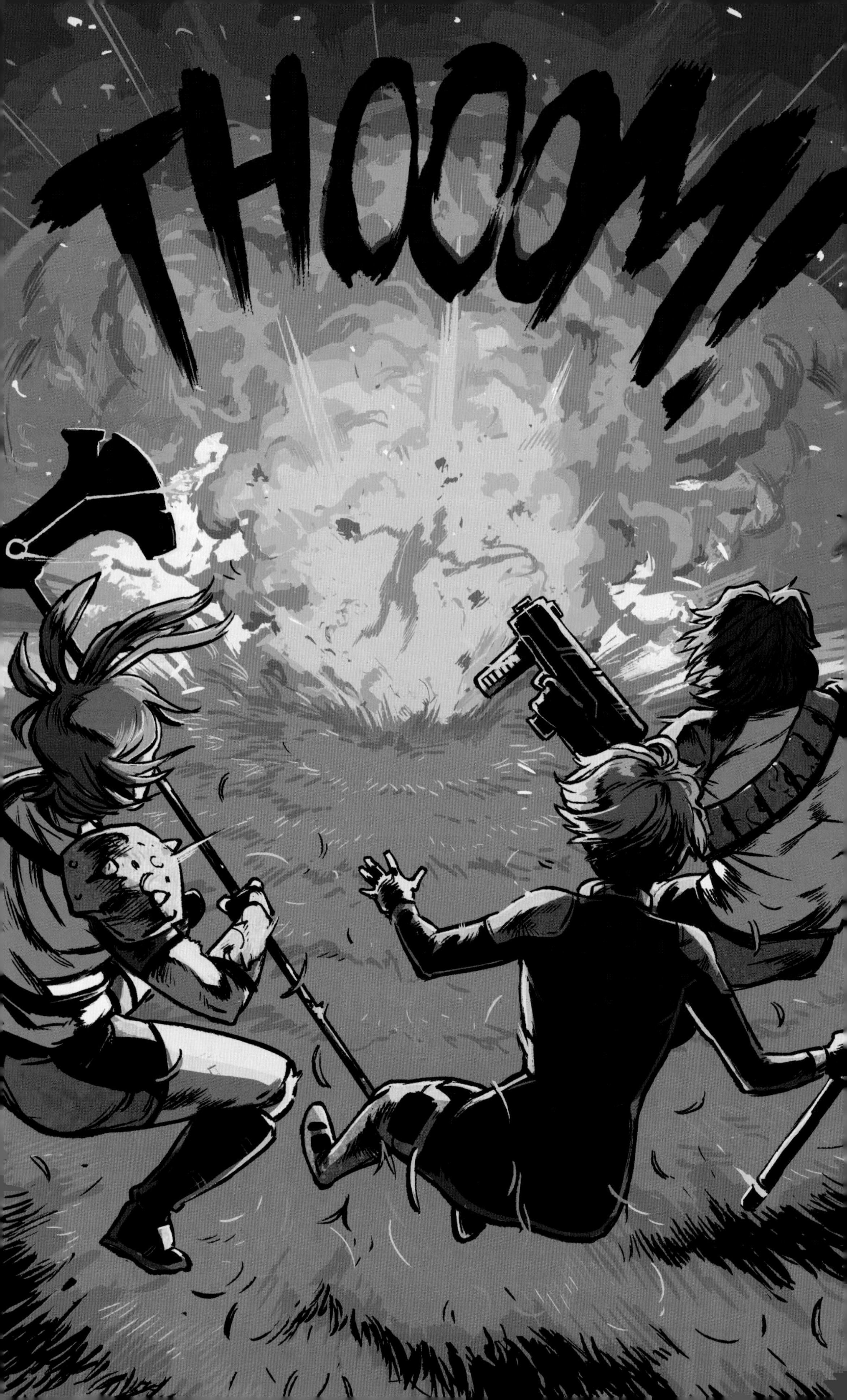
THOOOM!!

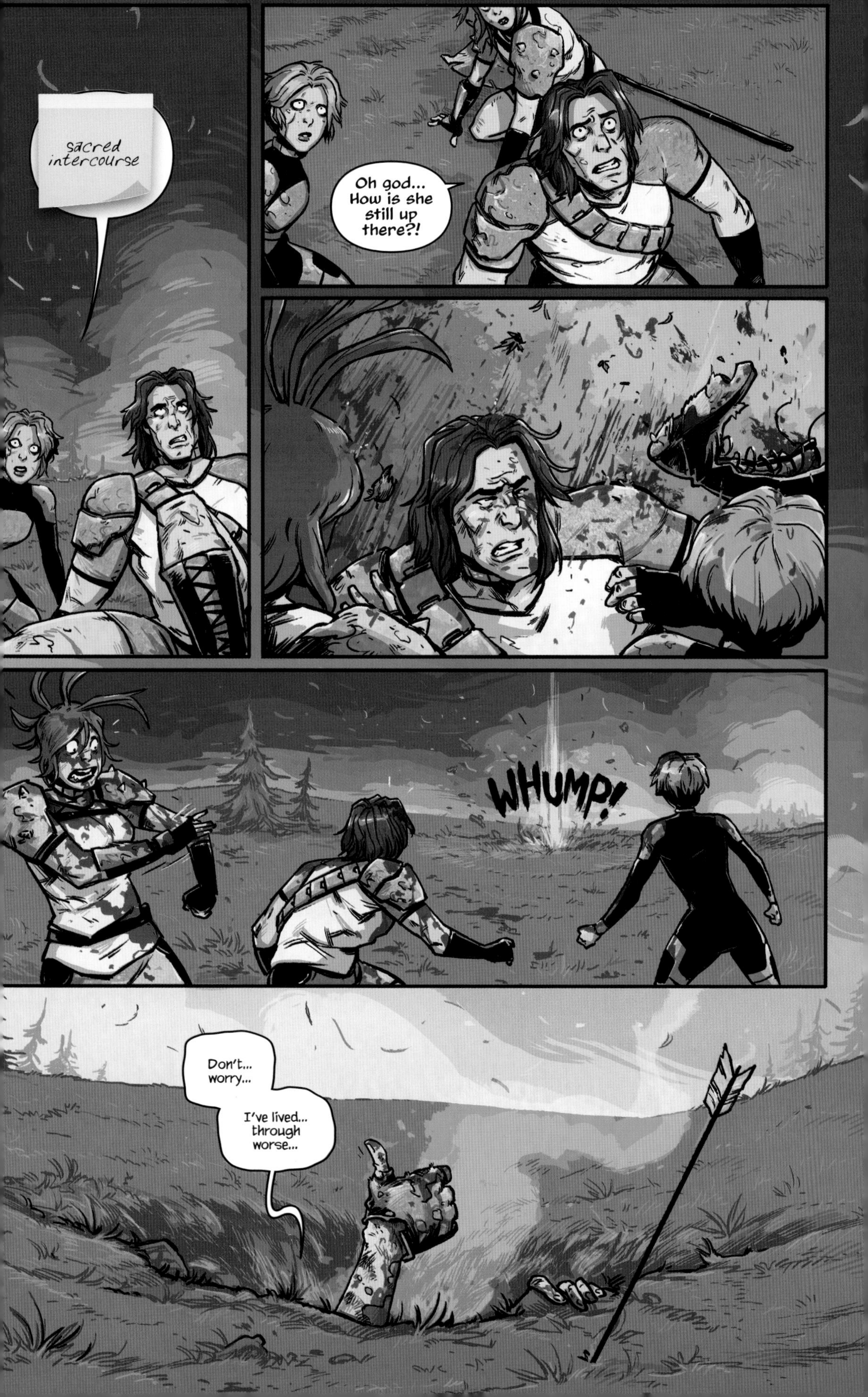
sacred intercourse
Oh god... How is she still up there?!
WHUMP!
Don't... worry...
I've lived... through worse...

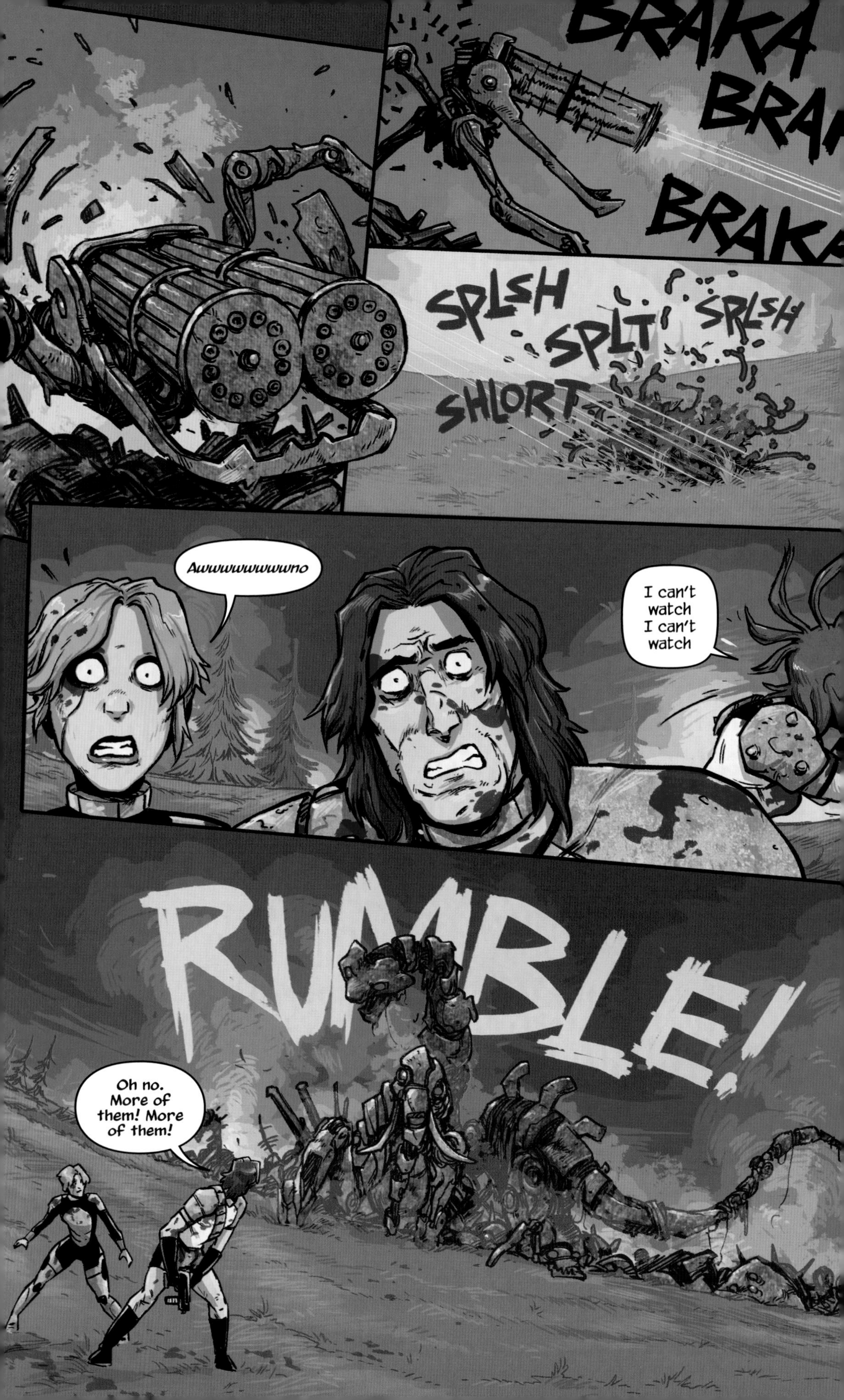
BRAKA
BRAK
BRAKA
SPLSH
SPLT
SPLSH
SHLORT
Awwwwwwwwno
I can't watch I can't watch
RUMBLE!
Oh no. More of them! More of them!

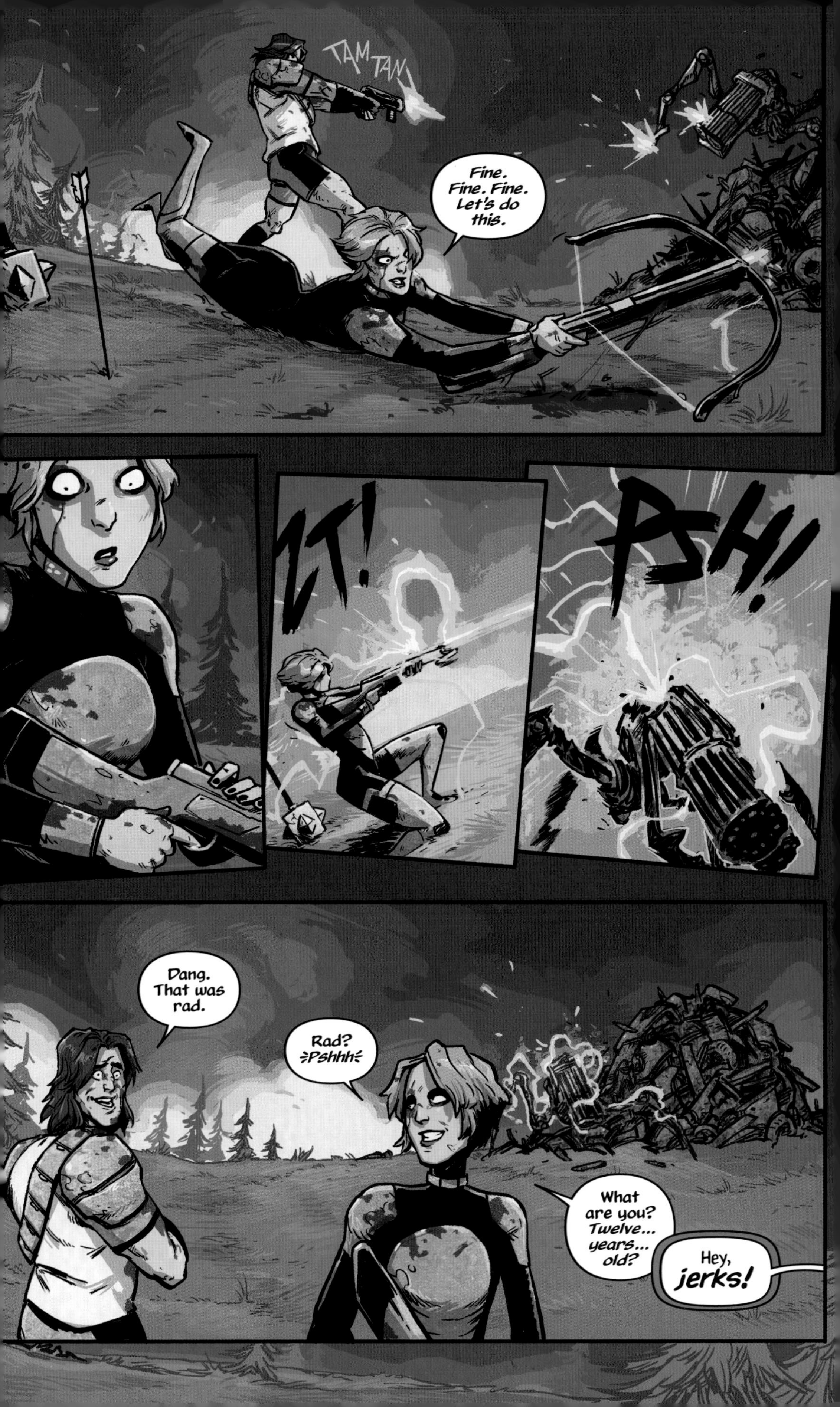
TAM TAN
Fine. Fine. Fine. Let's do this.
ZT!
PSH!
Dang. That was rad.
Rad? Pshhh
What are you? Twelve... years... old?
Hey, jerks!

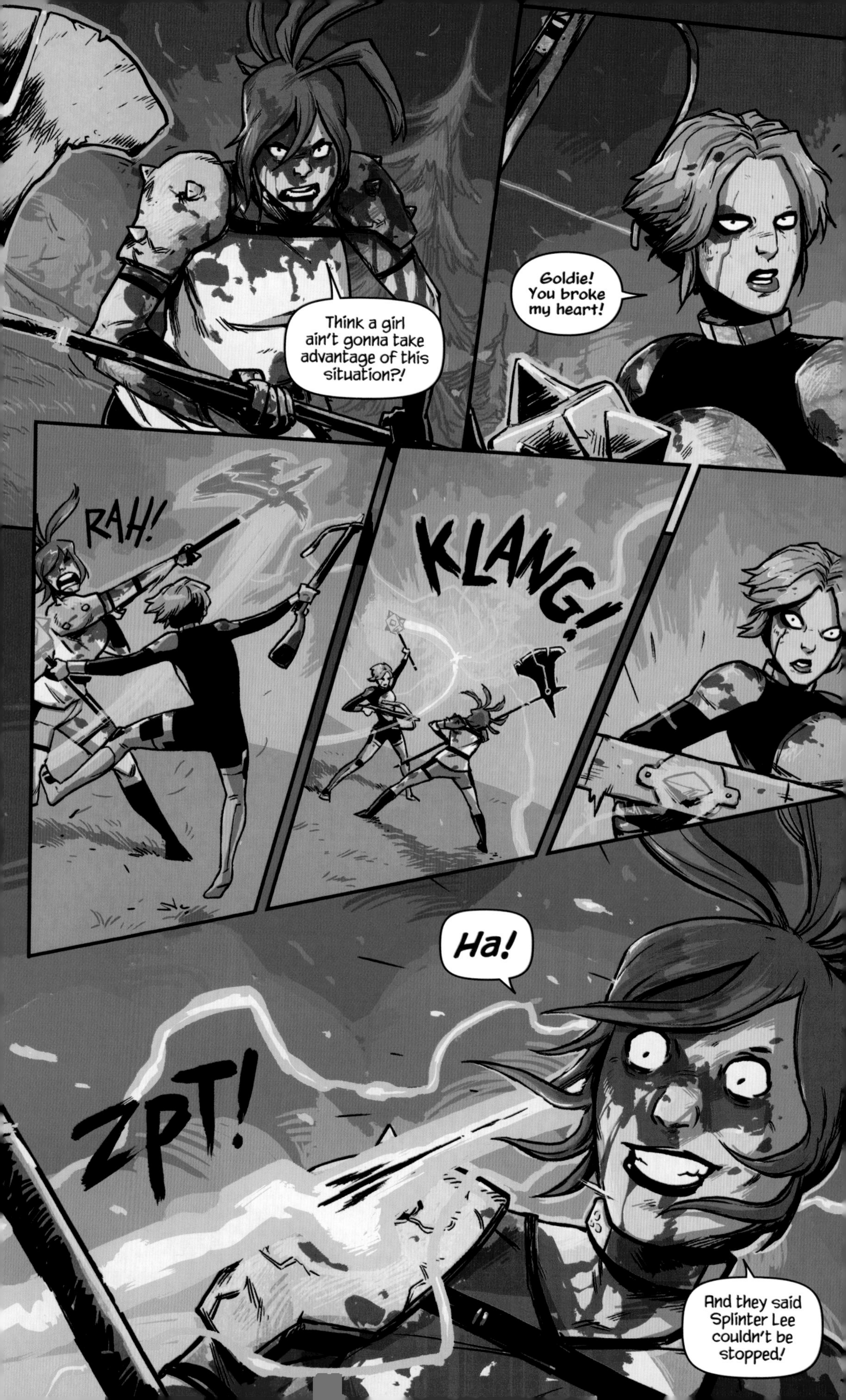
Think a girl ain't gonna take advantage of this situation?!
Goldie! You broke my heart!
RAH!
KLANG!
Ha!
ZPT!
And they said Splinter Lee couldn't be stopped!

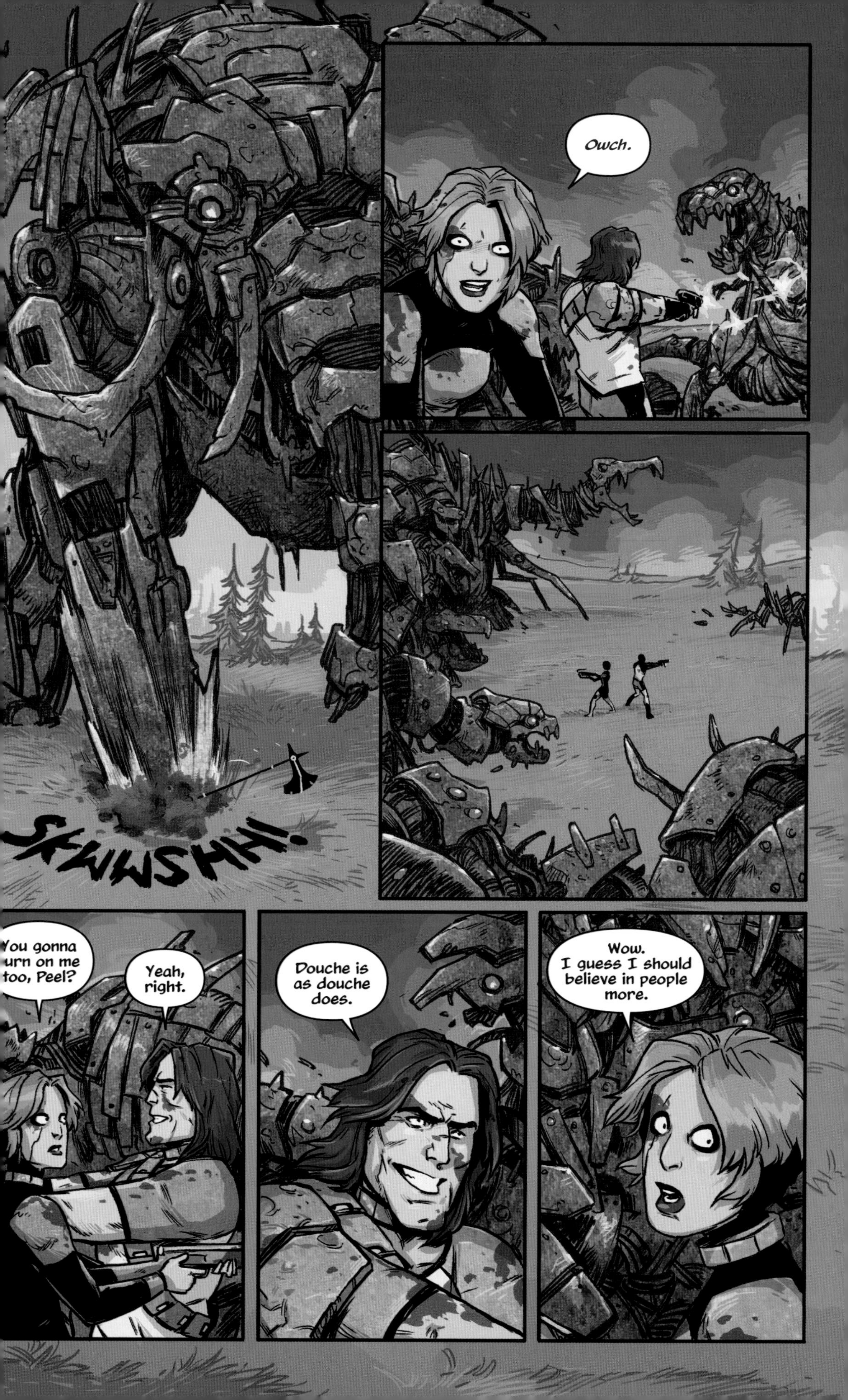
SKWWSHH!
Owch.
You gonna urn on me too, Peel?
Yeah, right.
Douche is as douche does.
Wow. I guess I should believe in people more.

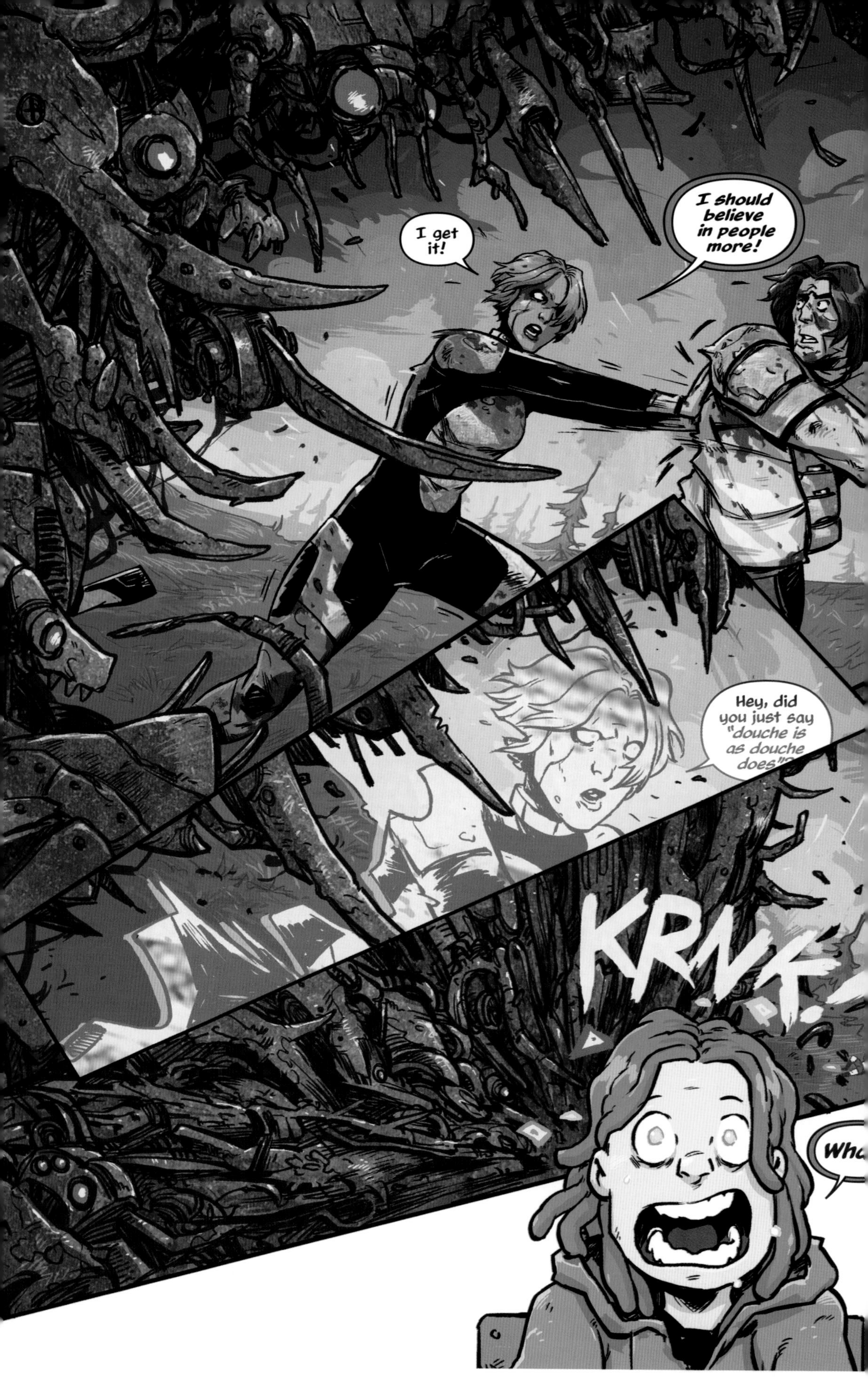
I get it!
I should believe in people more!
Hey, did you just say "douche is as douche does"
KRNK!
Wha

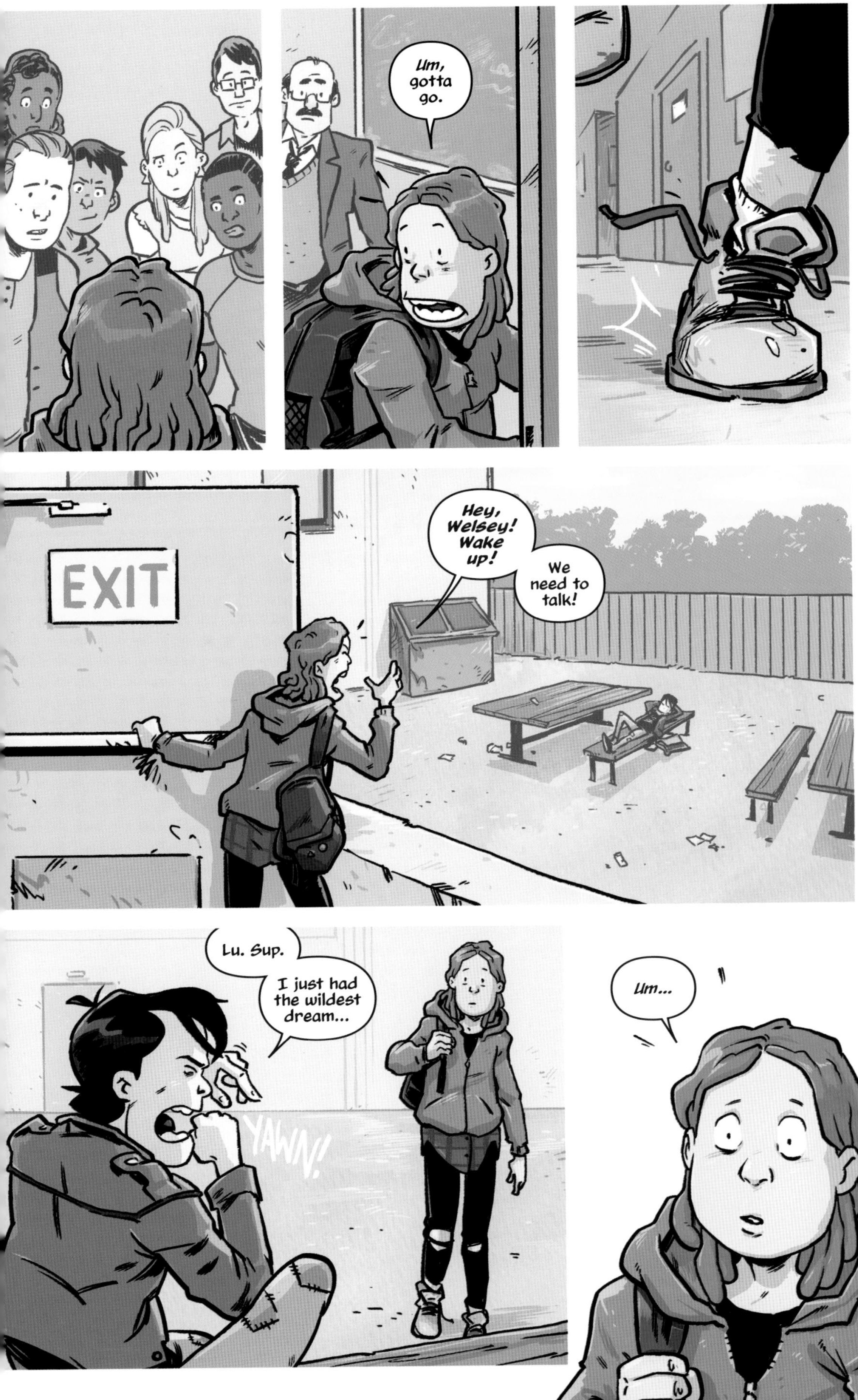

Um, gotta go.
EXIT
Hey, Welsey! Wake up!
We need to talk!
Lu. Sup.
I just had the wildest dream...
YAWN!
Um...

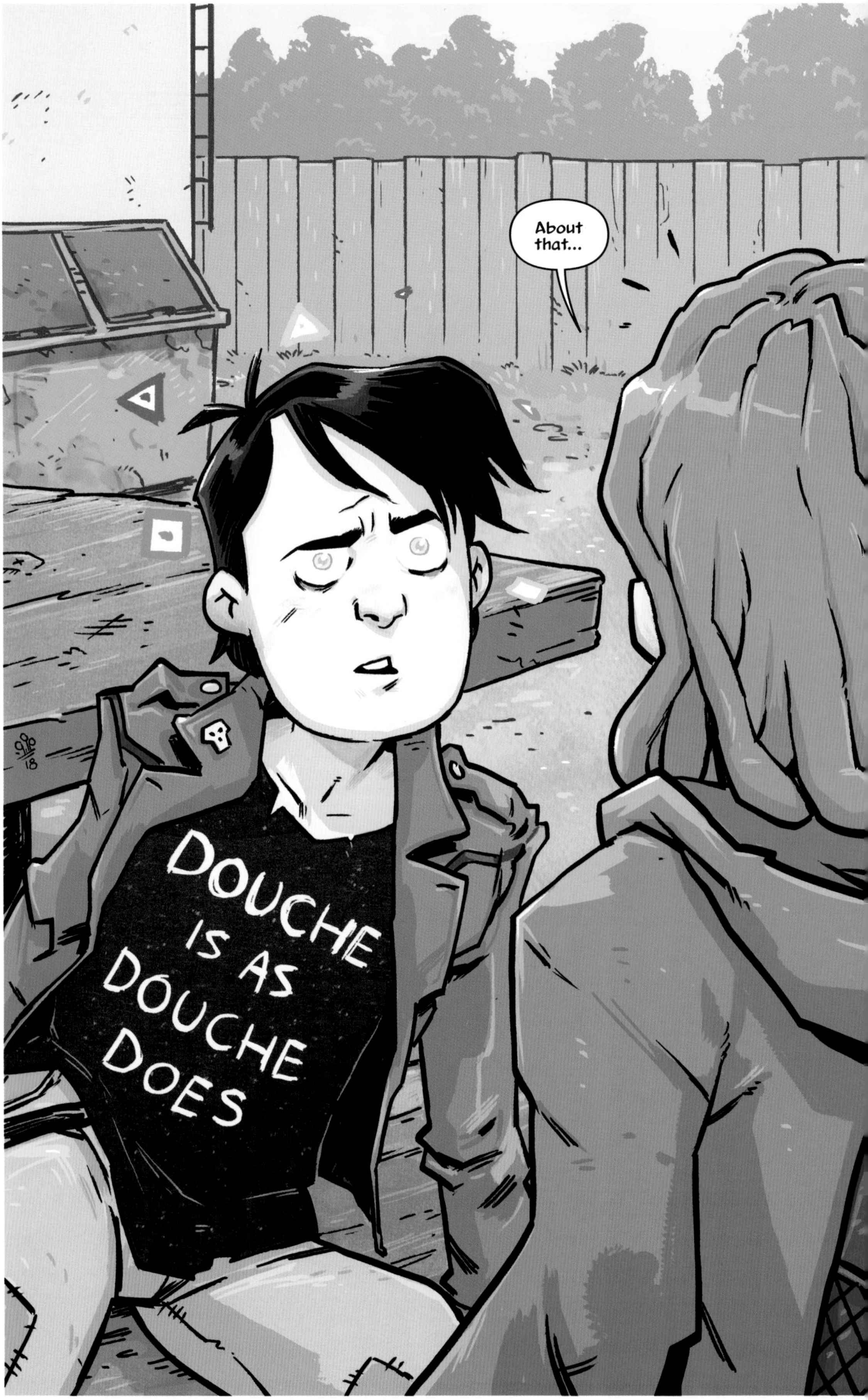
About that...
DOUCHE IS AS DOUCHE DOES

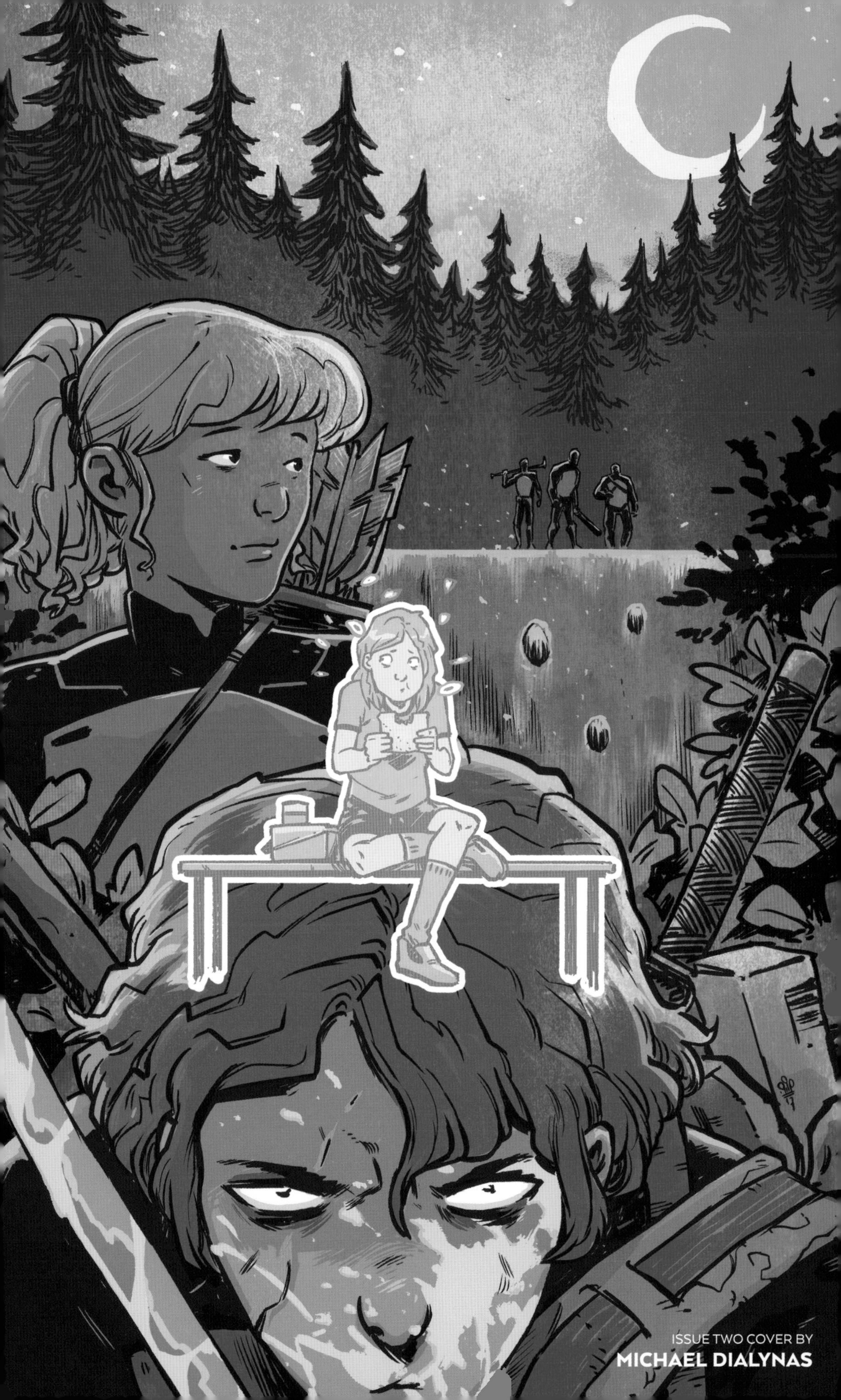

ISSUE TWO COVER BY
MICHAEL DIALYNAS

CHAPTER
THREE

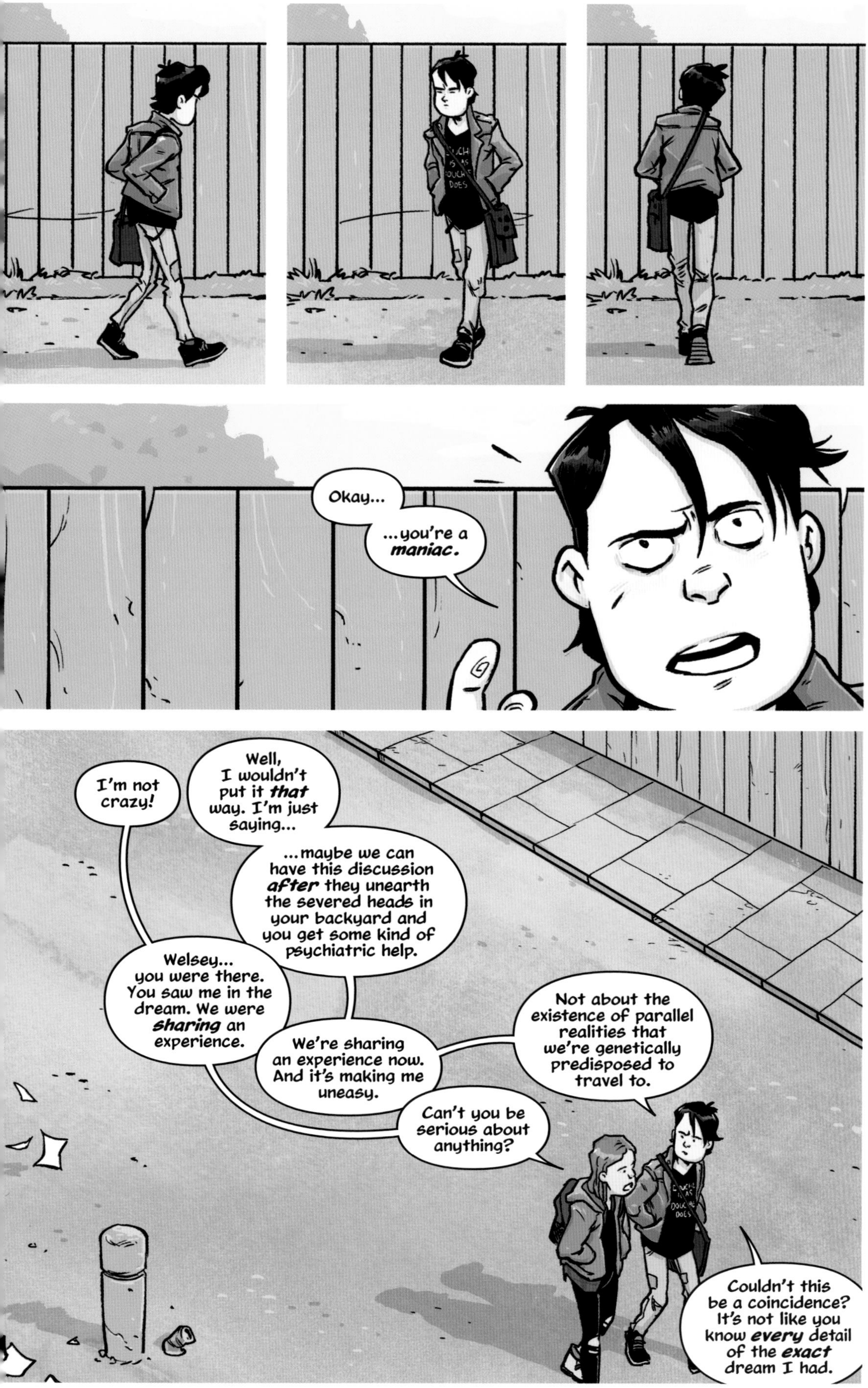
Okay...
...you're a *maniac.*
I'm not crazy!
Well, I wouldn't put it *that* way. I'm just saying...
...maybe we can have this discussion *after* they unearth the severed heads in your backyard and you get some kind of psychiatric help.
Welsey... you were there. You saw me in the dream. We were *sharing* an experience.
We're sharing an experience now. And it's making me uneasy.
Not about the existence of parallel realities that we're genetically predisposed to travel to.
Can't you be serious about anything?
Couldn't this be a coincidence? It's not like you know *every* detail of the *exact* dream I had.

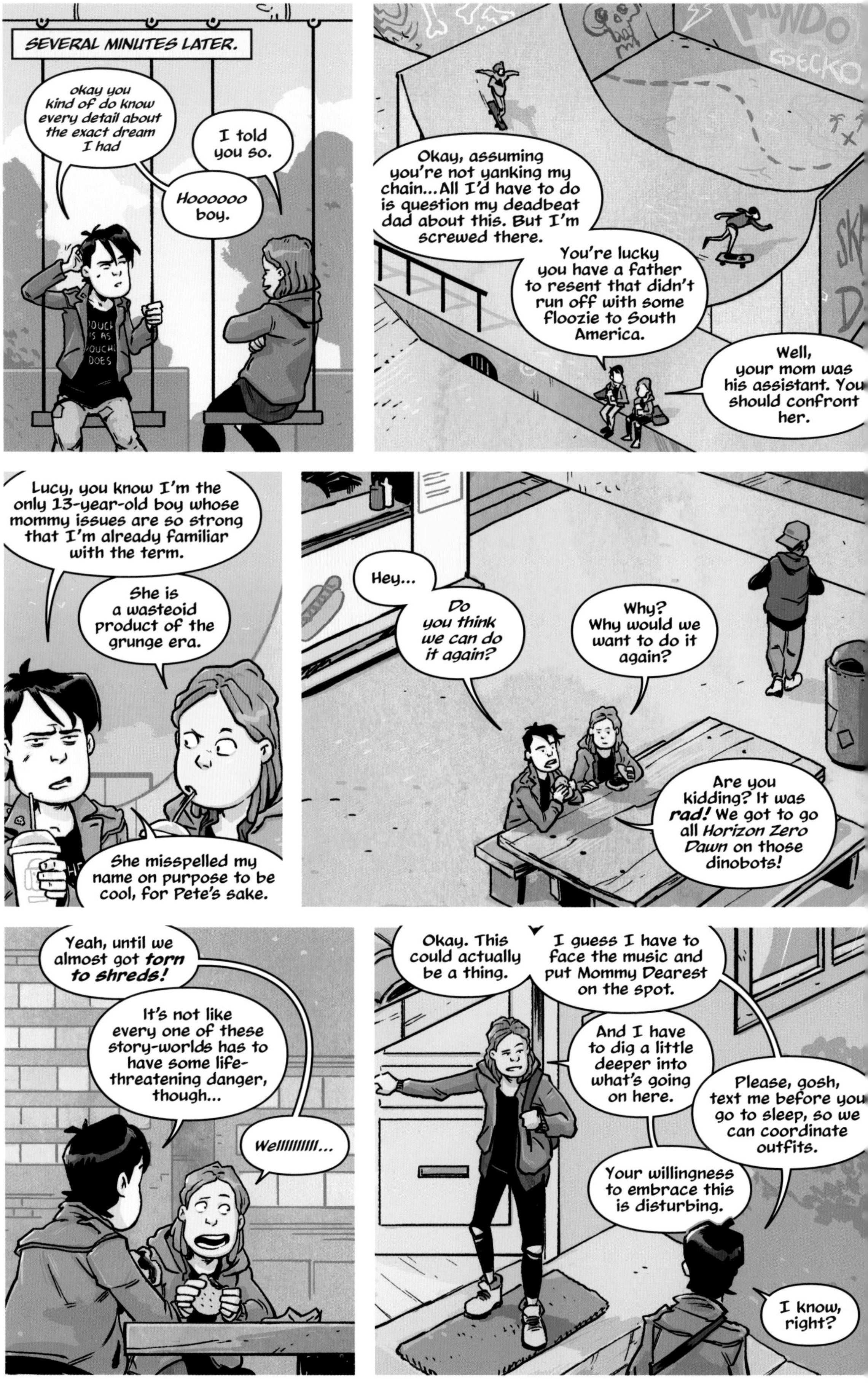
SEVERAL MINUTES LATER.
okay you kind of do know every detail about the exact dream I had
I told you so.
Hoooooo boy.
DOUCHE IS AS DOUCHE DOES
Okay, assuming you're not yanking my chain... All I'd have to do is question my deadbeat dad about this. But I'm screwed there.
You're lucky you have a father to resent that didn't run off with some floozie to South America.
Well, your mom was his assistant. You should confront her.
Lucy, you know I'm the only 13-year-old boy whose mommy issues are so strong that I'm already familiar with the term.
She is a wasteoid product of the grunge era.
She misspelled my name on purpose to be cool, for Pete's sake.
Hey...
Do you think we can do it again?
Why? Why would we want to do it again?
Are you kidding? It was rad! We got to go all Horizon Zero Dawn on those dinobots!
Yeah, until we almost got torn to shreds!
It's not like every one of these story-worlds has to have some life-threatening danger, though...
Wellllllllll...
Okay. This could actually be a thing.
I guess I have to face the music and put Mommy Dearest on the spot.
And I have to dig a little deeper into what's going on here.
Please, gosh, text me before you go to sleep, so we can coordinate outfits.
Your willingness to embrace this is disturbing.
I know, right?

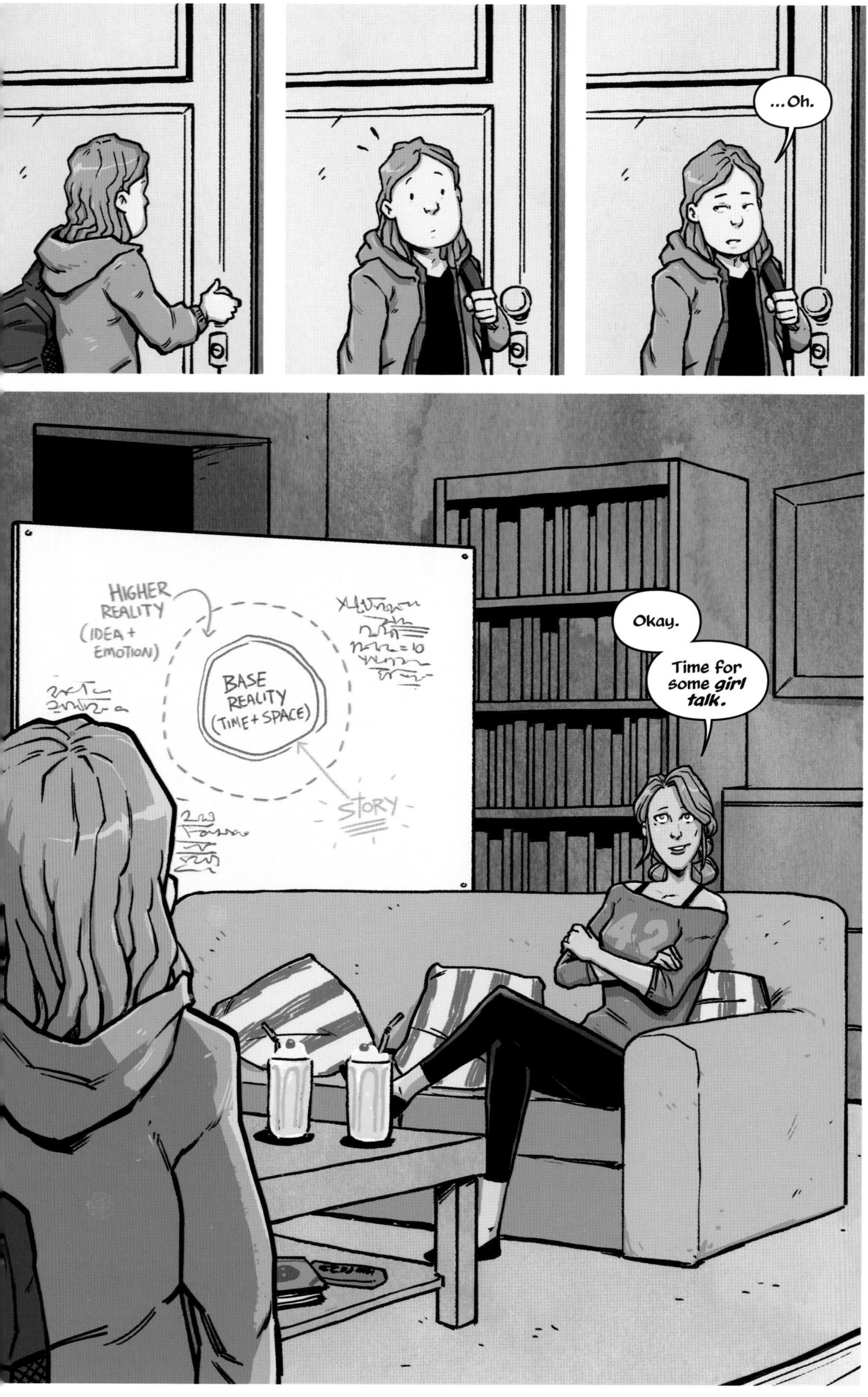
...Oh.
HIGHER REALITY (IDEA + EMOTION)
BASE REALITY (TIME + SPACE)
STORY
Okay.
Time for some *girl* *talk.*

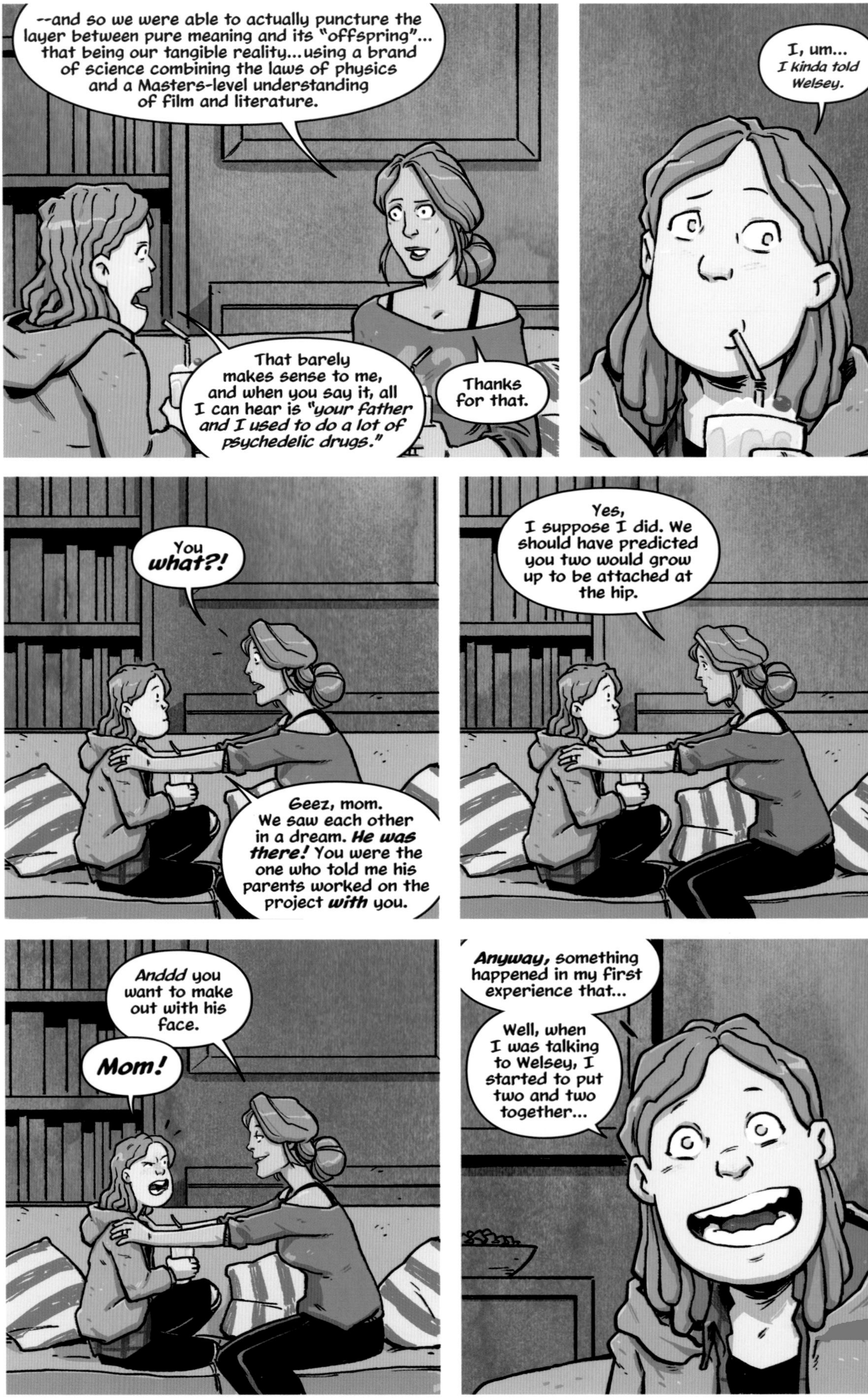
--and so we were able to actually puncture the layer between pure meaning and its "offspring"... that being our tangible reality...using a brand of science combining the laws of physics and a Masters-level understanding of film and literature.
That barely makes sense to me, and when you say it, all I can hear is "your father and I used to do a lot of psychedelic drugs."
Thanks for that.
I, um... I kinda told Welsey.
You what?!
Geez, mom. We saw each other in a dream. He was there! You were the one who told me his parents worked on the project with you.
Yes, I suppose I did. We should have predicted you two would grow up to be attached at the hip.
Anddd you want to make out with his face.
Mom!
Anyway, something happened in my first experience that...
Well, when I was talking to Welsey, I started to put two and two together...

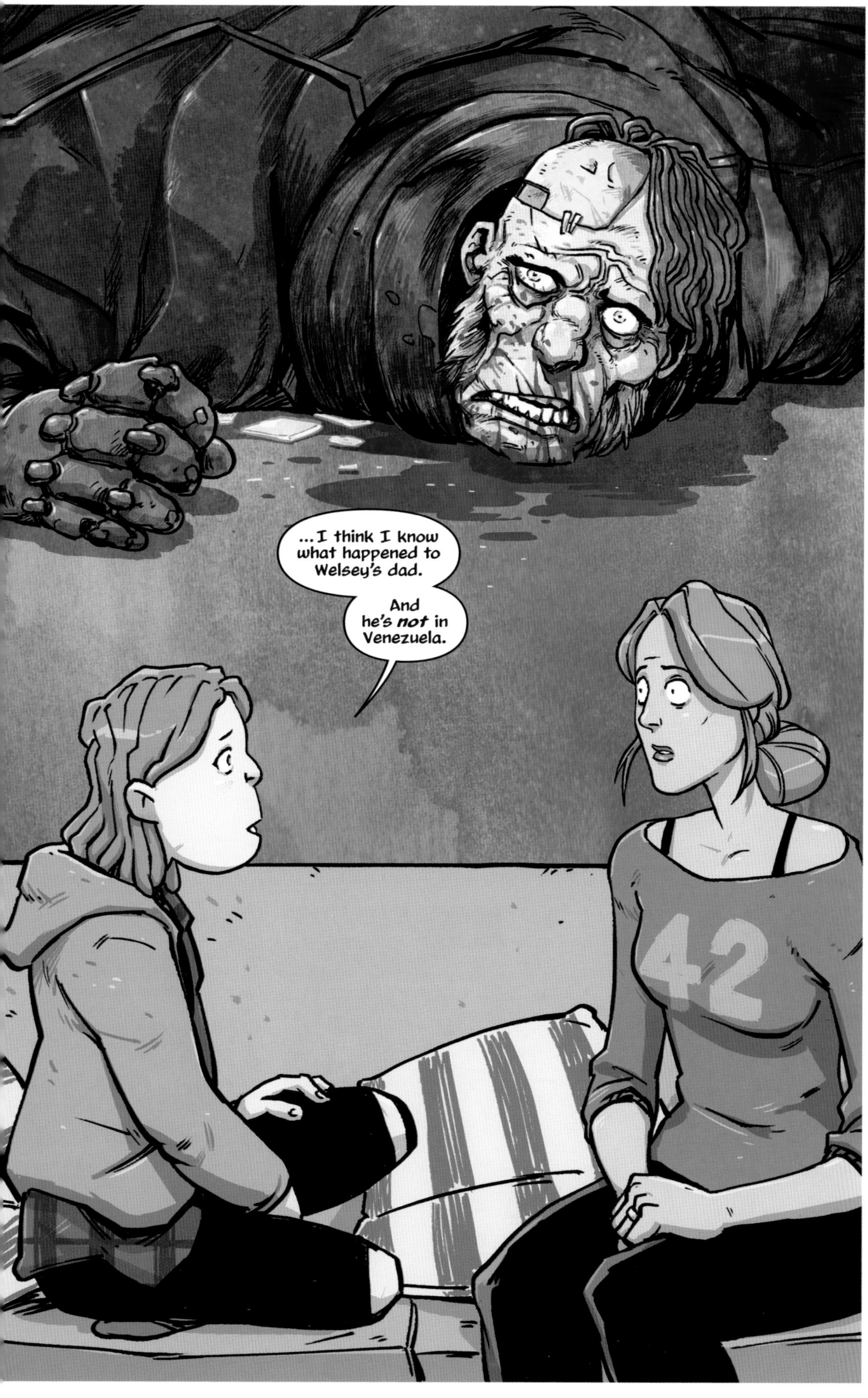
...I think I know what happened to Welsey's dad.
And he's *not* in Venezuela.

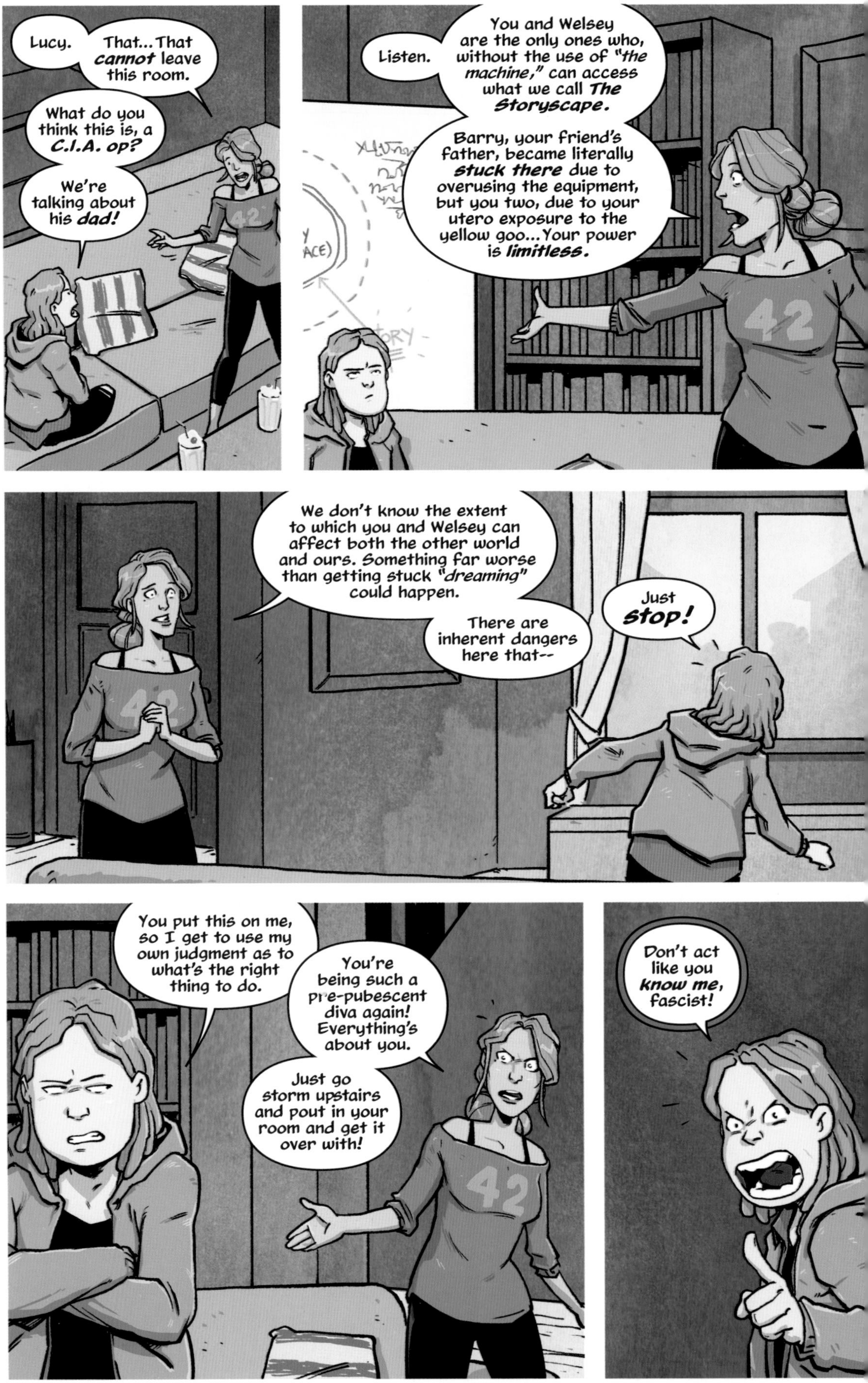
Lucy.
That... That *cannot* leave this room.
What do you think this is, a ***C.I.A. op?***
We're talking about his ***dad!***
Listen.
You and Welsey are the only ones who, without the use of *"the machine,"* can access what we call ***The Storyscape.***
Barry, your friend's father, became literally ***stuck there*** due to overusing the equipment, but you two, due to your utero exposure to the yellow goo... Your power is ***limitless.***
We don't know the extent to which you and Welsey can affect both the other world and ours. Something far worse than getting stuck *"dreaming"* could happen.
There are inherent dangers here that--
Just ***stop!***
You put this on me, so I get to use my own judgment as to what's the right thing to do.
You're being such a pre-pubescent diva again! Everything's about you.
Just go storm upstairs and pout in your room and get it over with!
Don't act like you ***know me***, fascist!

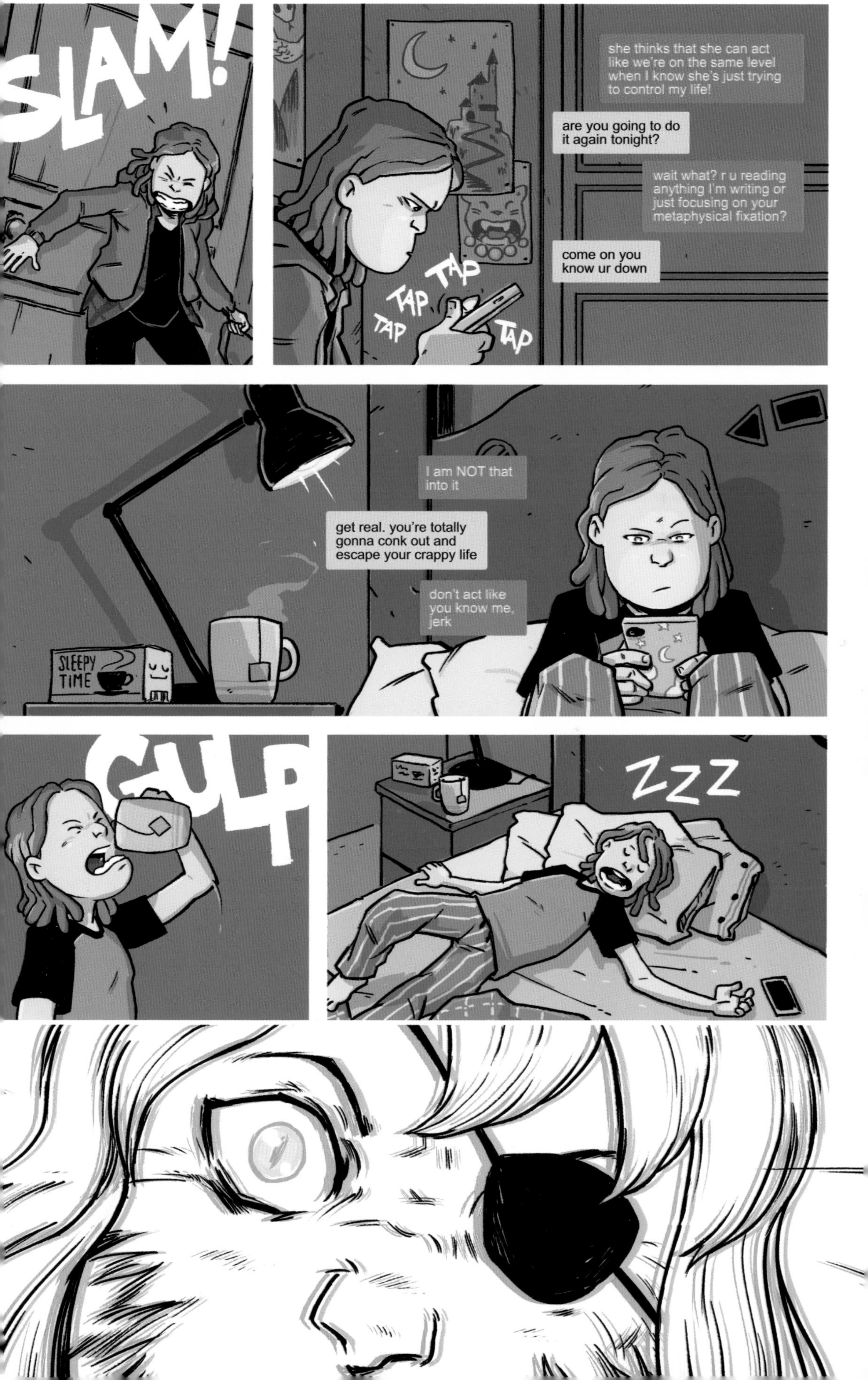
SLAM!
she thinks that she can act like we're on the same level when I know she's just trying to control my life!
are you going to do it again tonight?
wait what? r u reading anything I'm writing or just focusing on your metaphysical fixation?
come on you know ur down
TAP TAP TAP TAP
I am NOT that into it
get real. you're totally gonna conk out and escape your crappy life
don't act like you know me, jerk
SLEEPY TIME
GULP
ZZZ

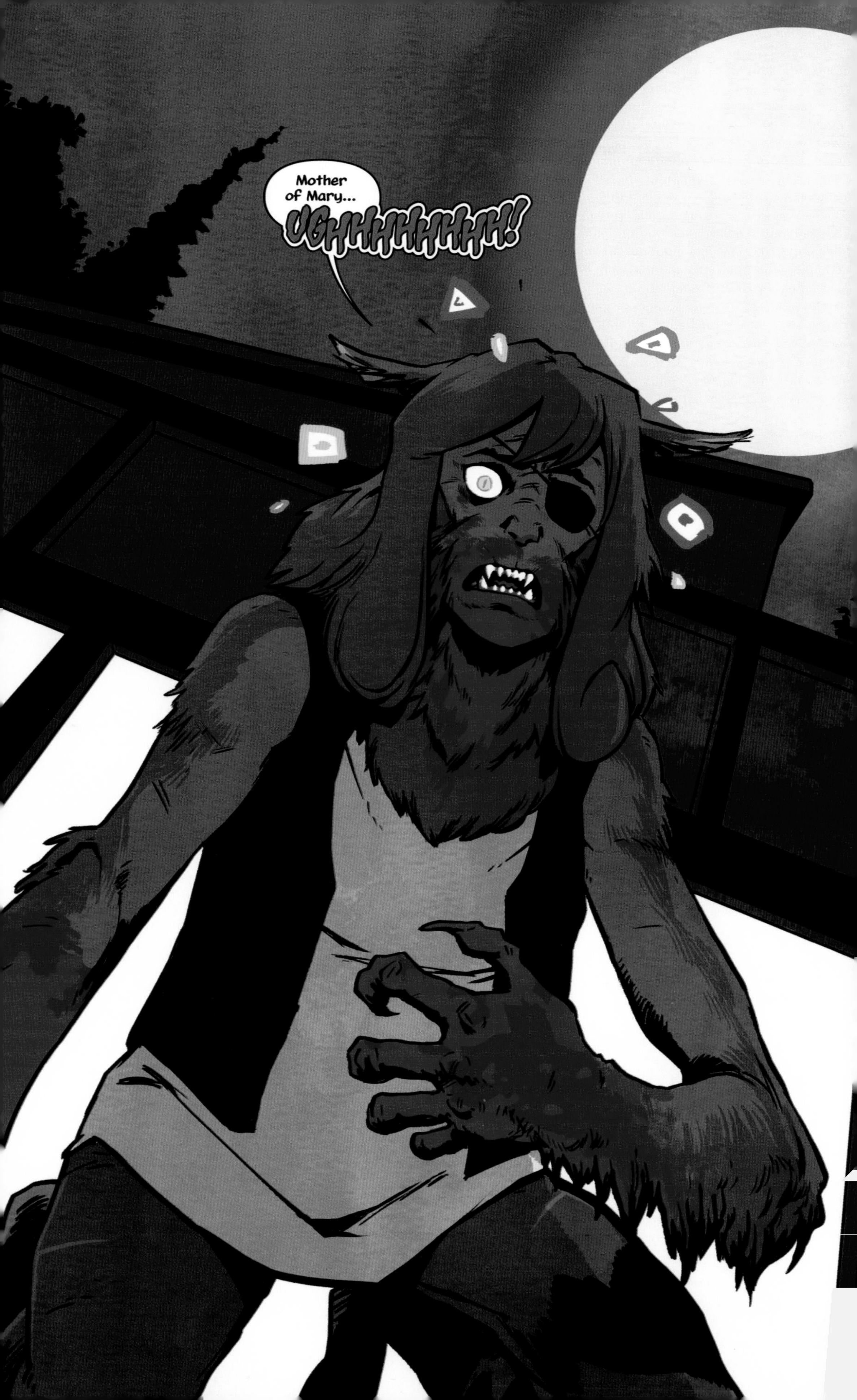
Mother of Mary...
UGHHHHHHHHH!

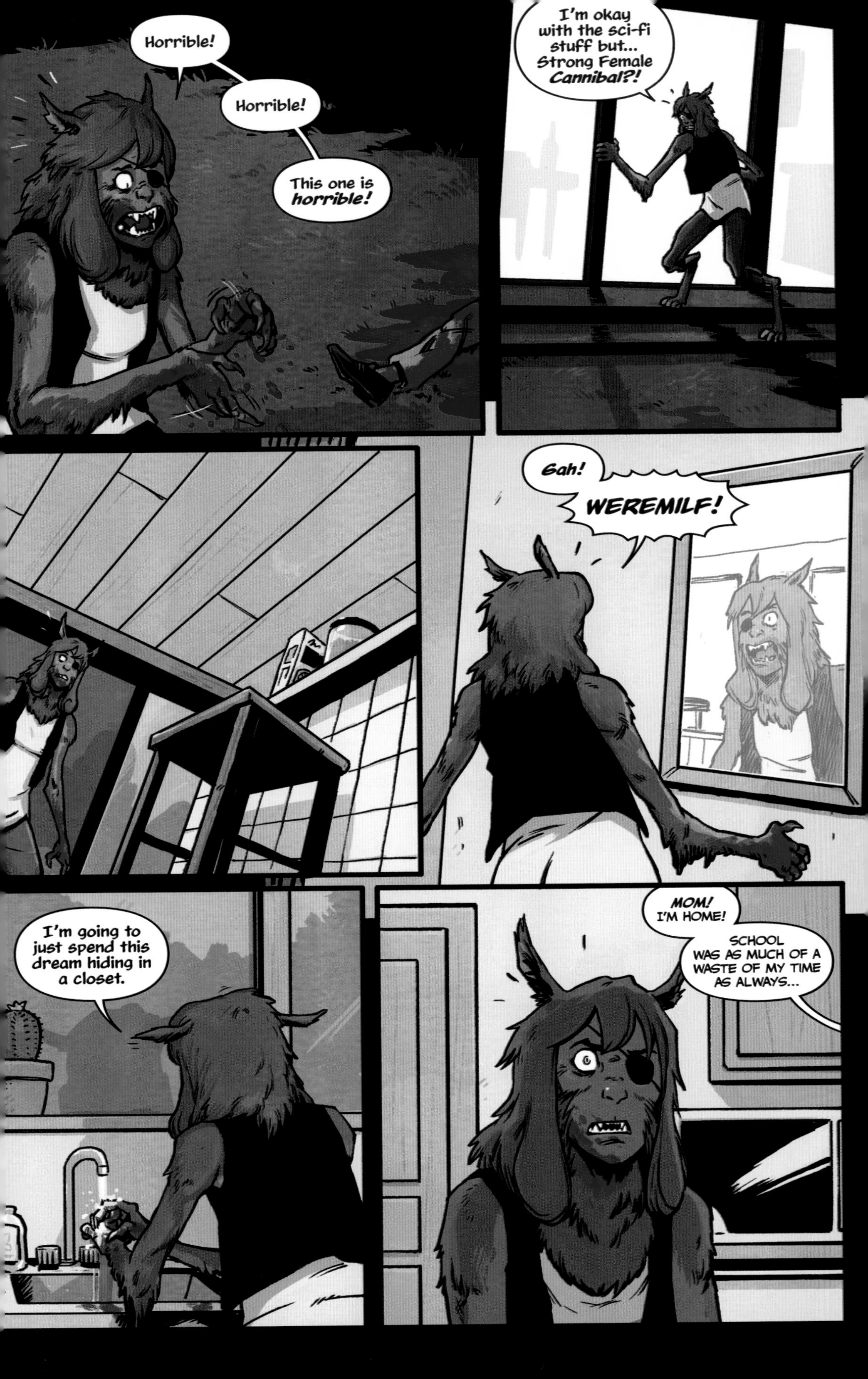
Horrible!
Horrible!
This one is *horrible!*
I'm okay with the sci-fi stuff but... Strong Female *Cannibal?!*
Gah!
WEREMILF!
I'm going to just spend this dream hiding in a closet.
MOM! I'M HOME!
SCHOOL WAS AS MUCH OF A WASTE OF MY TIME AS ALWAYS...

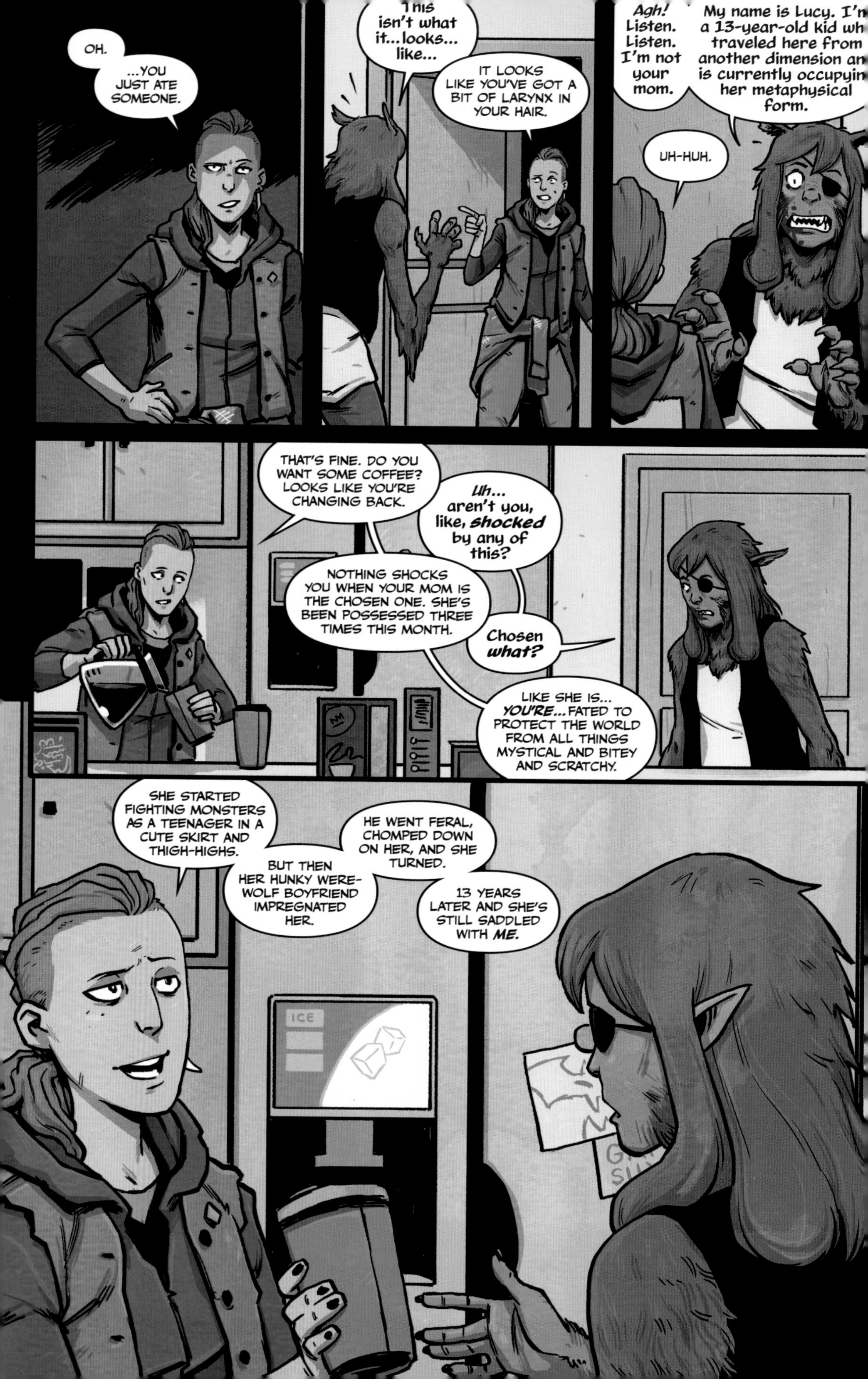
OH.
...YOU JUST ATE SOMEONE.
This isn't what it...looks... like...
IT LOOKS LIKE YOU'VE GOT A BIT OF LARYNX IN YOUR HAIR.
Agh! Listen. Listen. I'm not your mom.
My name is Lucy. I'm a 13-year-old kid who traveled here from another dimension and is currently occupying her metaphysical form.
UH-HUH.
THAT'S FINE. DO YOU WANT SOME COFFEE? LOOKS LIKE YOU'RE CHANGING BACK.
Uh... aren't you, like, shocked by any of this?
NOTHING SHOCKS YOU WHEN YOUR MOM IS THE CHOSEN ONE. SHE'S BEEN POSSESSED THREE TIMES THIS MONTH.
Chosen what?
LIKE SHE IS... YOU'RE... FATED TO PROTECT THE WORLD FROM ALL THINGS MYSTICAL AND BITEY AND SCRATCHY.
SHE STARTED FIGHTING MONSTERS AS A TEENAGER IN A CUTE SKIRT AND THIGH-HIGHS.
BUT THEN HER HUNKY WERE-WOLF BOYFRIEND IMPREGNATED HER.
HE WENT FERAL, CHOMPED DOWN ON HER, AND SHE TURNED.
13 YEARS LATER AND SHE'S STILL SADDLED WITH ME.
ICE

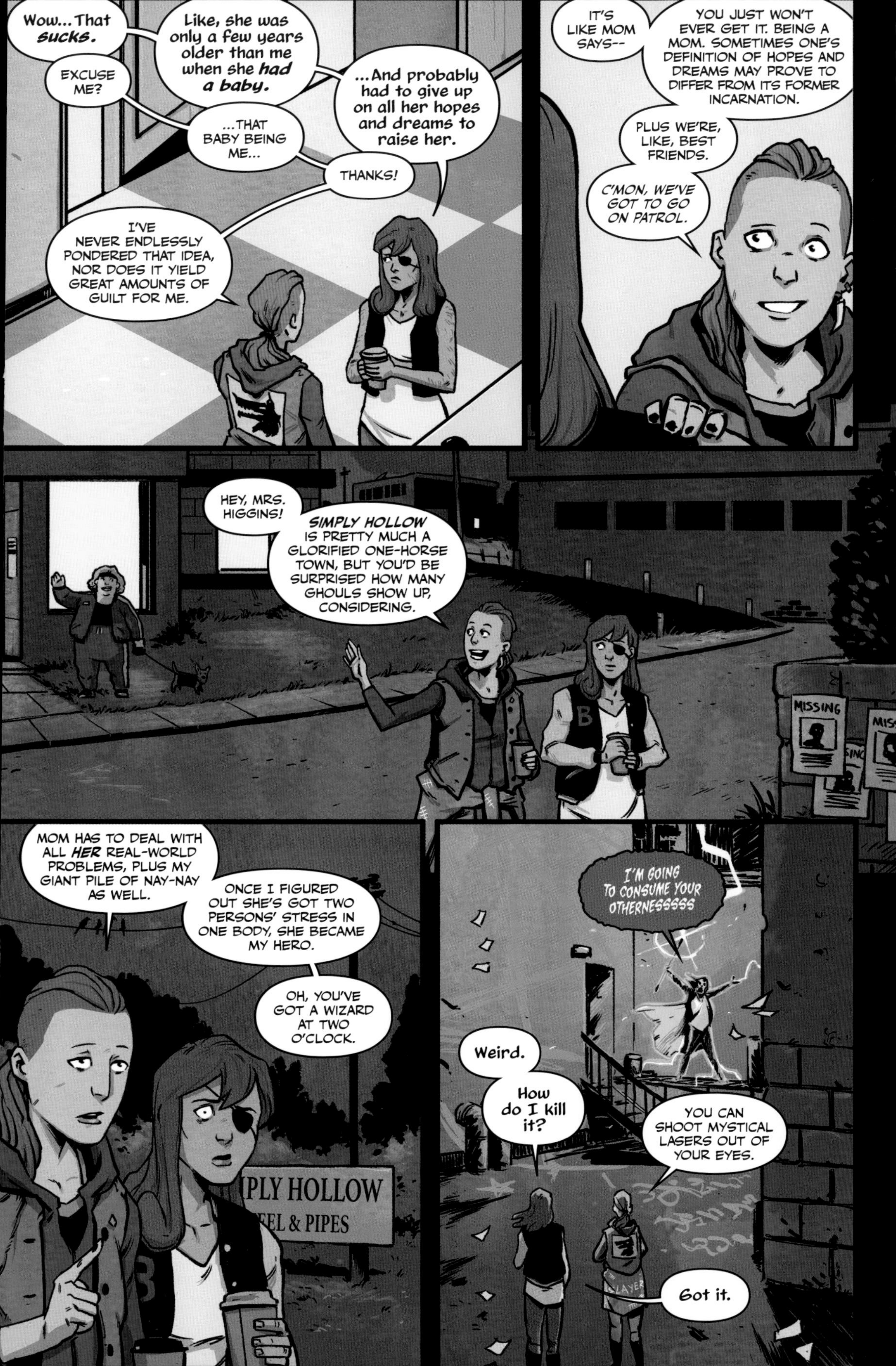
Wow... That sucks.
Like, she was only a few years older than me when she had a baby.
EXCUSE ME?
...THAT BABY BEING ME...
...And probably had to give up on all her hopes and dreams to raise her.
THANKS!
I'VE NEVER ENDLESSLY PONDERED THAT IDEA, NOR DOES IT YIELD GREAT AMOUNTS OF GUILT FOR ME.
IT'S LIKE MOM SAYS--
YOU JUST WON'T EVER GET IT. BEING A MOM. SOMETIMES ONE'S DEFINITION OF HOPES AND DREAMS MAY PROVE TO DIFFER FROM ITS FORMER INCARNATION.
PLUS WE'RE, LIKE, BEST FRIENDS.
C'MON, WE'VE GOT TO GO ON PATROL.
HEY, MRS. HIGGINS!
SIMPLY HOLLOW IS PRETTY MUCH A GLORIFIED ONE-HORSE TOWN, BUT YOU'D BE SURPRISED HOW MANY GHOULS SHOW UP, CONSIDERING.
MISSING
MOM HAS TO DEAL WITH ALL HER REAL-WORLD PROBLEMS, PLUS MY GIANT PILE OF NAY-NAY AS WELL.
ONCE I FIGURED OUT SHE'S GOT TWO PERSONS' STRESS IN ONE BODY, SHE BECAME MY HERO.
OH, YOU'VE GOT A WIZARD AT TWO O'CLOCK.
PLY HOLLOW
EEL & PIPES
I'M GOING TO CONSUME YOUR OTHERNESSSSS
Weird.
How do I kill it?
YOU CAN SHOOT MYSTICAL LASERS OUT OF YOUR EYES.
Got it.

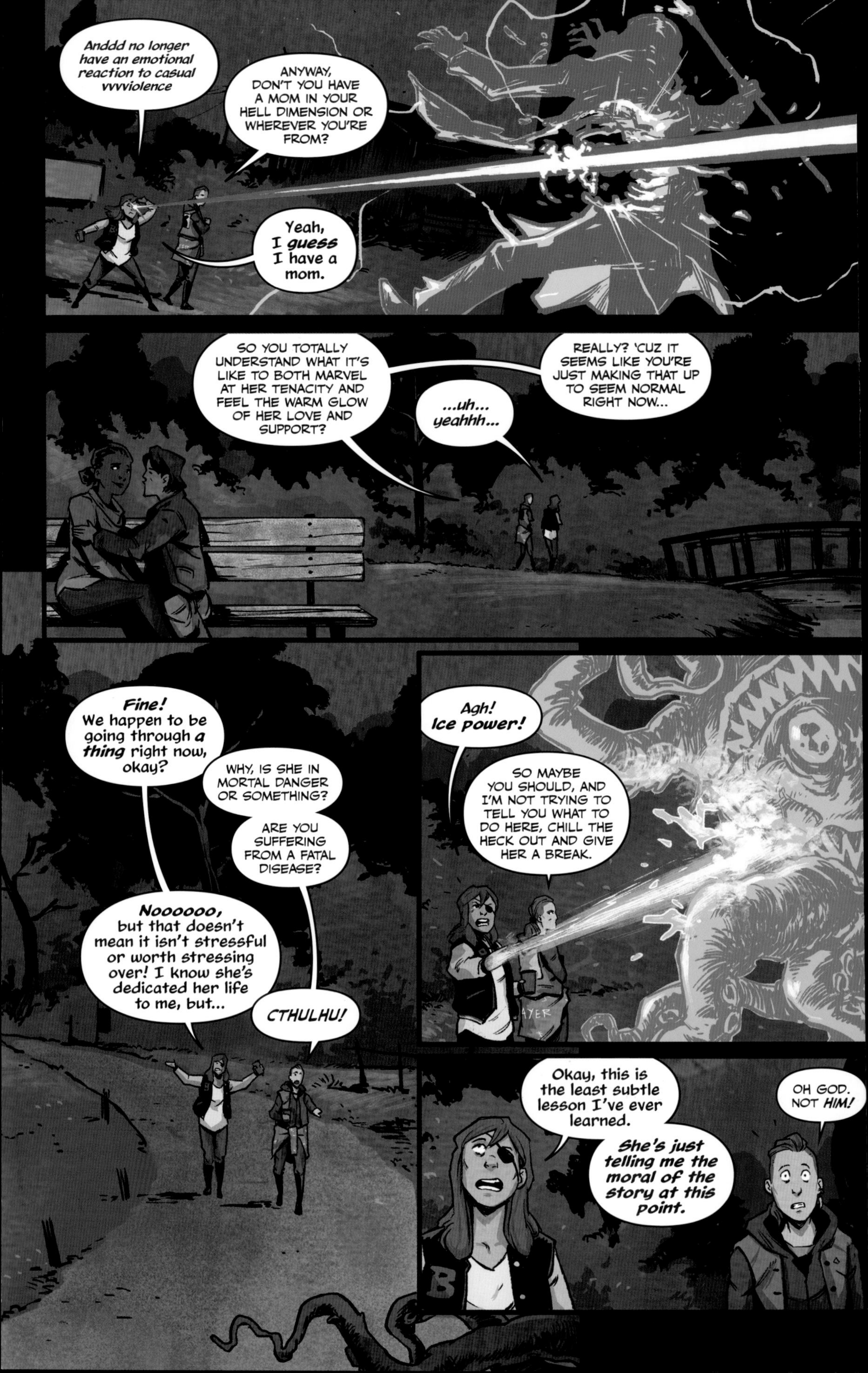
Anddd no longer have an emotional reaction to casual vvvviolence
ANYWAY, DON'T YOU HAVE A MOM IN YOUR HELL DIMENSION OR WHEREVER YOU'RE FROM?
Yeah, I guess I have a mom.
SO YOU TOTALLY UNDERSTAND WHAT IT'S LIKE TO BOTH MARVEL AT HER TENACITY AND FEEL THE WARM GLOW OF HER LOVE AND SUPPORT?
...uh... yeahhh...
REALLY? 'CUZ IT SEEMS LIKE YOU'RE JUST MAKING THAT UP TO SEEM NORMAL RIGHT NOW...
Fine! We happen to be going through a thing right now, okay?
WHY, IS SHE IN MORTAL DANGER OR SOMETHING?
ARE YOU SUFFERING FROM A FATAL DISEASE?
Noooooo, but that doesn't mean it isn't stressful or worth stressing over! I know she's dedicated her life to me, but...
CTHULHU!
Agh! Ice power!
SO MAYBE YOU SHOULD, AND I'M NOT TRYING TO TELL YOU WHAT TO DO HERE, CHILL THE HECK OUT AND GIVE HER A BREAK.
Okay, this is the least subtle lesson I've ever learned.
She's just telling me the moral of the story at this point.
OH GOD. NOT HIM!

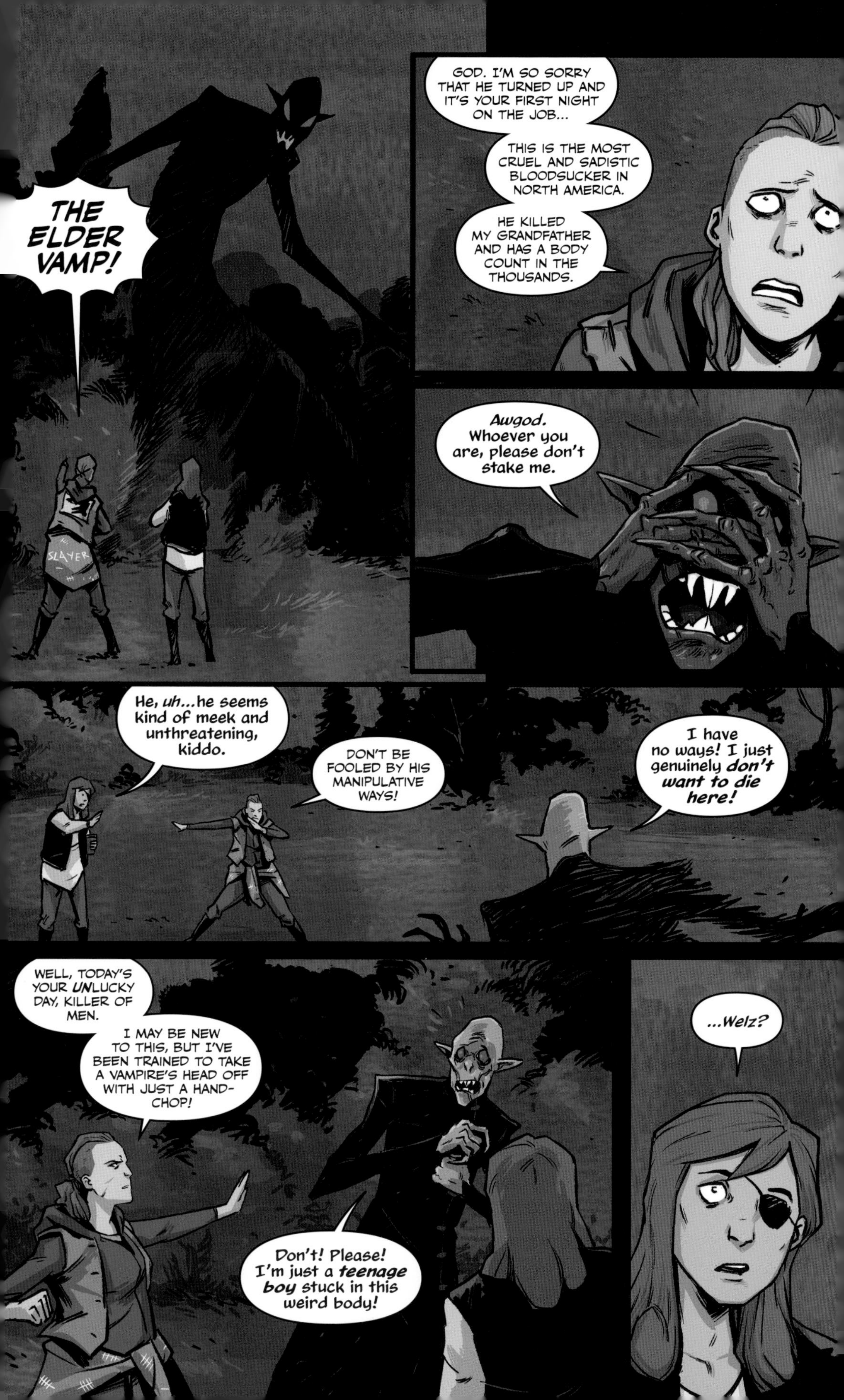
THE ELDER VAMP!
GOD. I'M SO SORRY THAT HE TURNED UP AND IT'S YOUR FIRST NIGHT ON THE JOB...
THIS IS THE MOST CRUEL AND SADISTIC BLOODSUCKER IN NORTH AMERICA.
HE KILLED MY GRANDFATHER AND HAS A BODY COUNT IN THE THOUSANDS.
SLAYER
Awgod. Whoever you are, please don't stake me.
He, uh...he seems kind of meek and unthreatening, kiddo.
DON'T BE FOOLED BY HIS MANIPULATIVE WAYS!
I have no ways! I just genuinely don't want to die here!
WELL, TODAY'S YOUR UNLUCKY DAY, KILLER OF MEN.
I MAY BE NEW TO THIS, BUT I'VE BEEN TRAINED TO TAKE A VAMPIRE'S HEAD OFF WITH JUST A HAND-CHOP!
Don't! Please! I'm just a teenage boy stuck in this weird body!
...Welz?

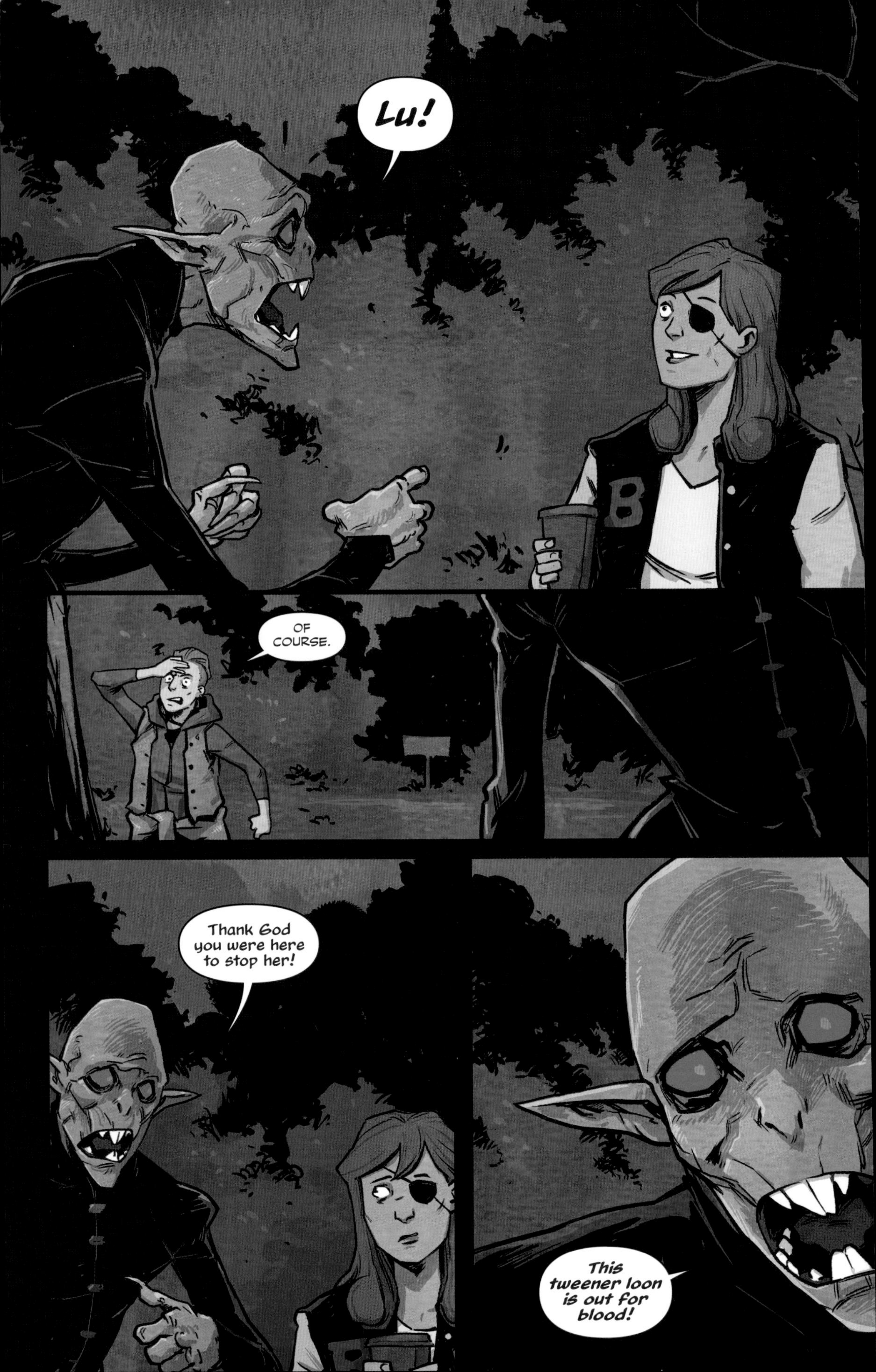
Lu!
OF COURSE.
Thank God you were here to stop her!
This tweener loon is out for blood!

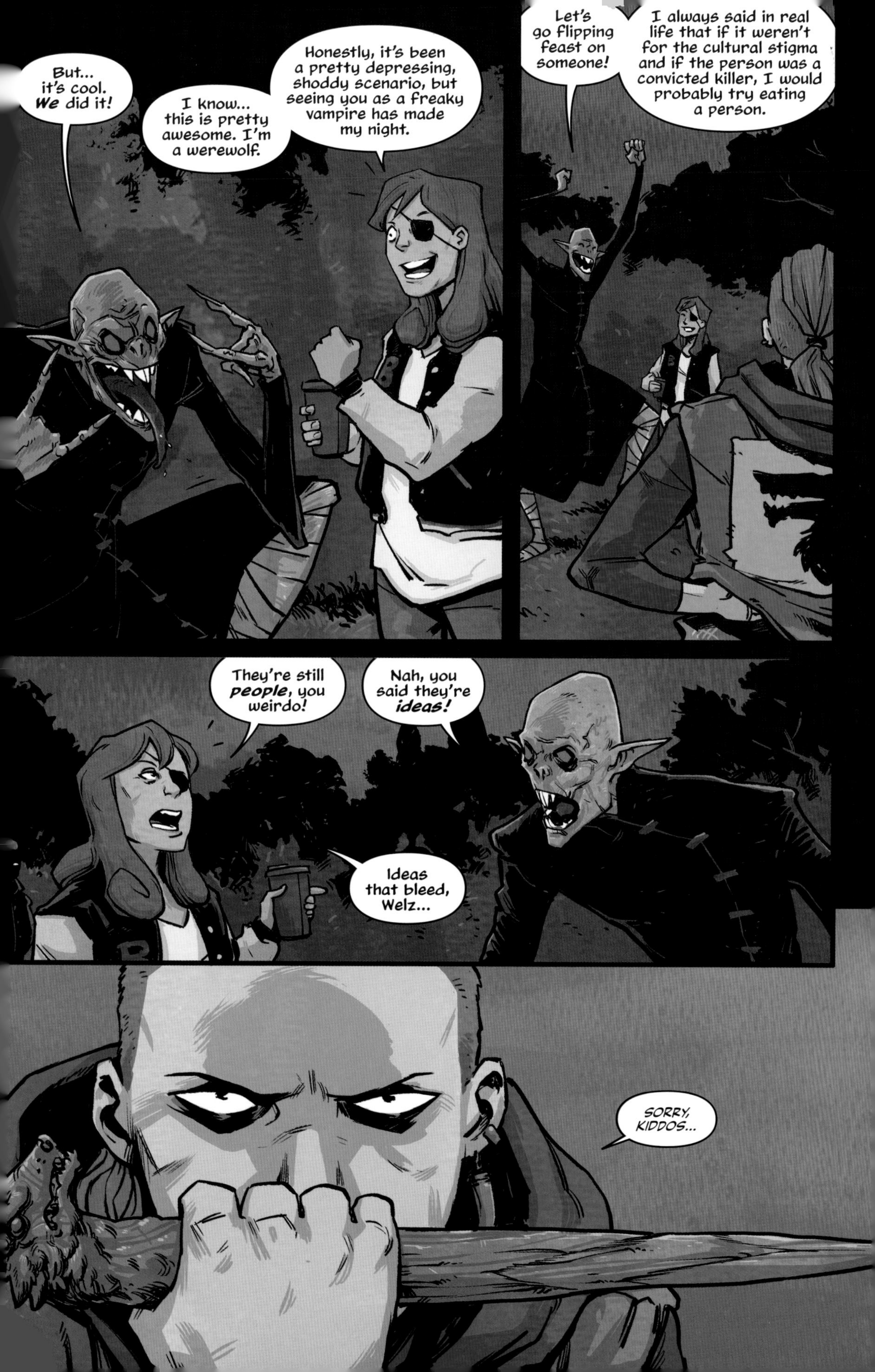
But... it's cool. We did it!
I know... this is pretty awesome. I'm a werewolf.
Honestly, it's been a pretty depressing, shoddy scenario, but seeing you as a freaky vampire has made my night.
Let's go flipping feast on someone!
I always said in real life that if it weren't for the cultural stigma and if the person was a convicted killer, I would probably try eating a person.
They're still people, you weirdo!
Nah, you said they're ideas!
Ideas that bleed, Welz...
SORRY, KIDDOS...

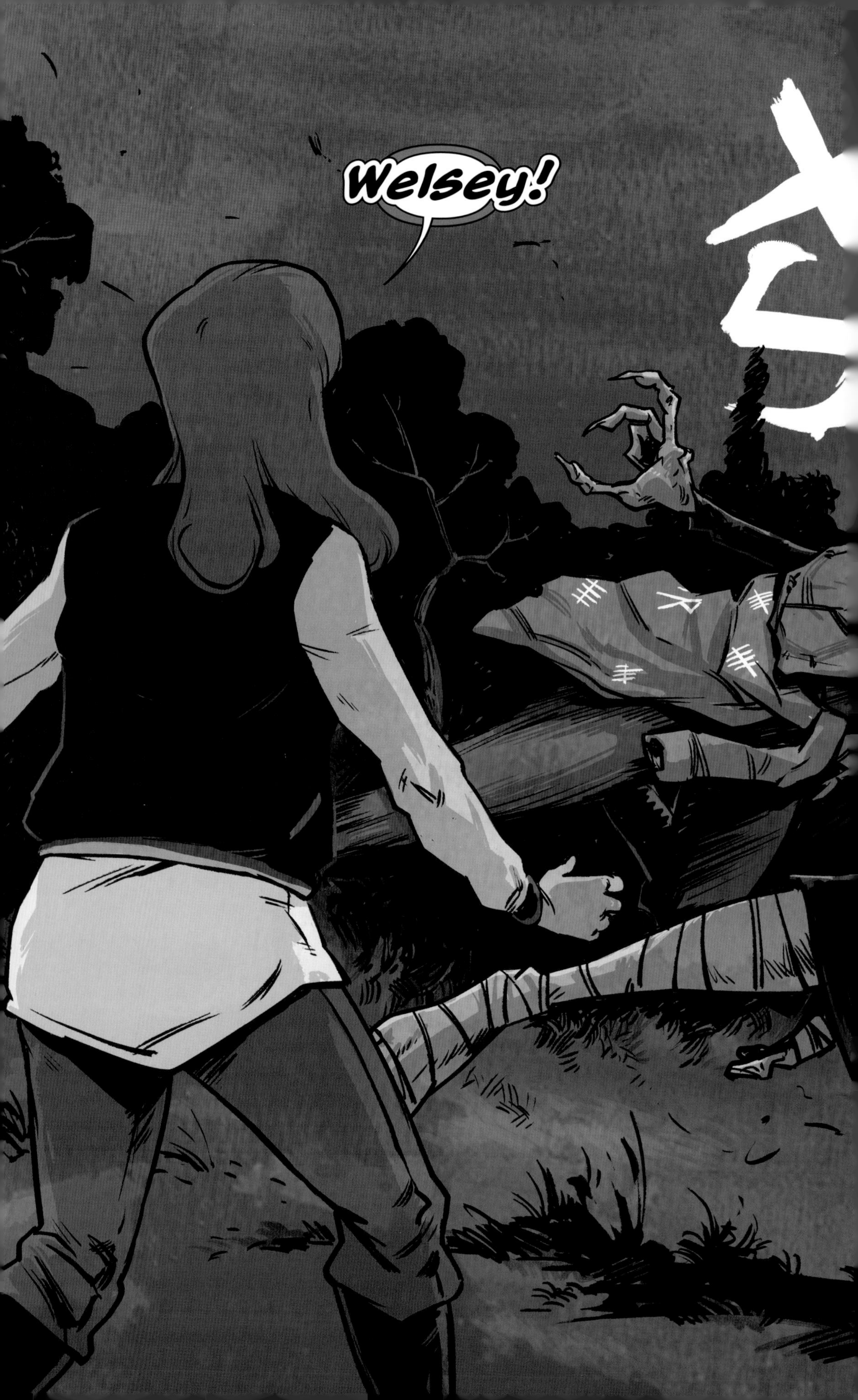
Welsey!

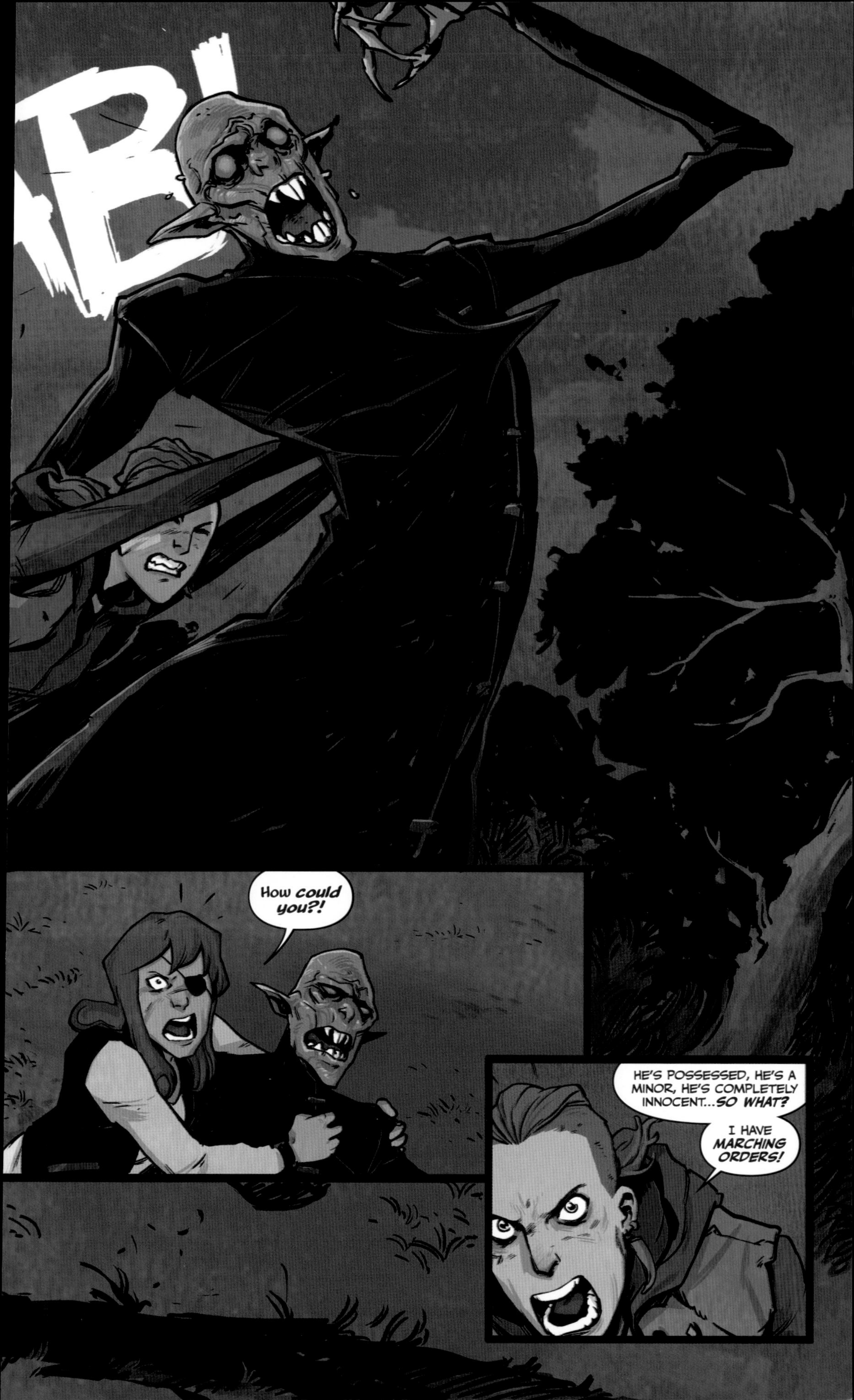
How could you?!
HE'S POSSESSED, HE'S A MINOR, HE'S COMPLETELY INNOCENT...SO WHAT?
I HAVE MARCHING ORDERS!

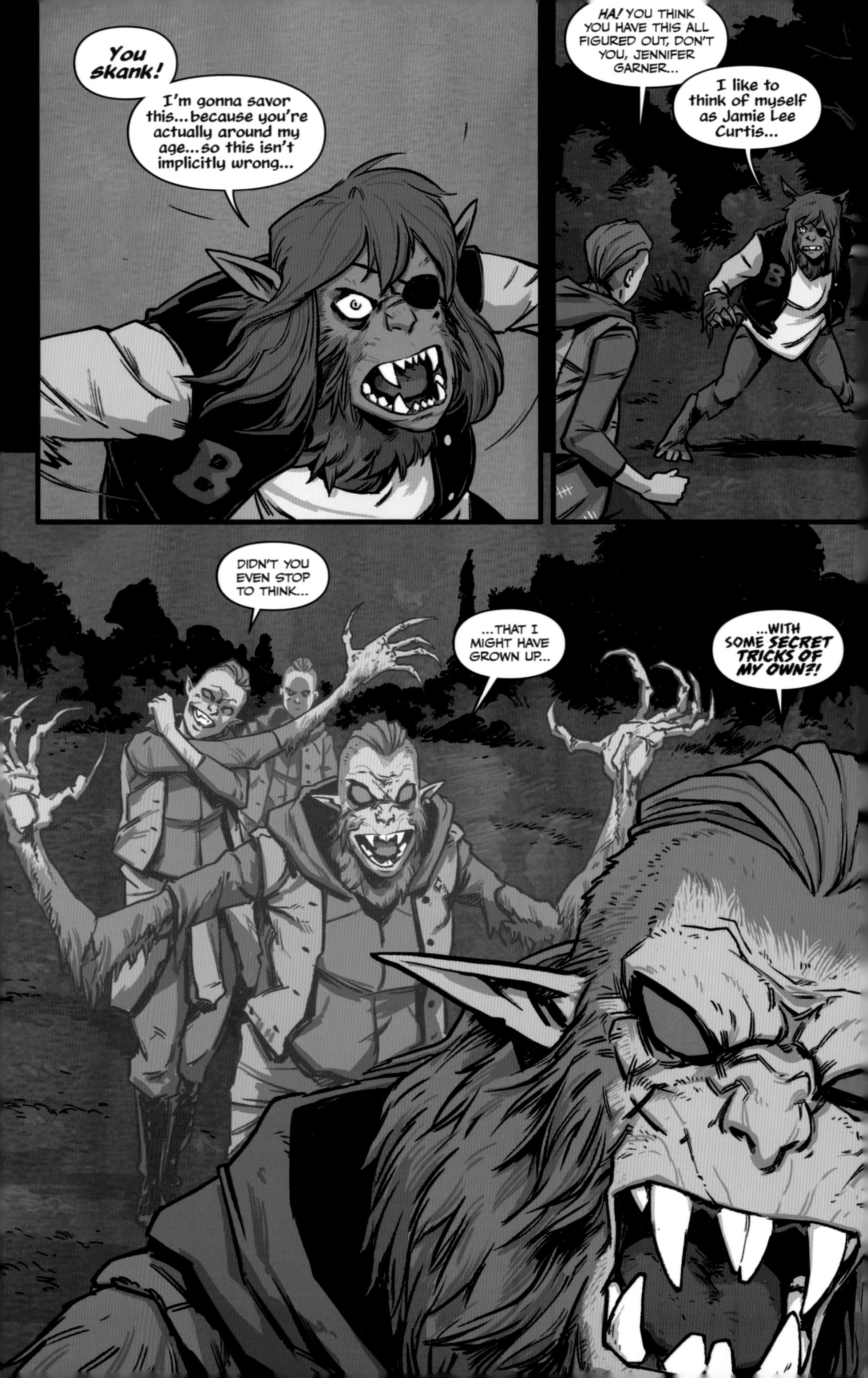
You skank!
I'm gonna savor this...because you're actually around my age...so this isn't implicitly wrong...
HA! YOU THINK YOU HAVE THIS ALL FIGURED OUT, DON'T YOU, JENNIFER GARNER...
I like to think of myself as Jamie Lee Curtis...
DIDN'T YOU EVEN STOP TO THINK...
...THAT I MIGHT HAVE GROWN UP...
...WITH SOME SECRET TRICKS OF MY OWN?!

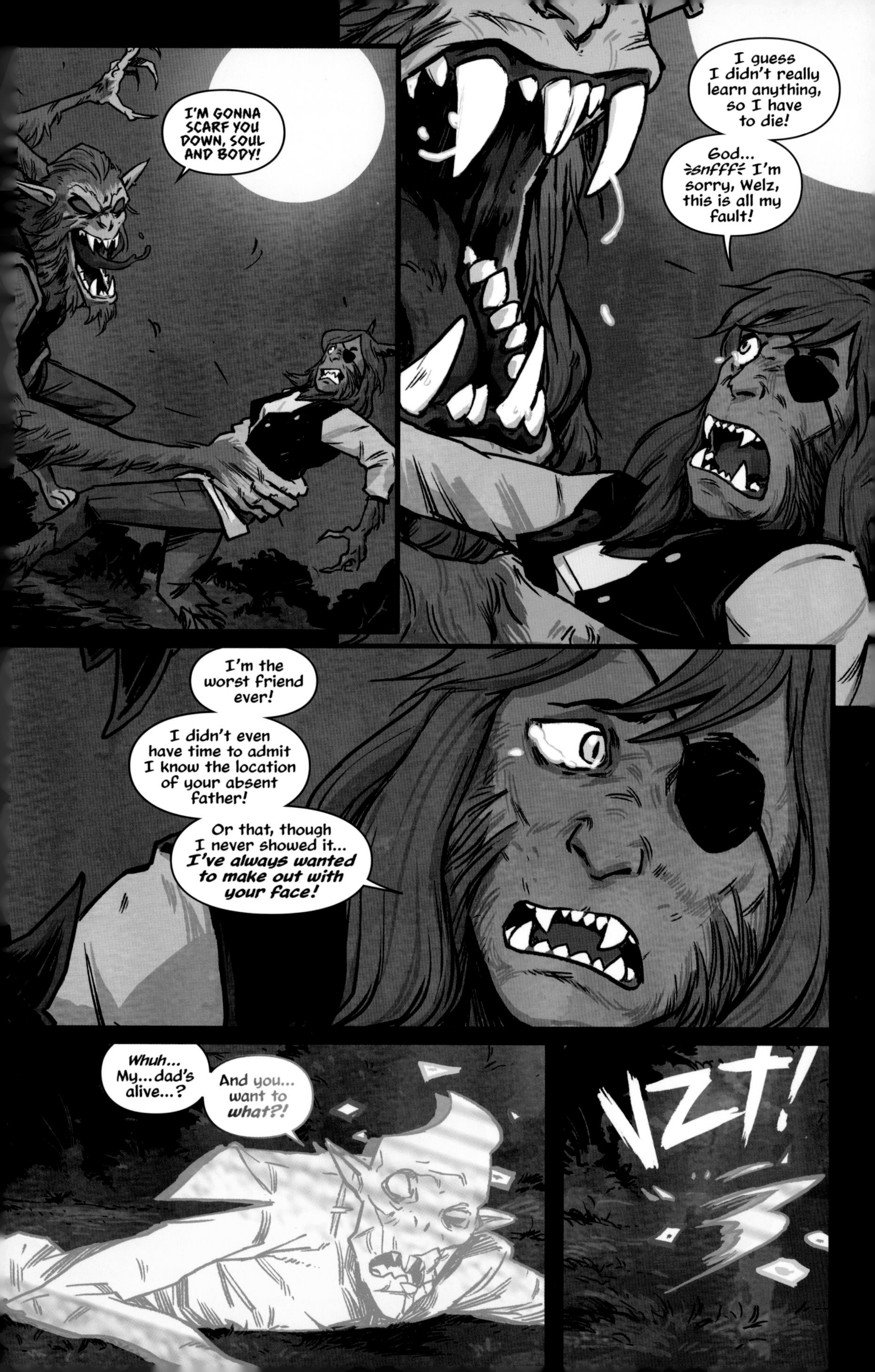

I'M GONNA SCARF YOU DOWN, SOUL AND BODY!
I guess I didn't really learn anything, so I have to die!
God... ≠snfff≠ I'm sorry, Welz, this is all my fault!
I'm the worst friend ever!
I didn't even have time to admit I know the location of your absent father!
Or that, though I never showed it... I've always wanted to make out with your face!
Whuh... My...dad's alive...?
And you... want to what?!
VZT!

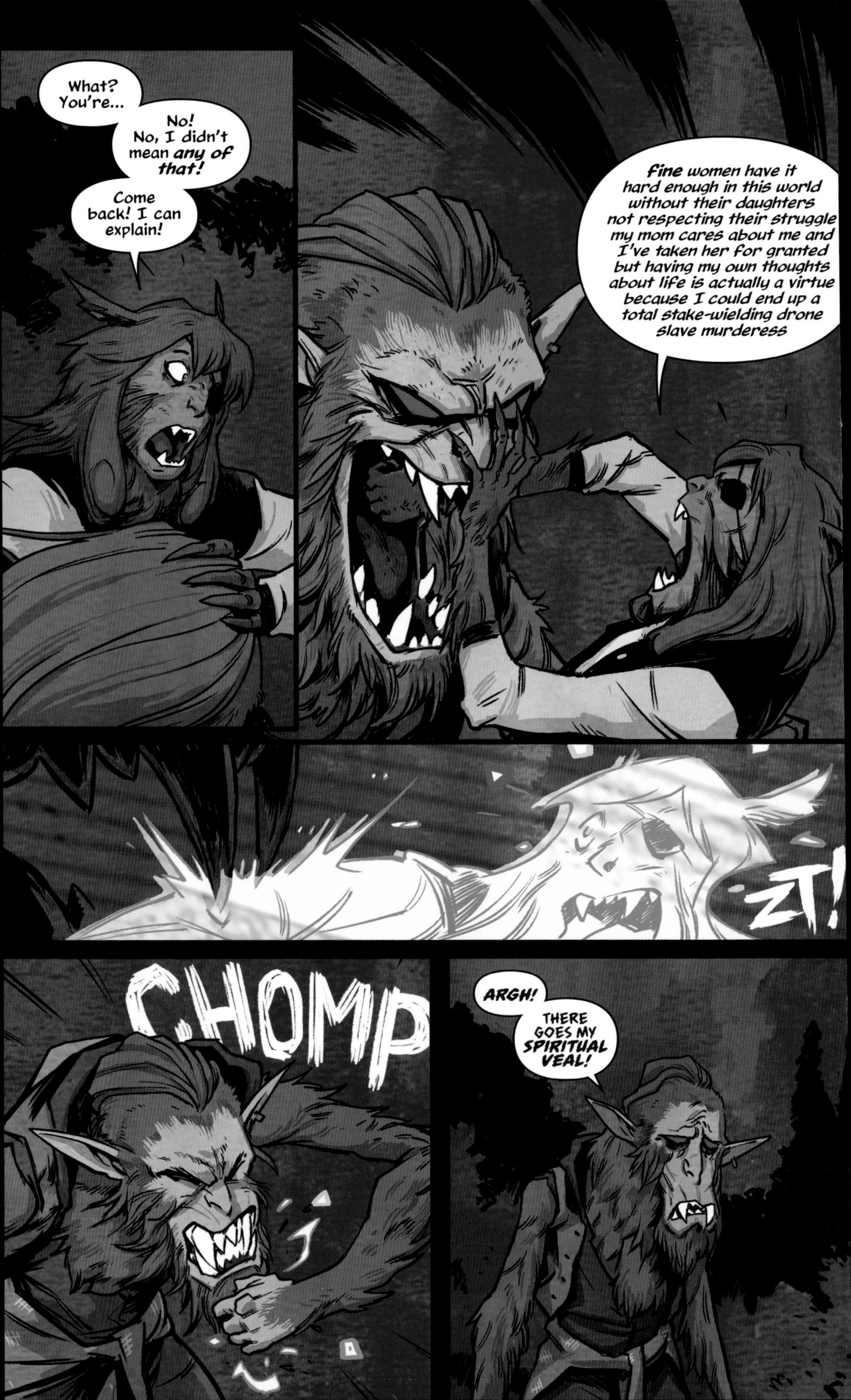
What? You're...
No! No, I didn't mean any of that!
Come back! I can explain!
fine women have it hard enough in this world without their daughters not respecting their struggle my mom cares about me and I've taken her for granted but having my own thoughts about life is actually a virtue because I could end up a total stake-wielding drone slave murderess
ZT!
CHOMP
ARGH!
THERE GOES MY SPIRITUAL VEAL!

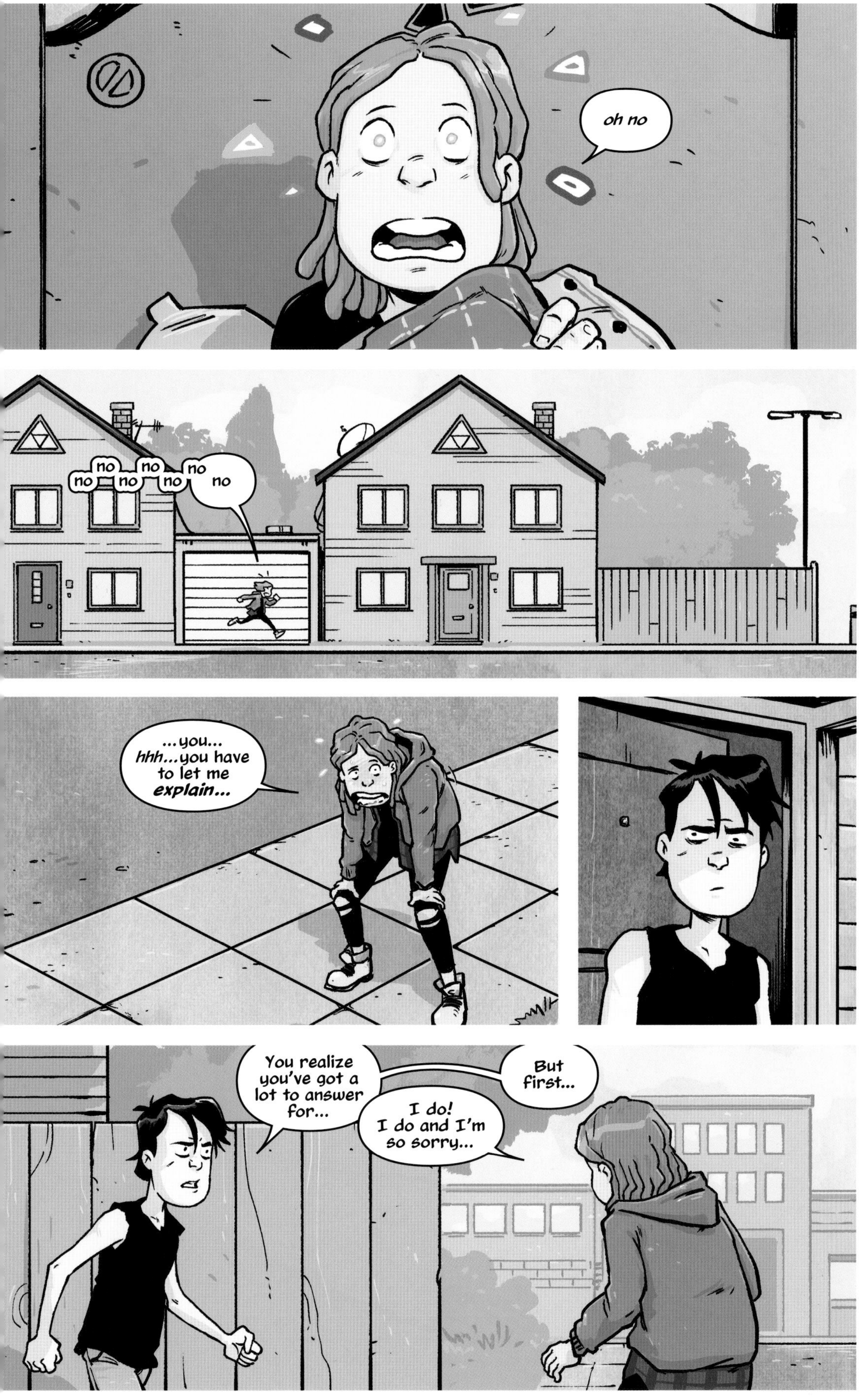
oh no
no no no no no no no
...you...
hhh...you have
to let me
explain...
You realize
you've got a
lot to answer
for...
I do!
I do and I'm
so sorry...
But
first...

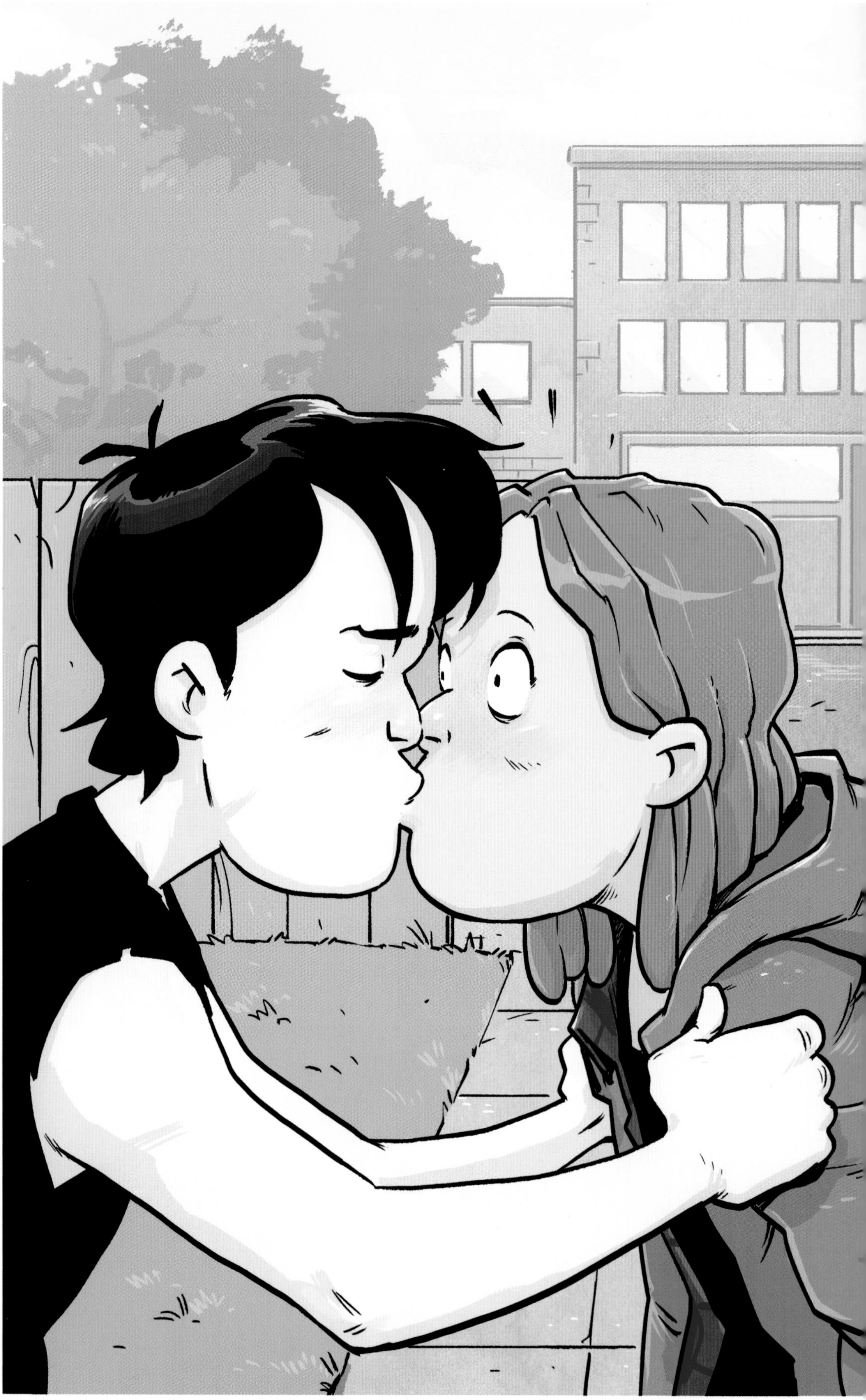

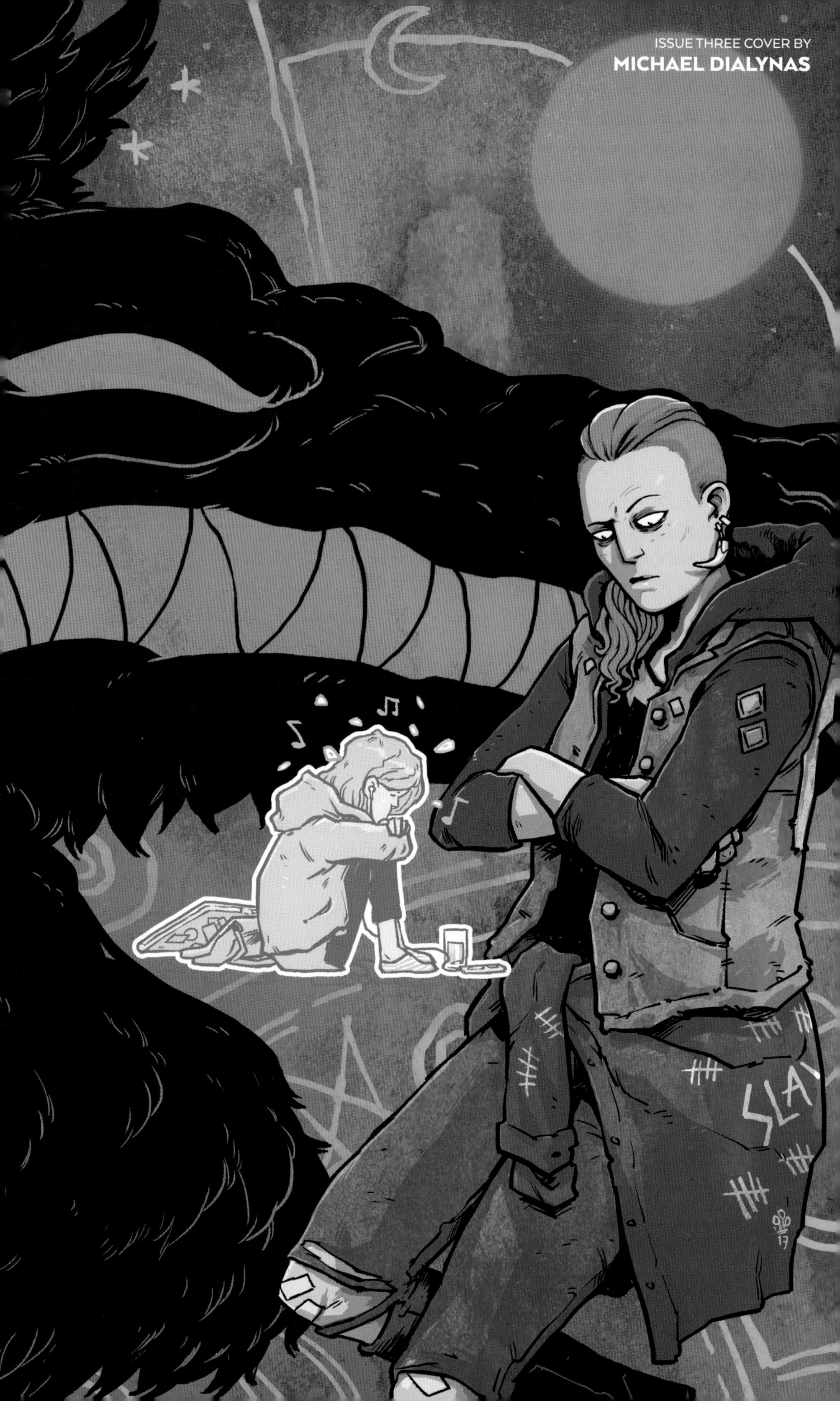

ISSUE THREE COVER BY
MICHAEL DIALYNAS

CHAPTER
FOUR

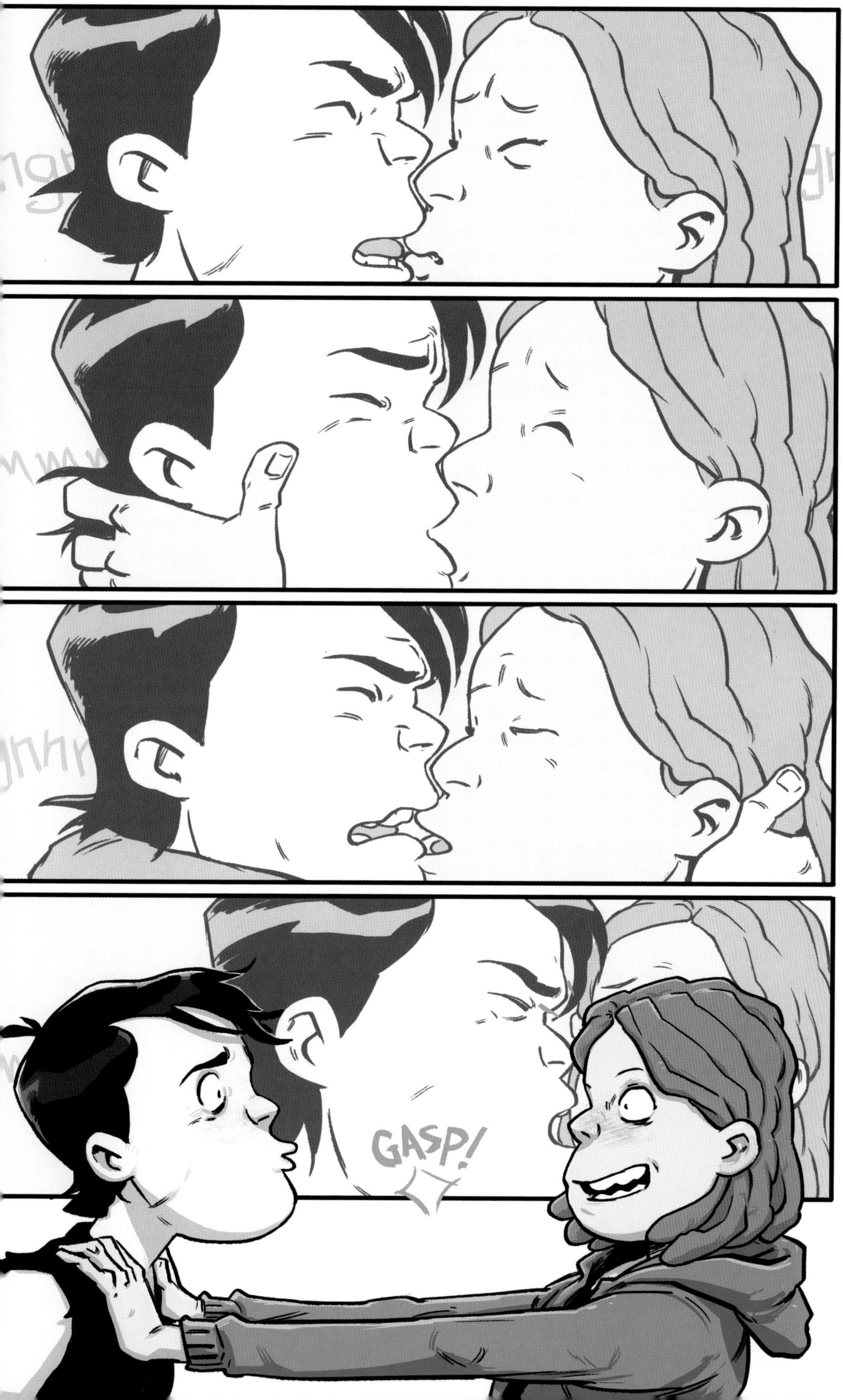
GASP!

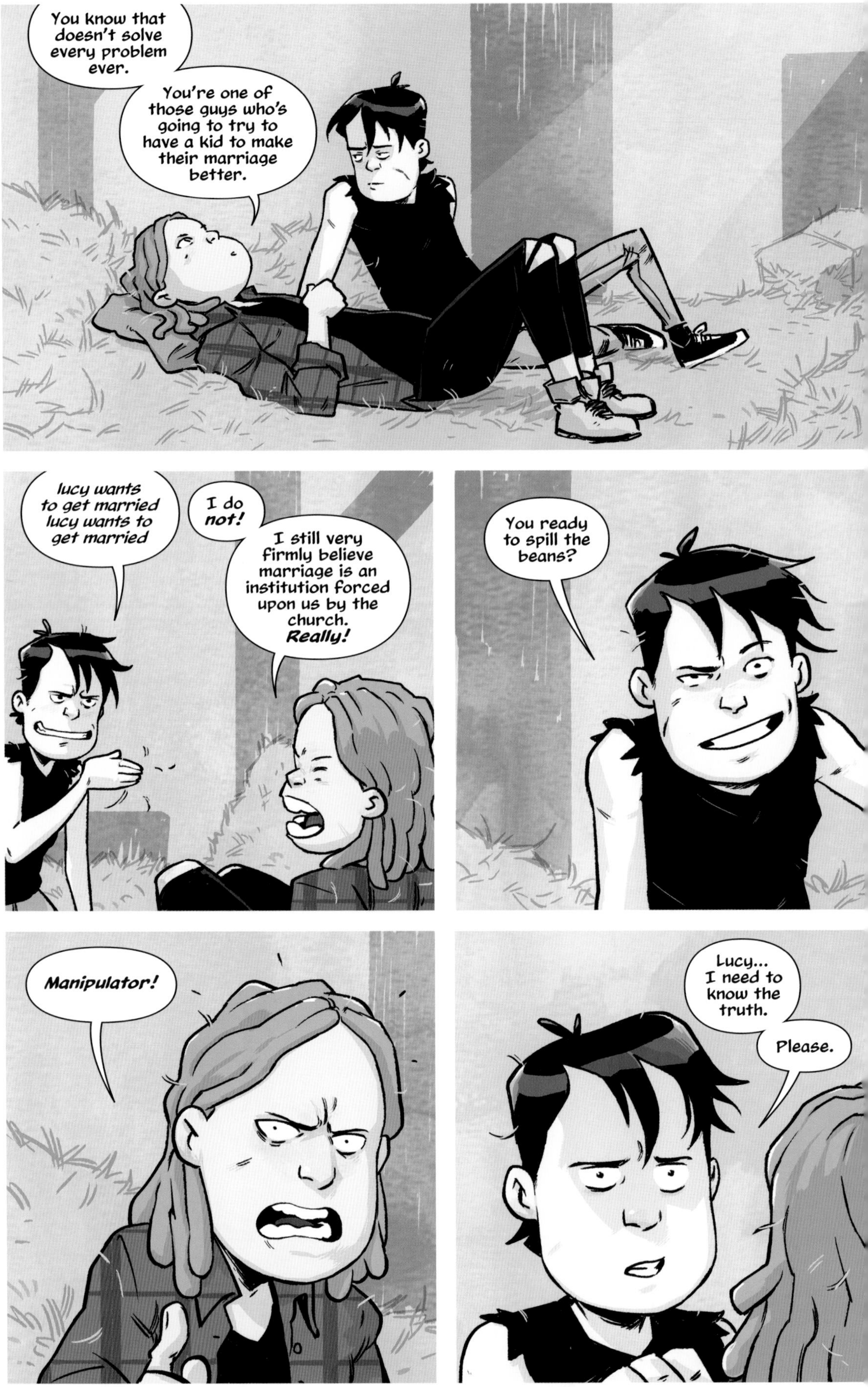
You know that doesn't solve every problem ever.
You're one of those guys who's going to try to have a kid to make their marriage better.
lucy wants to get married lucy wants to get married
I do *not!*
I still very firmly believe marriage is an institution forced upon us by the church. ***Really!***
You ready to spill the beans?
Manipulator!
Lucy... I need to know the truth.
Please.

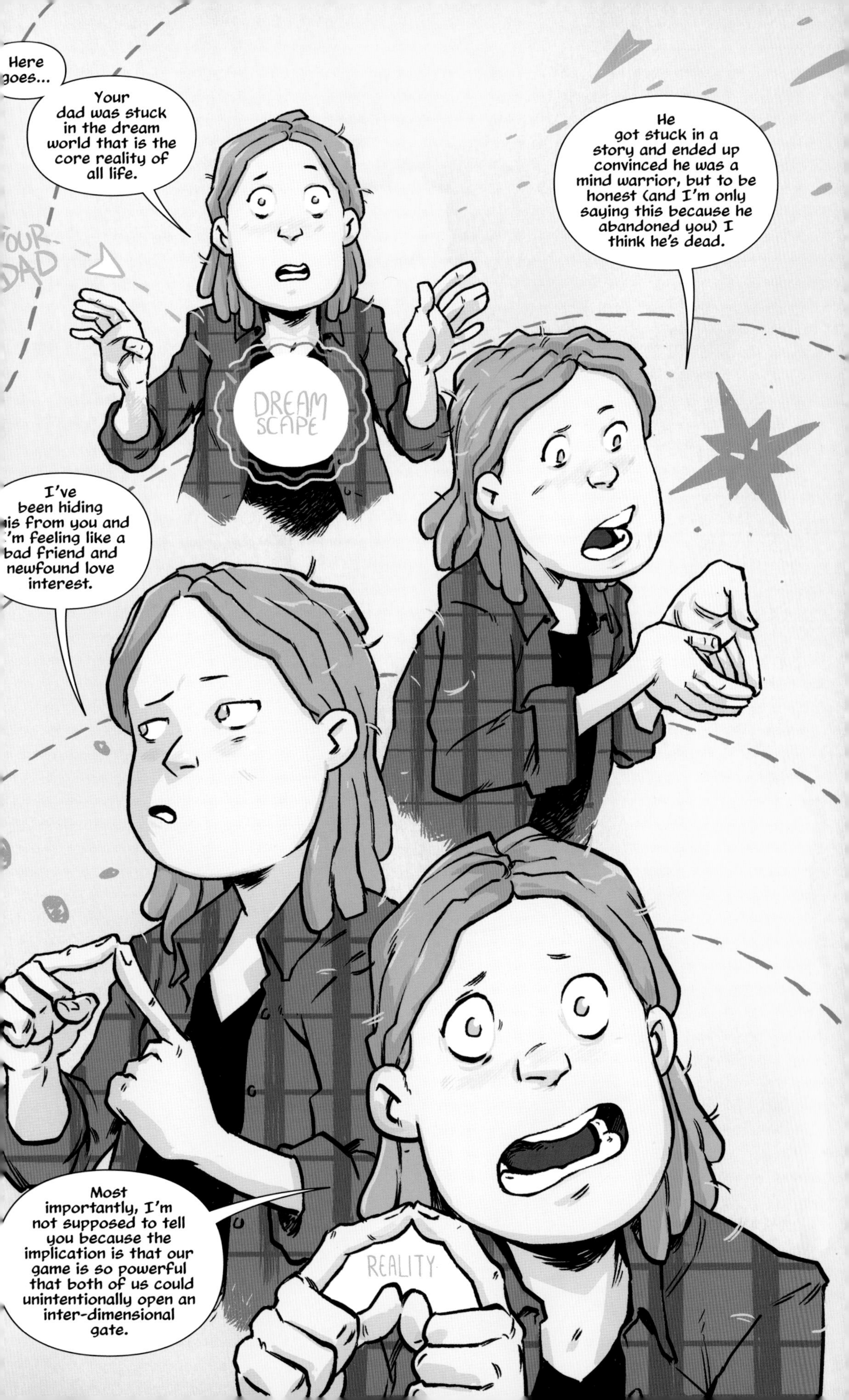

Here goes...
Your dad was stuck in the dream world that is the core reality of all life.
OUR DAD
DREAM SCAPE
He got stuck in a story and ended up convinced he was a mind warrior, but to be honest (and I'm only saying this because he abandoned you) I think he's dead.
I've been hiding is from you and 'm feeling like a bad friend and newfound love interest.
Most importantly, I'm not supposed to tell you because the implication is that our game is so powerful that both of us could unintentionally open an inter-dimensional gate.
REALITY

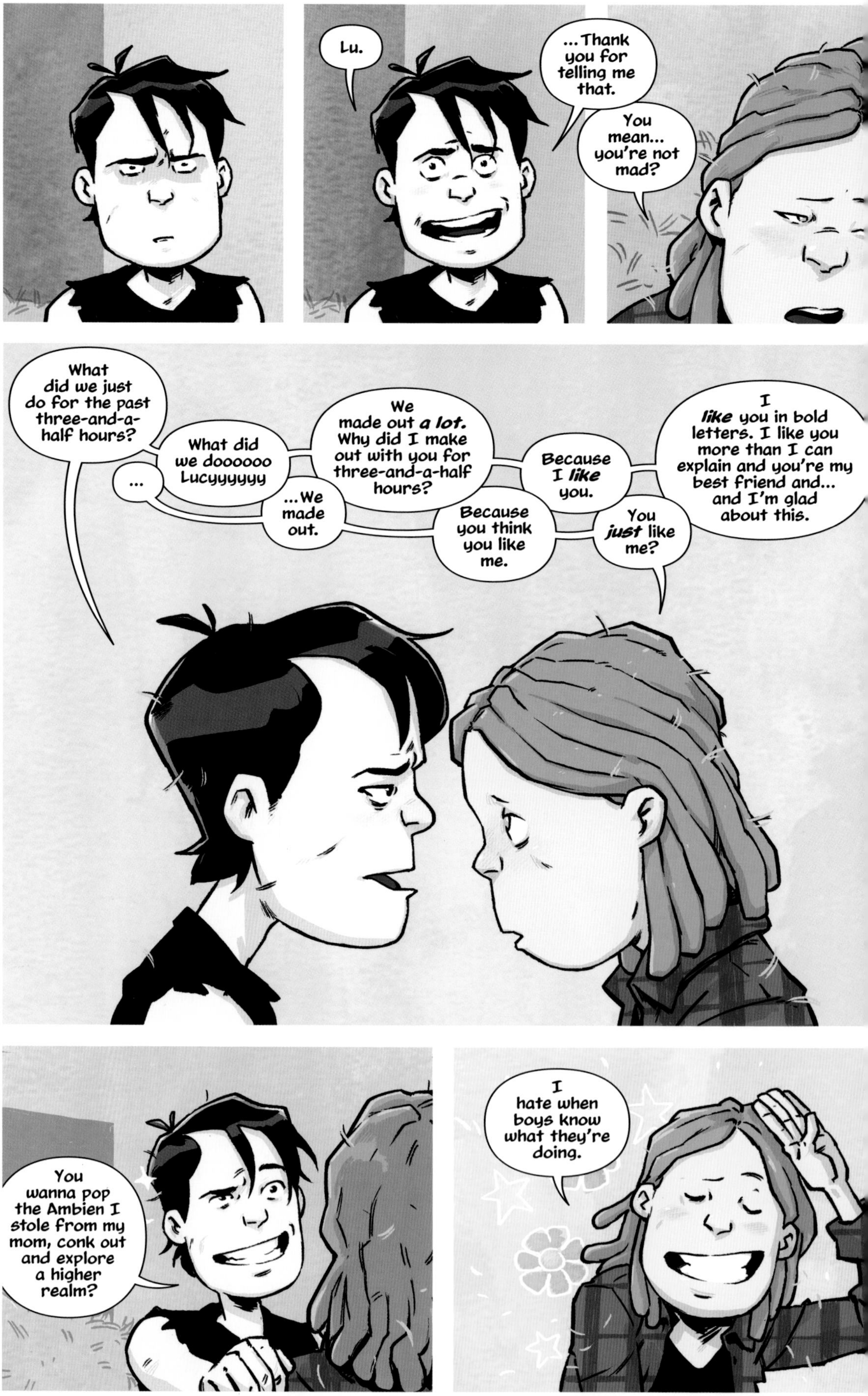
Lu.
...Thank you for telling me that.
You mean... you're not mad?
What did we just do for the past three-and-a-half hours?
...
What did we doooooo Lucyyyyyy
...We made out.
We made out a lot. Why did I make out with you for three-and-a-half hours?
Because you think you like me.
Because I like you.
You just like me?
I like you in bold letters. I like you more than I can explain and you're my best friend and... and I'm glad about this.
You wanna pop the Ambien I stole from my mom, conk out and explore a higher realm?
I hate when boys know what they're doing.

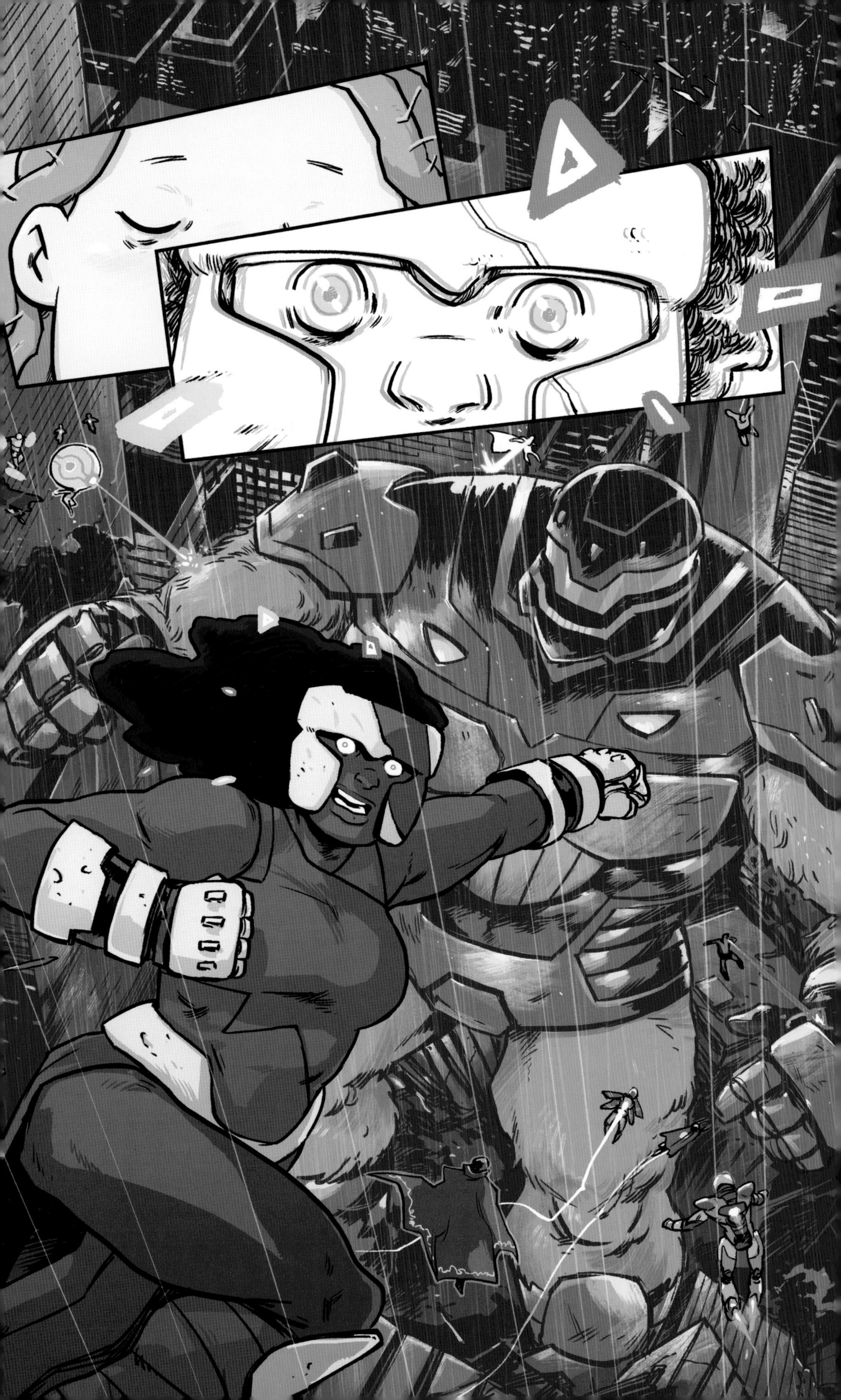

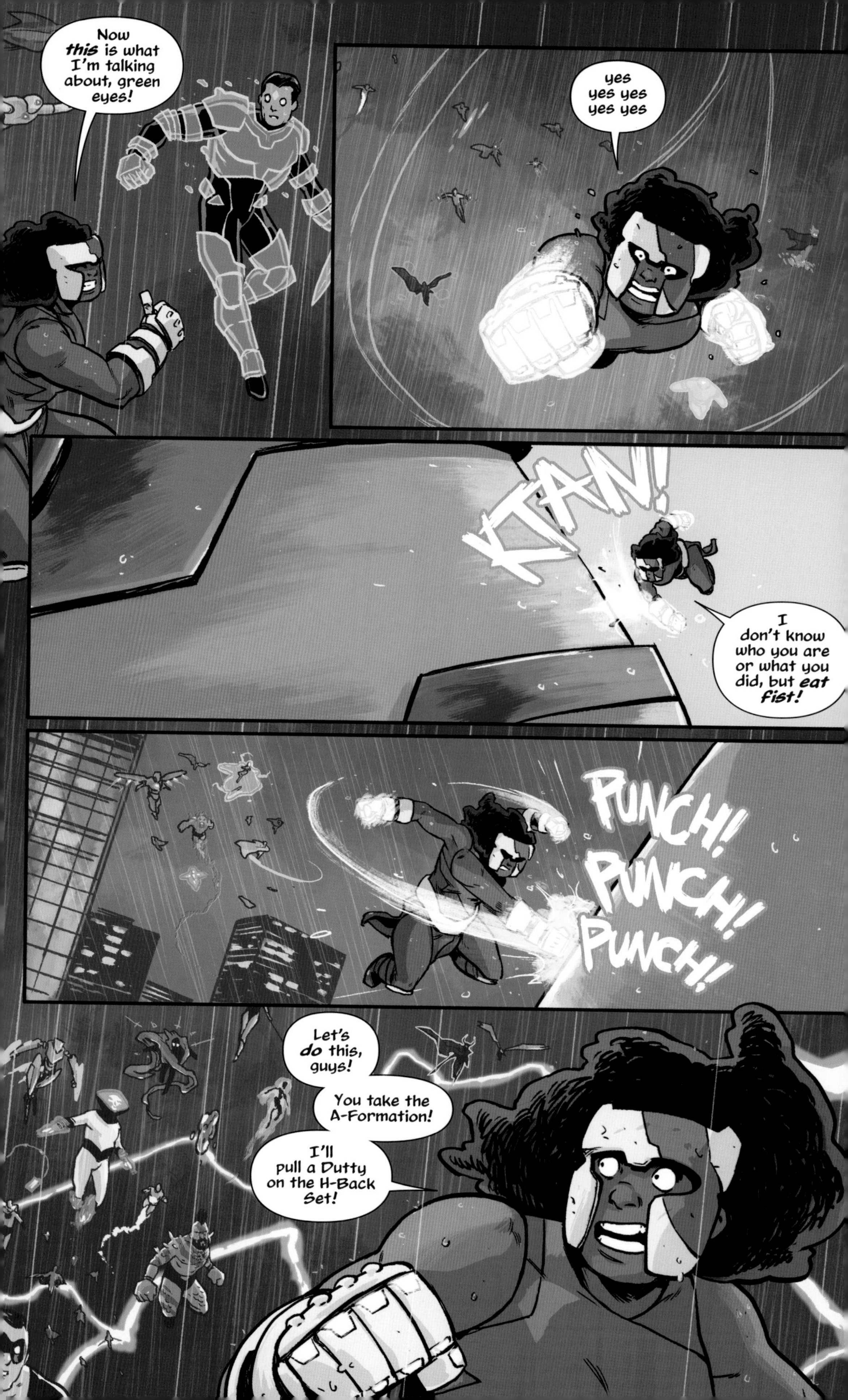
Now *this* is what I'm talking about, green eyes!
yes yes yes yes yes
KTAN!
I don't know who you are or what you did, but *eat fist!*
PUNCH! PUNCH! PUNCH!
Let's *do* this, guys!
You take the A-Formation!
I'll pull a Dutty on the H-Back Set!

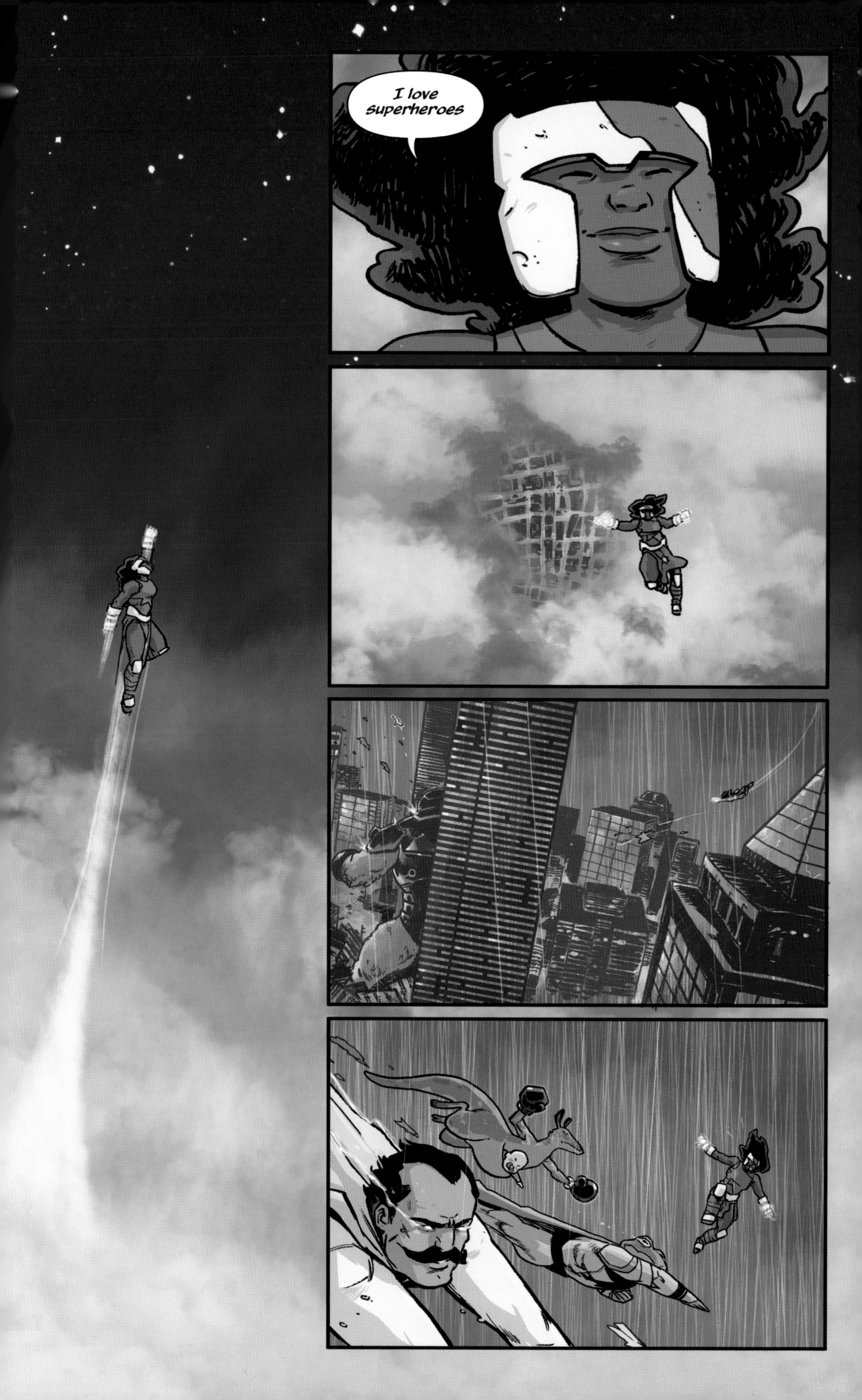
I love superheroes

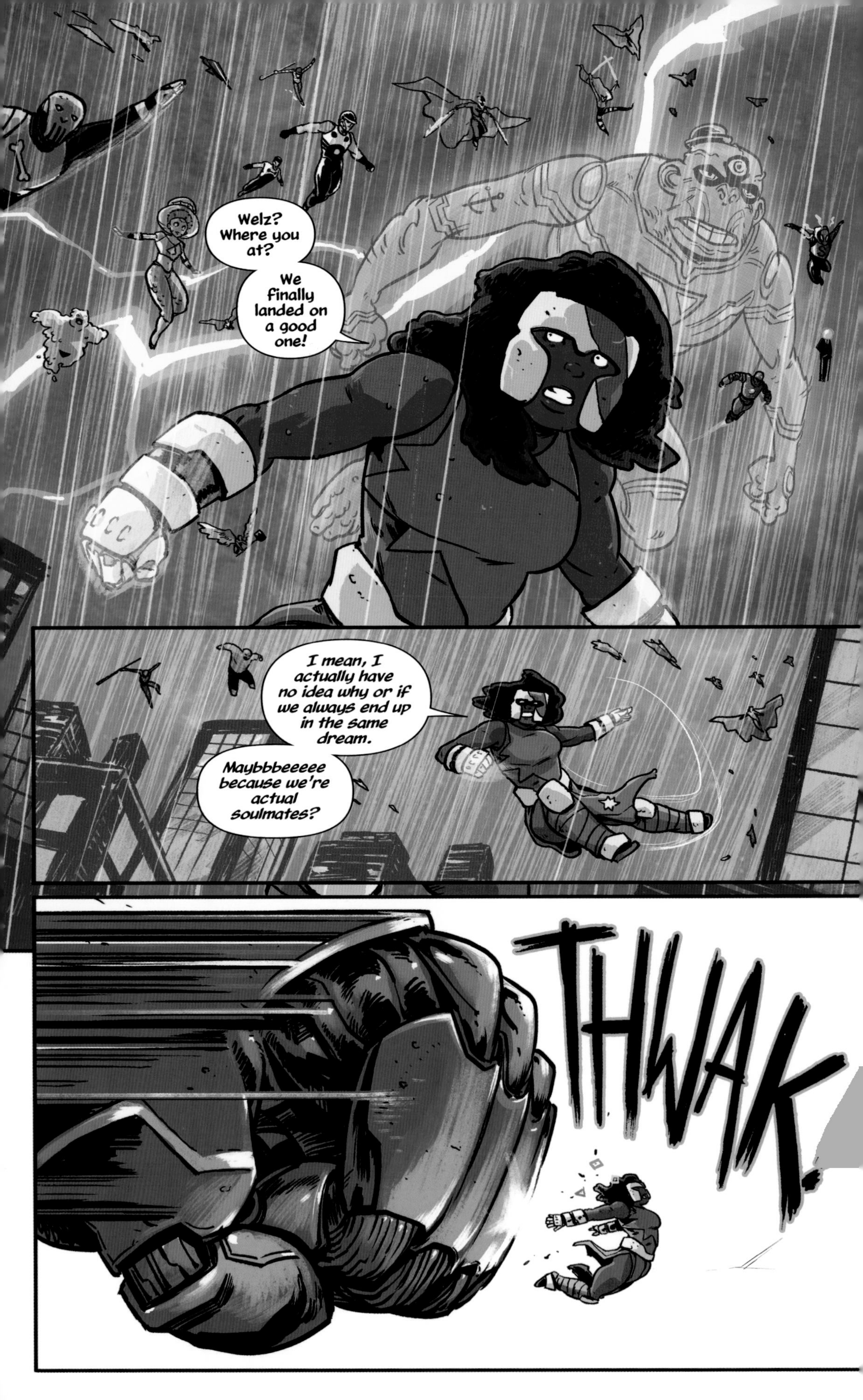
Welz? Where you at?
We finally landed on a good one!
I mean, I actually have no idea why or if we always end up in the same dream.
Maybbbeeeee because we're actual soulmates?
THWAK.

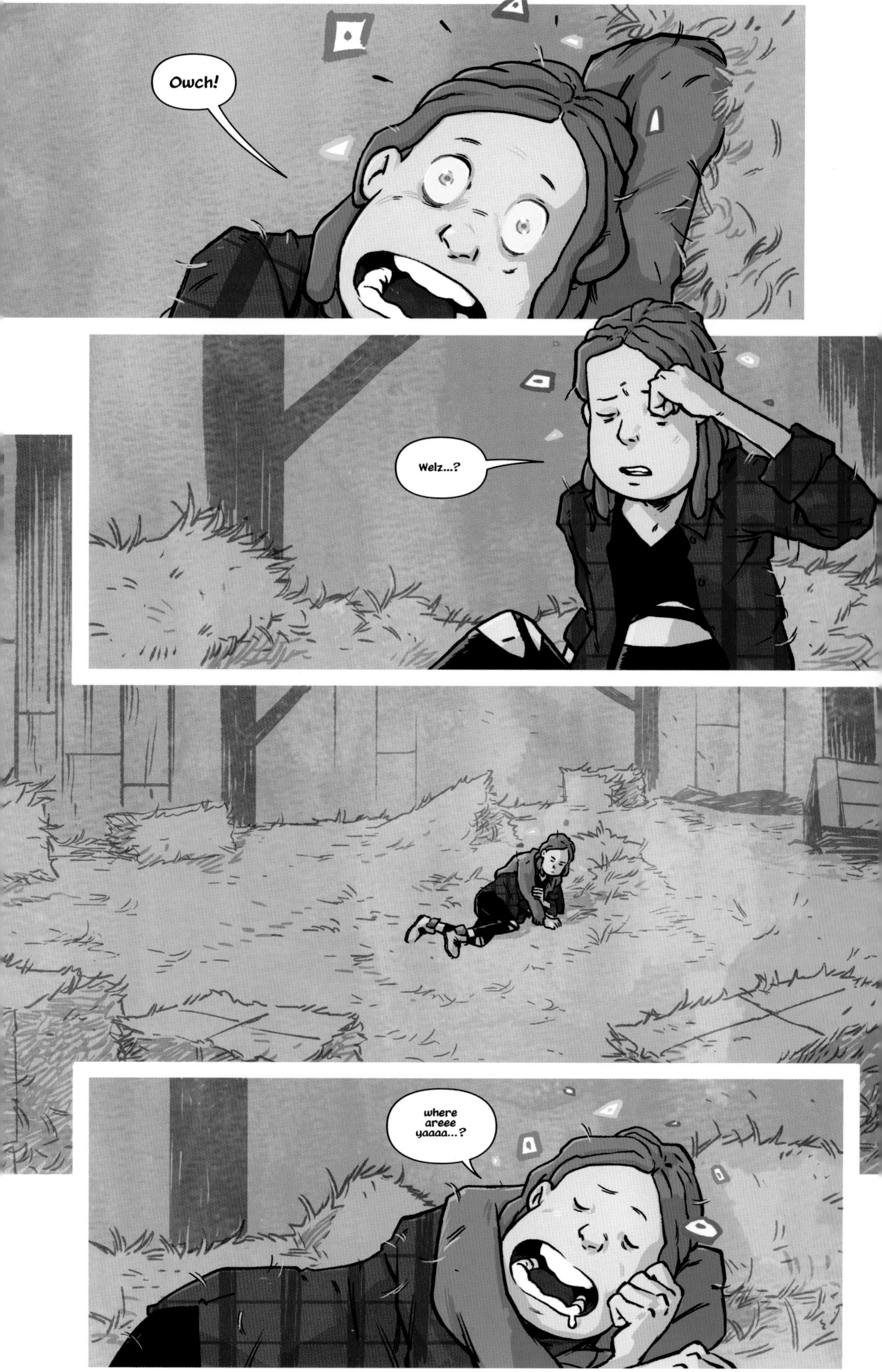
Owch!
Welz...?
where areee yaaaa...?

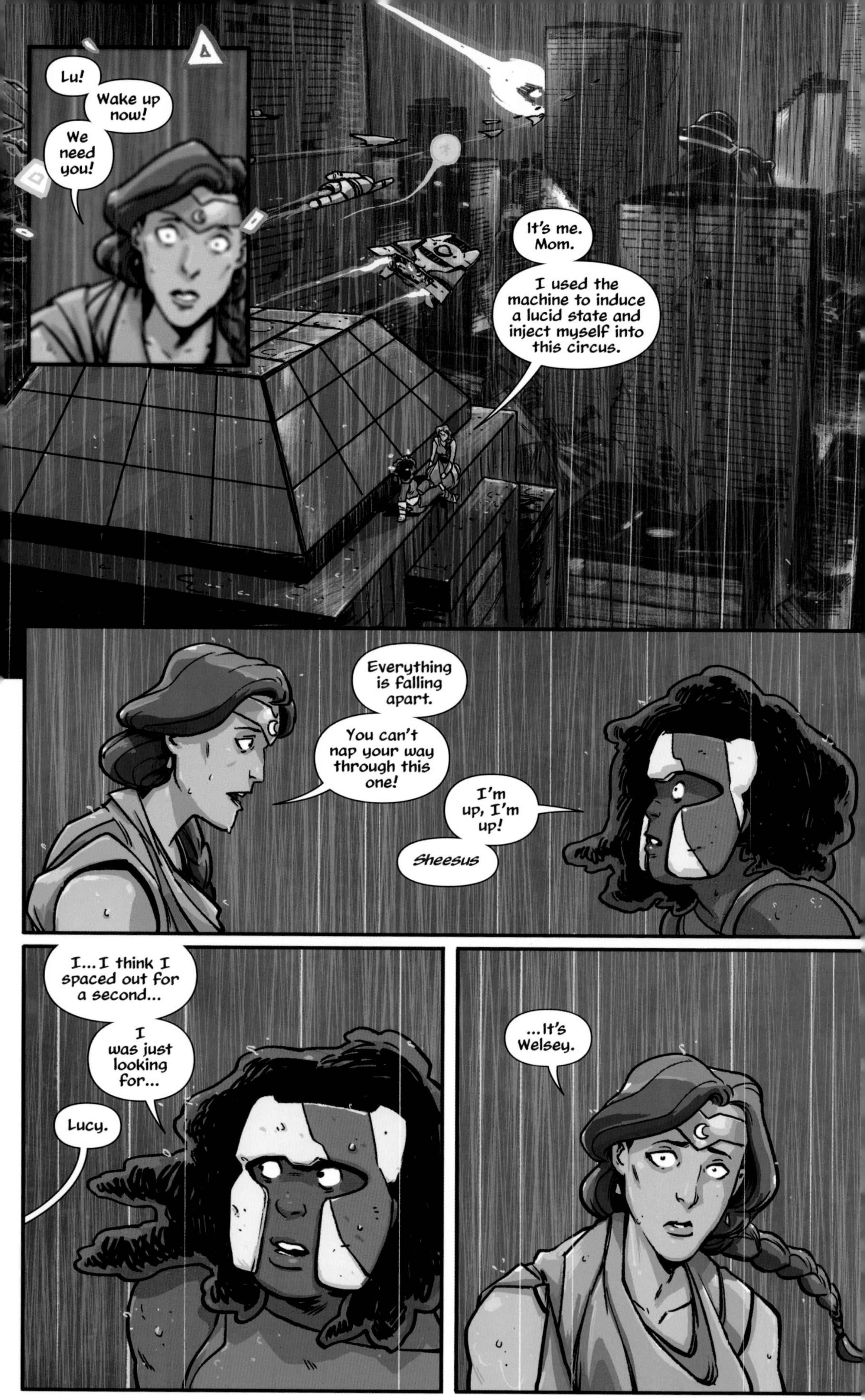
Lu!
Wake up now!
We need you!
It's me. Mom.
I used the machine to induce a lucid state and inject myself into this circus.
Everything is falling apart.
You can't nap your way through this one!
I'm up, I'm up!
Sheesus
I... I think I spaced out for a second...
I was just looking for...
Lucy.
...It's Welsey.

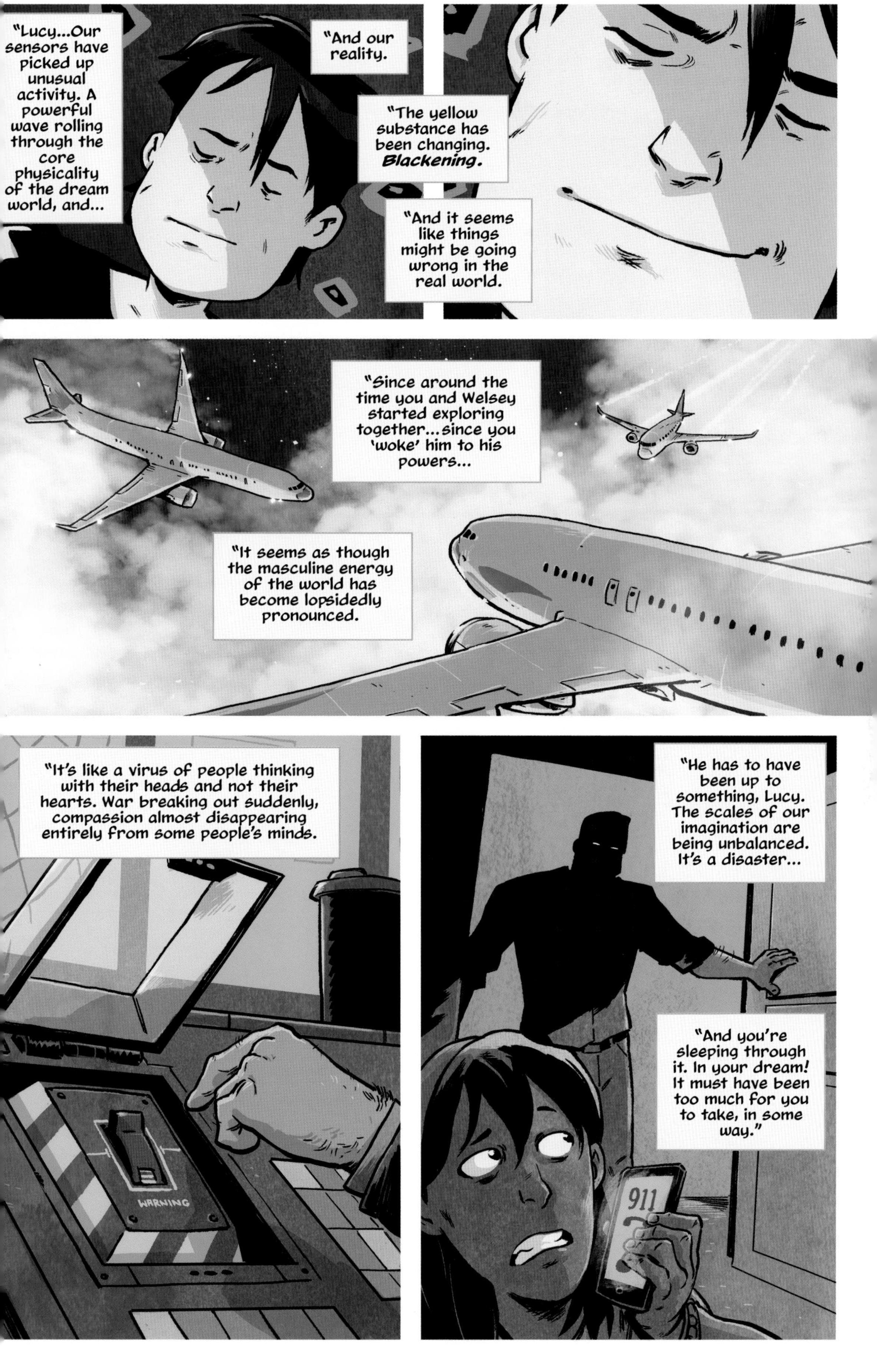
"Lucy...Our sensors have picked up unusual activity. A powerful wave rolling through the core physicality of the dream world, and...
"And our reality.
"The yellow substance has been changing. *Blackening.*
"And it seems like things might be going wrong in the real world.
"Since around the time you and Welsey started exploring together...since you 'woke' him to his powers...
"It seems as though the masculine energy of the world has become lopsidedly pronounced.
"It's like a virus of people thinking with their heads and not their hearts. War breaking out suddenly, compassion almost disappearing entirely from some people's minds.
WARNING
"He has to have been up to something, Lucy. The scales of our imagination are being unbalanced. It's a disaster...
"And you're sleeping through it. In your dream! It must have been too much for you to take, in some way."
911

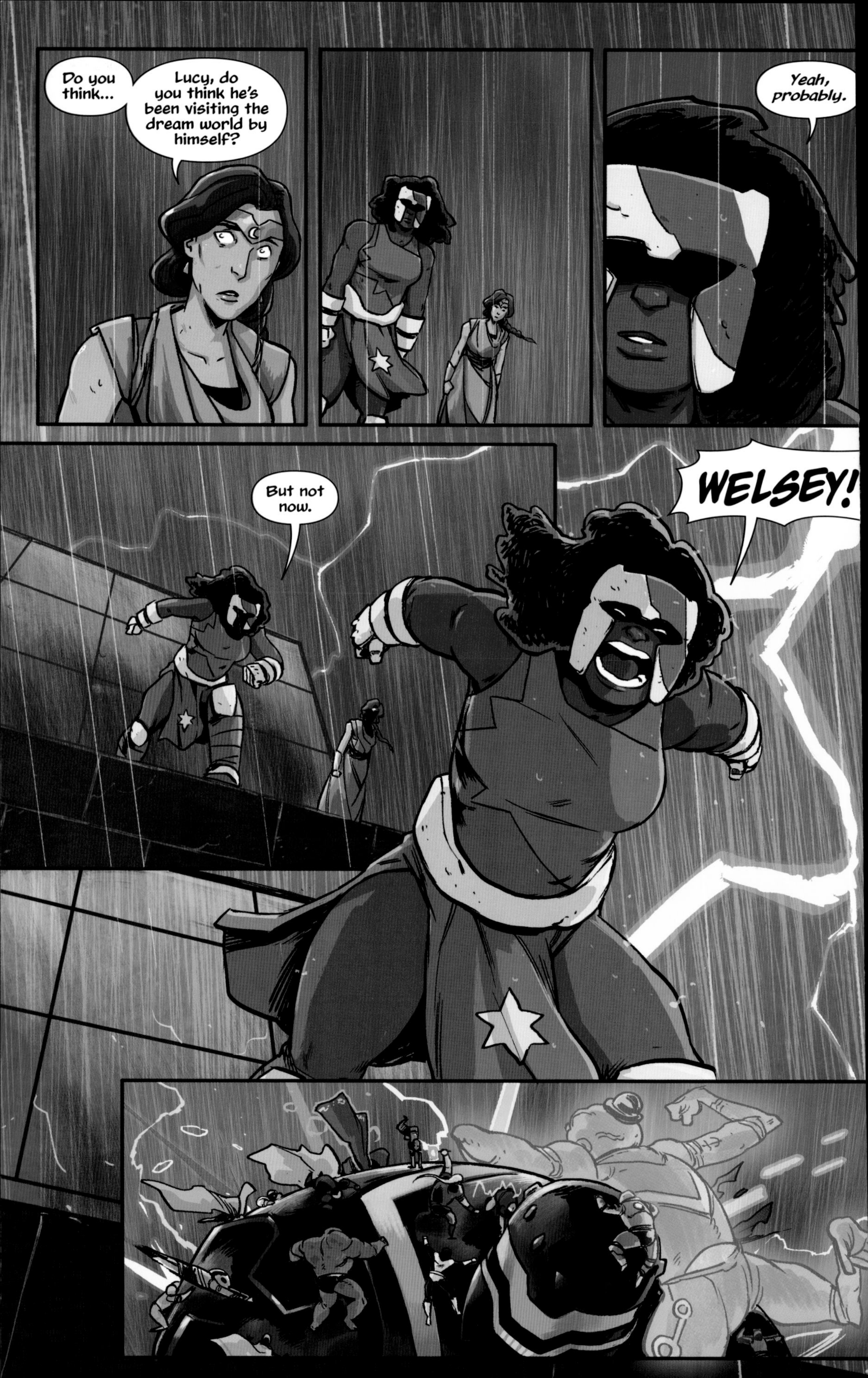
Do you think...
Lucy, do you think he's been visiting the dream world by himself?
Yeah, probably.
But not now.
WELSEY!

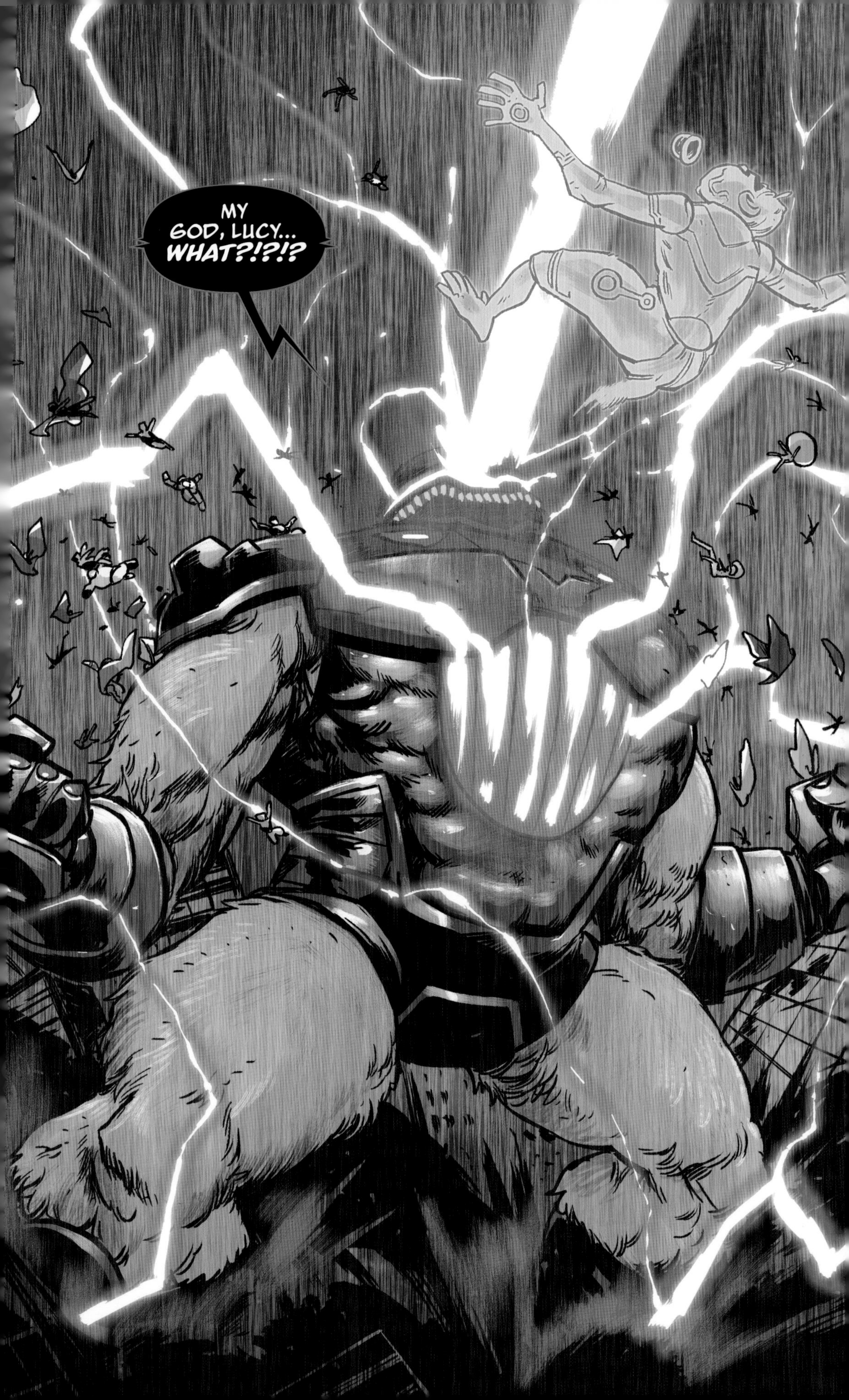
MY GOD, LUCY... WHAT?!?!?

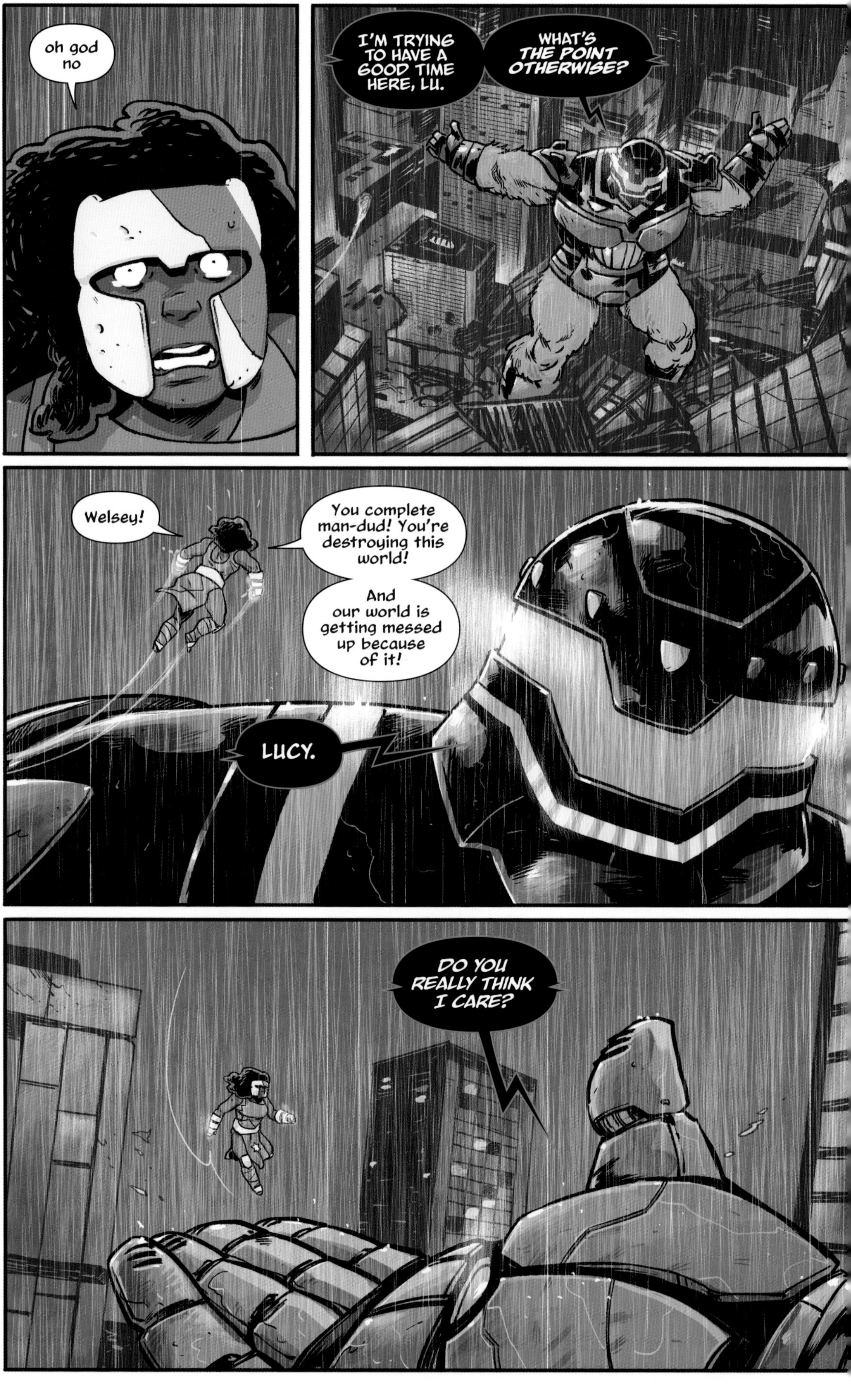
oh god no
I'M TRYING TO HAVE A GOOD TIME HERE, LU.
WHAT'S THE POINT OTHERWISE?
Welsey!
You complete man-dud! You're destroying this world!
And our world is getting messed up because of it!
LUCY.
DO YOU REALLY THINK I CARE?

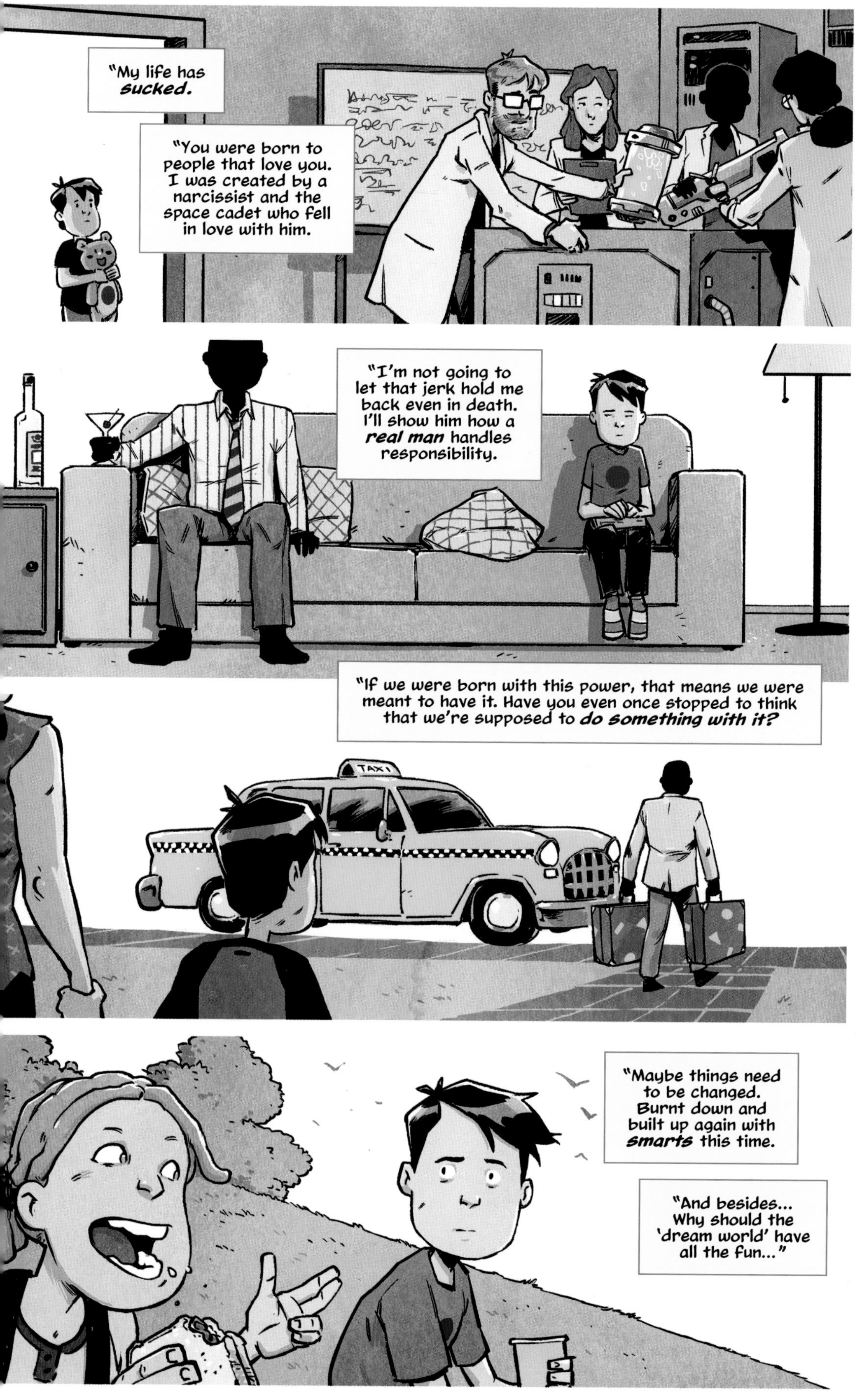
"My life has *sucked.*
"You were born to people that love you. I was created by a narcissist and the space cadet who fell in love with him.
"I'm not going to let that jerk hold me back even in death. I'll show him how a *real man* handles responsibility.
"If we were born with this power, that means we were meant to have it. Have you even once stopped to think that we're supposed to *do something with it?*
TAXI
"Maybe things need to be changed. Burnt down and built up again with *smarts* this time.
"And besides... Why should the 'dream world' have all the fun..."

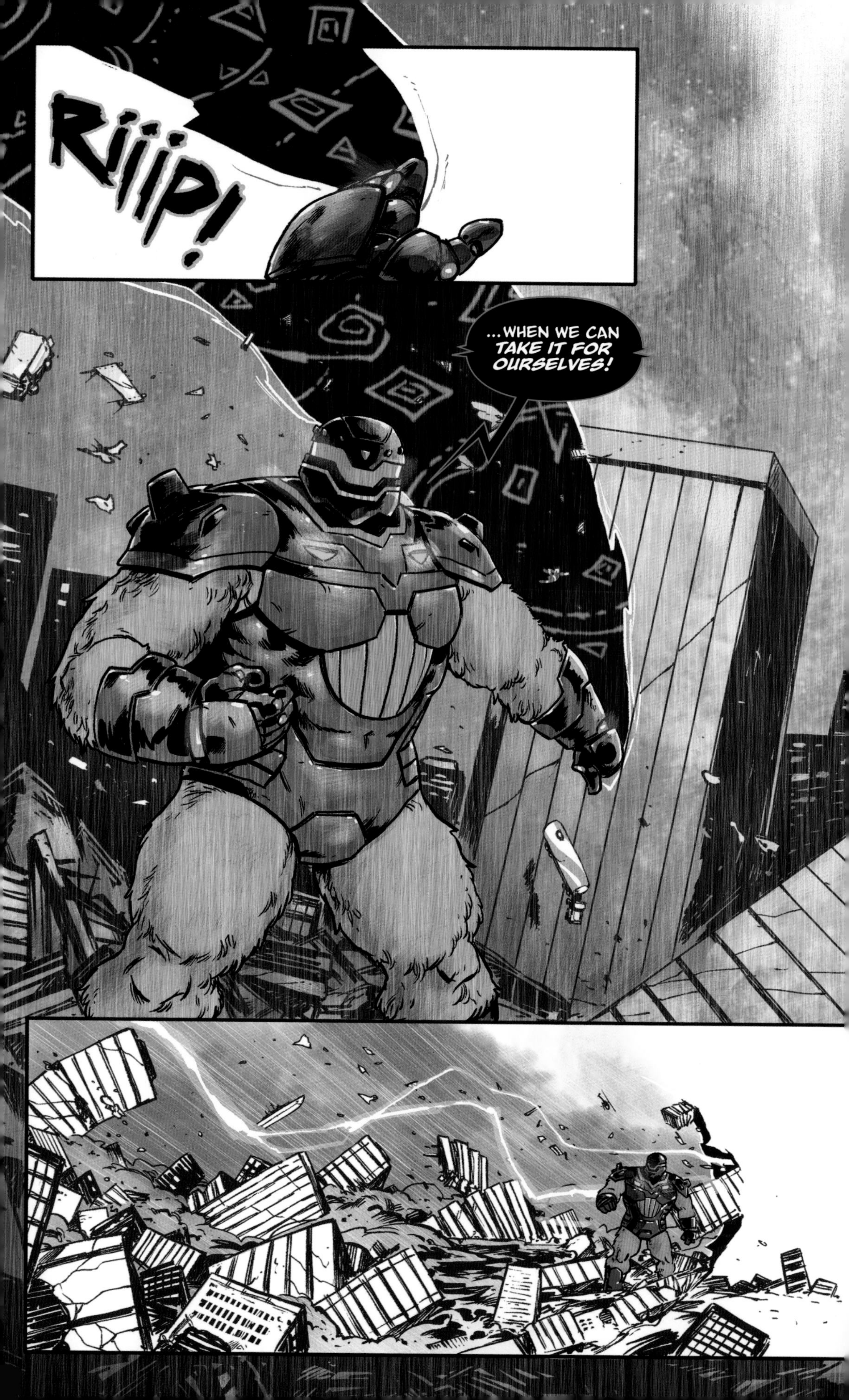
RIIIP!
...WHEN WE CAN TAKE IT FOR OURSELVES!

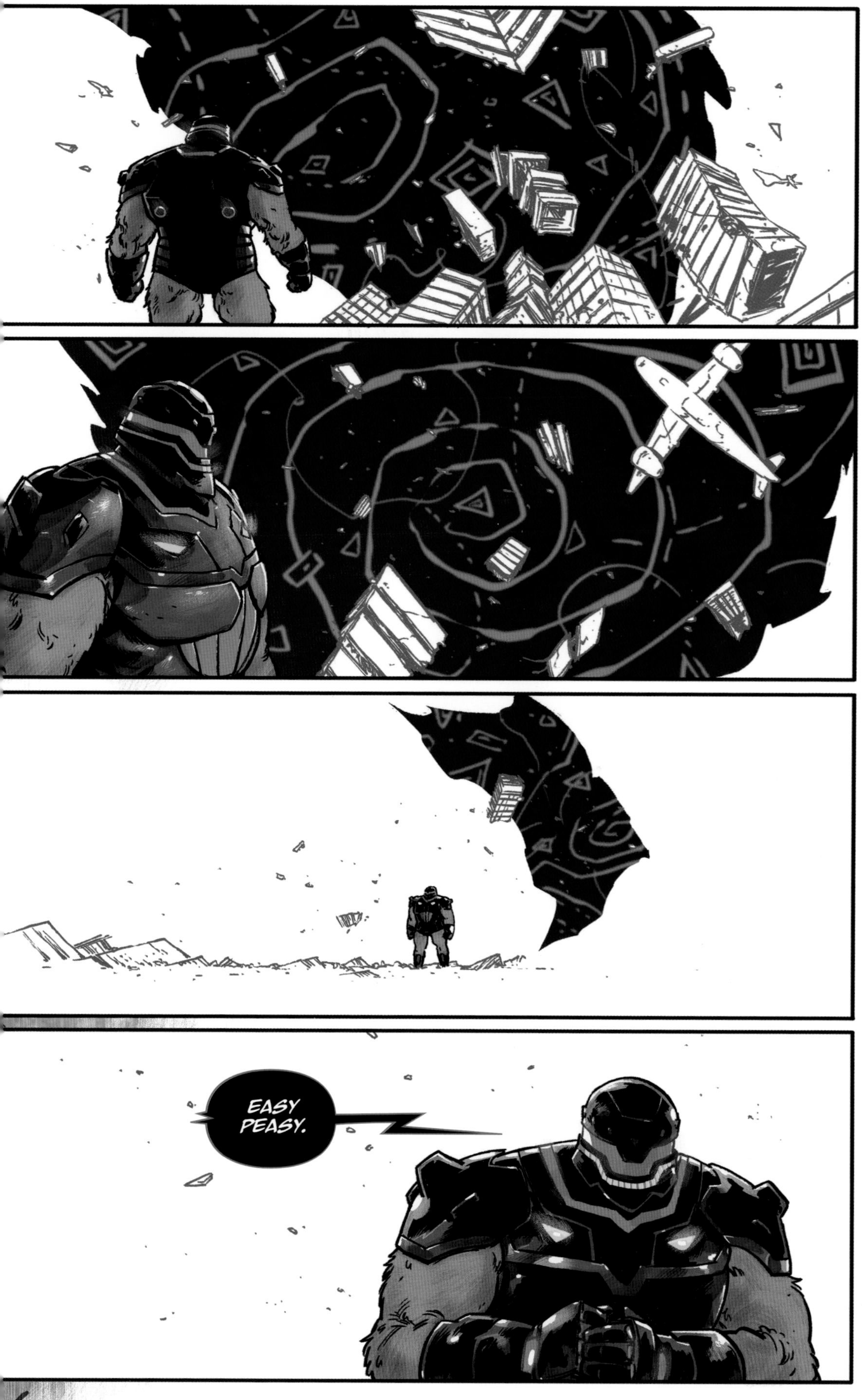
EASY PEASY.

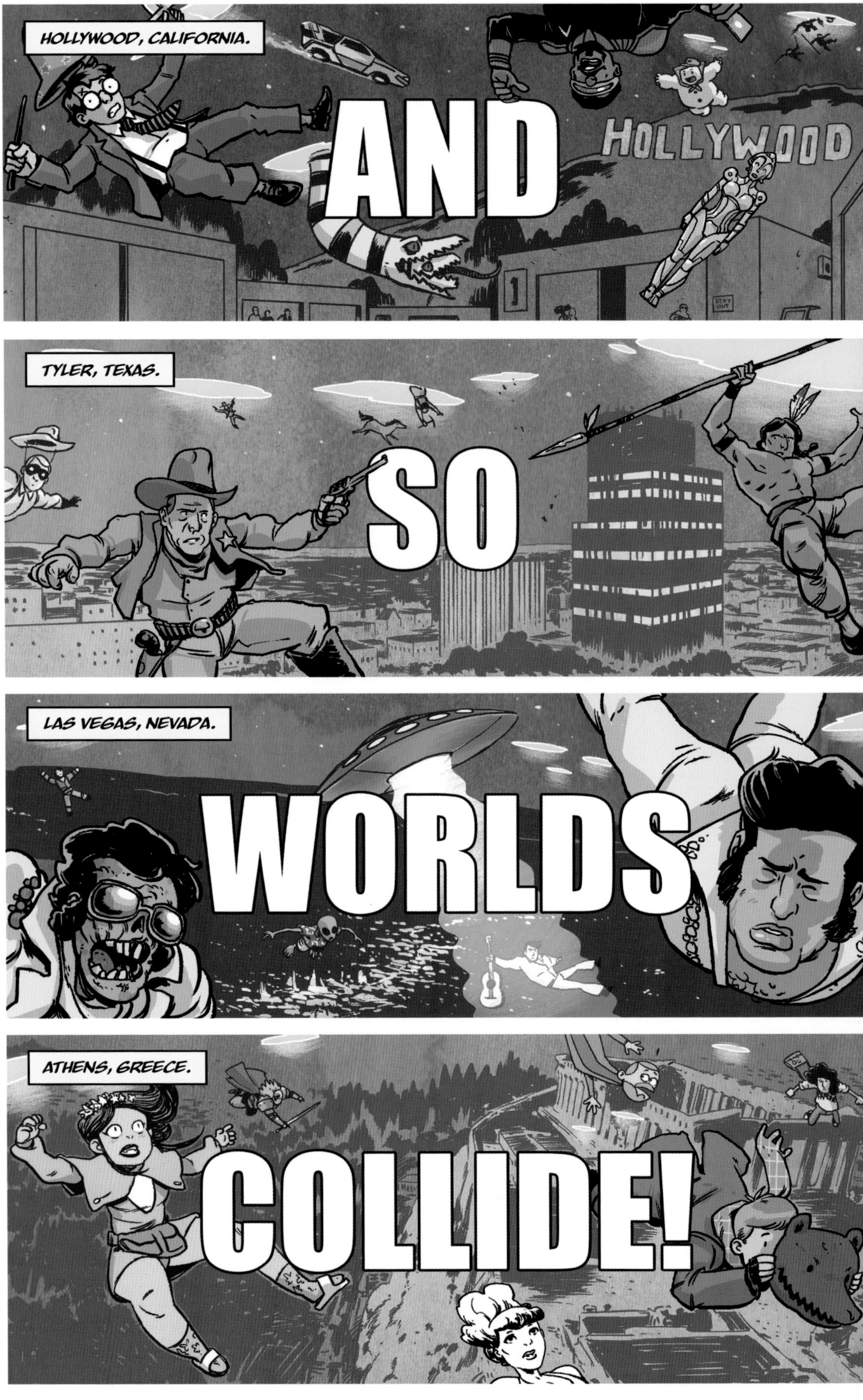
HOLLYWOOD, CALIFORNIA.
HOLLYWOOD
AND
STAY OUT
TYLER, TEXAS.
SO
LAS VEGAS, NEVADA.
WORLDS
ATHENS, GREECE.
COLLIDE!

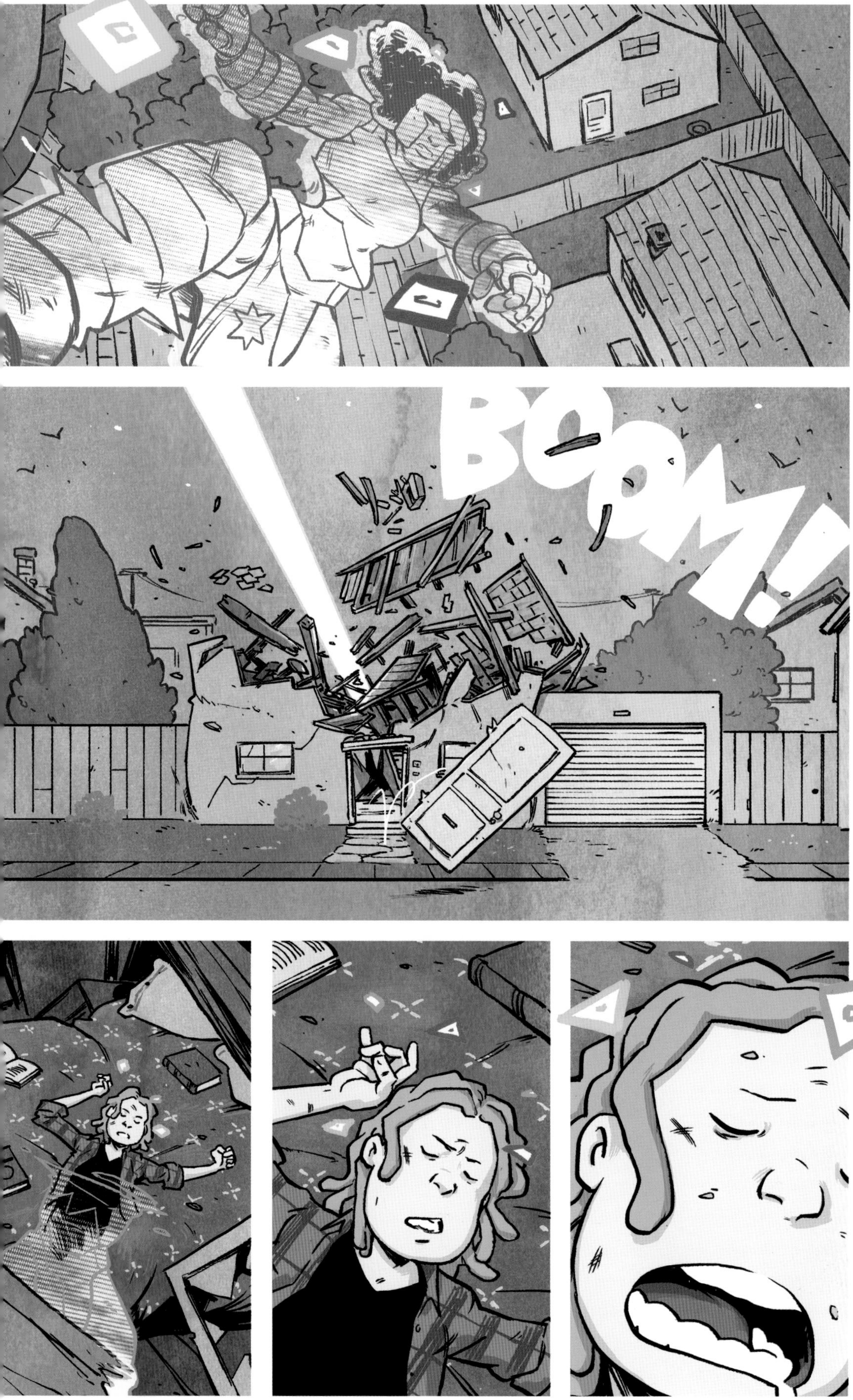
BOOM!!

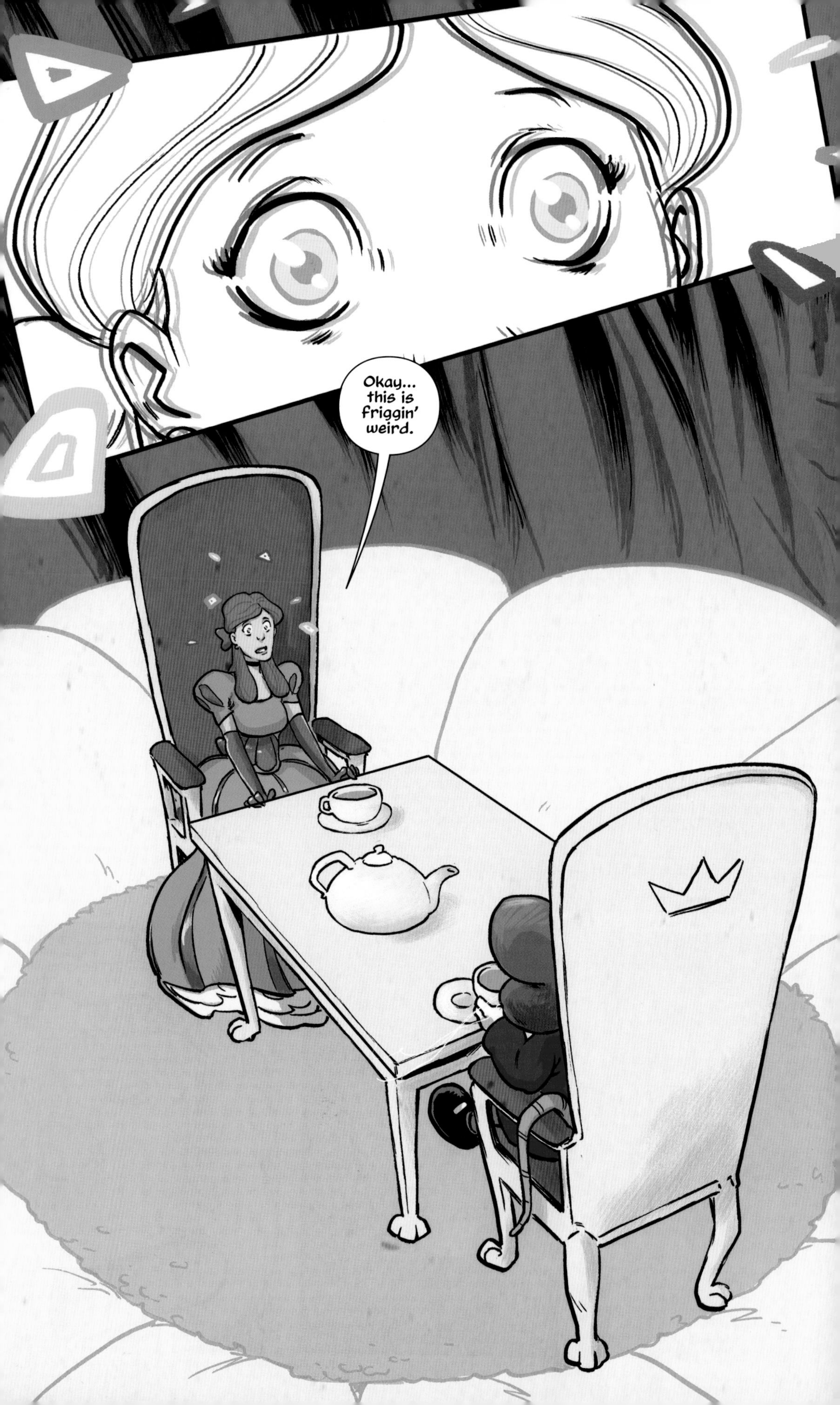
Okay... this is friggin' weird.

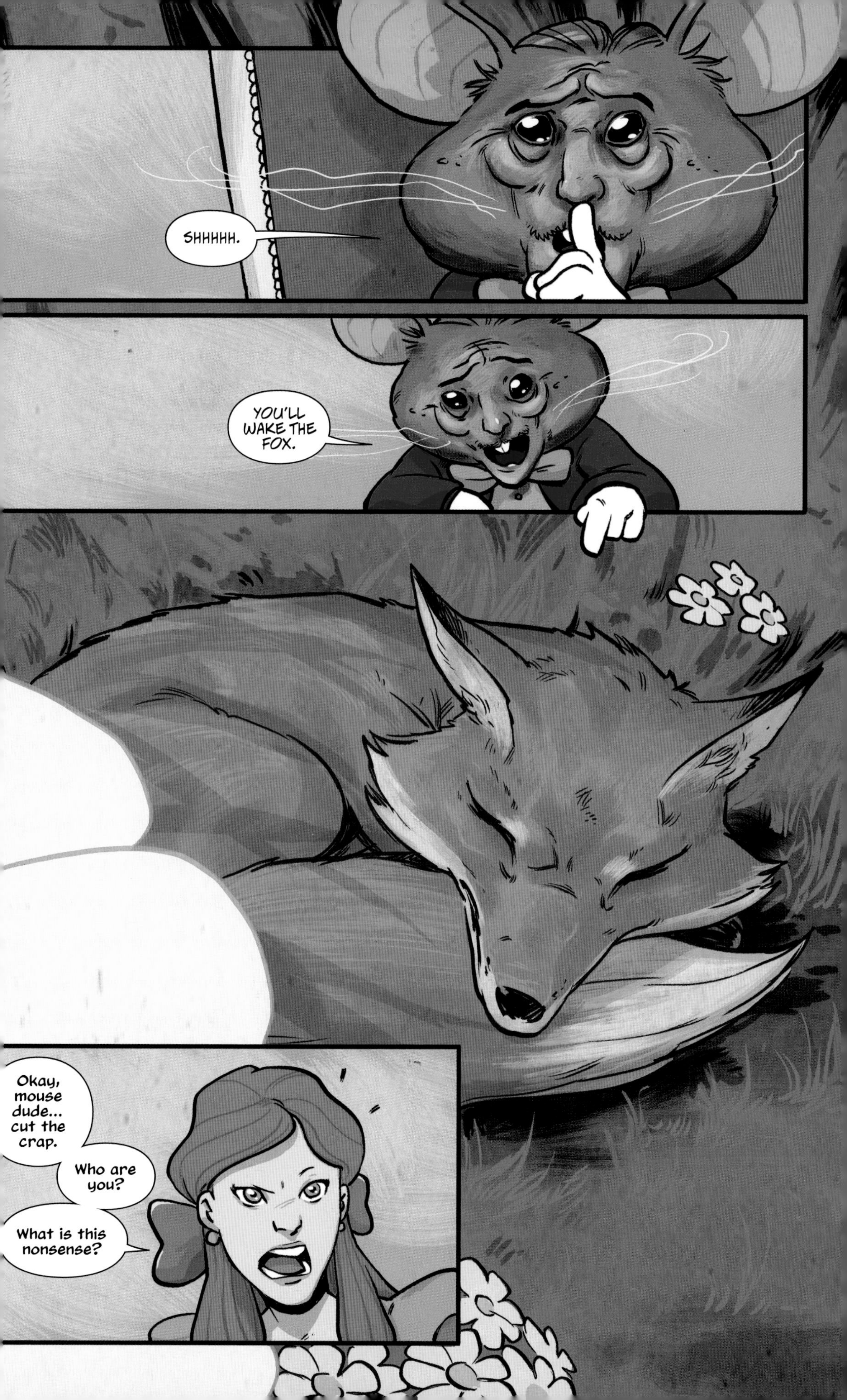
SHHHHH.
YOU'LL WAKE THE FOX.
Okay, mouse dude... cut the crap.
Who are you?
What is this nonsense?

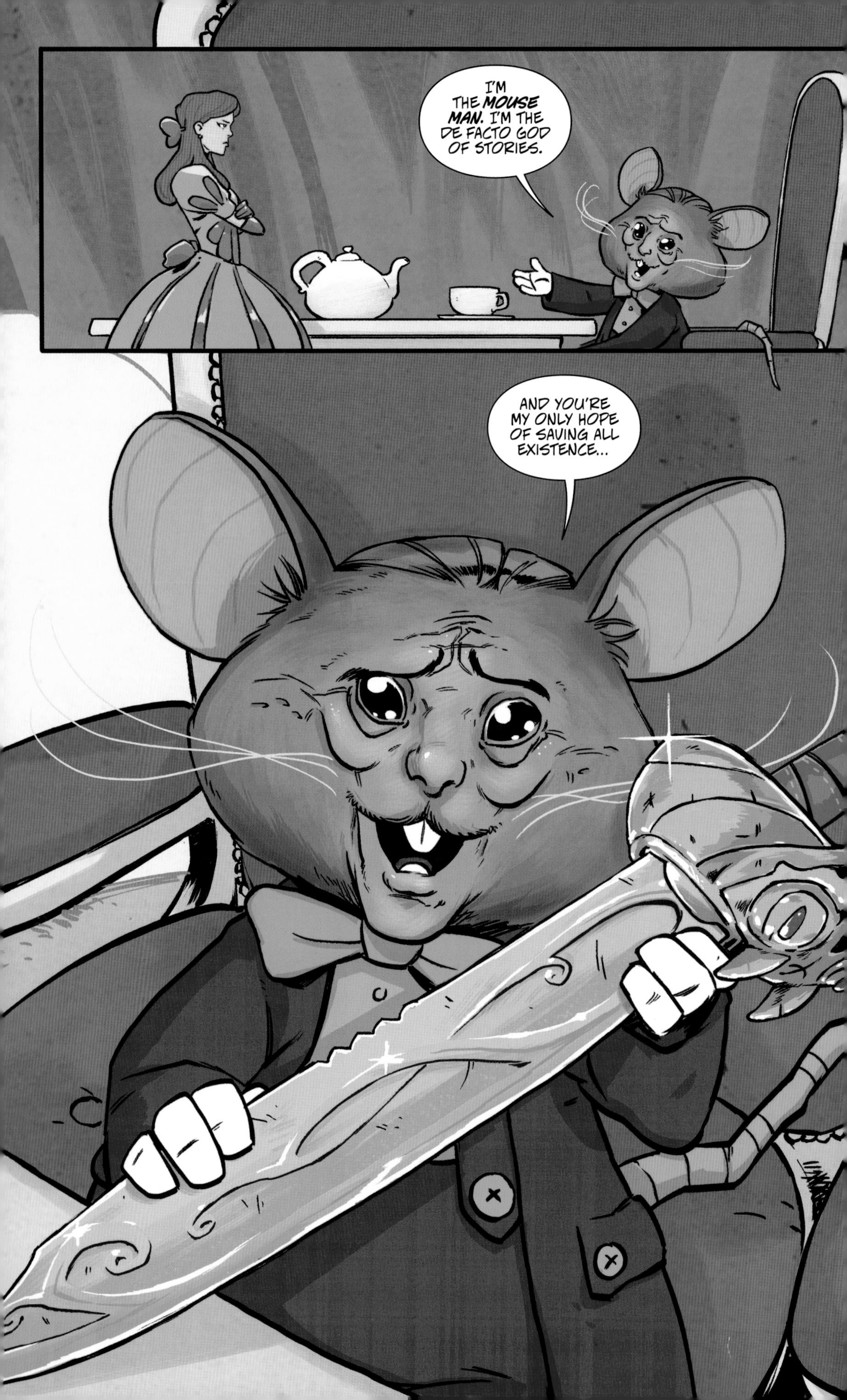
I'M THE **MOUSE MAN.** I'M THE DE FACTO GOD OF STORIES.
AND YOU'RE MY ONLY HOPE OF SAVING ALL EXISTENCE...

ISSUE FOUR COVER BY
MICHAEL DIALYNAS

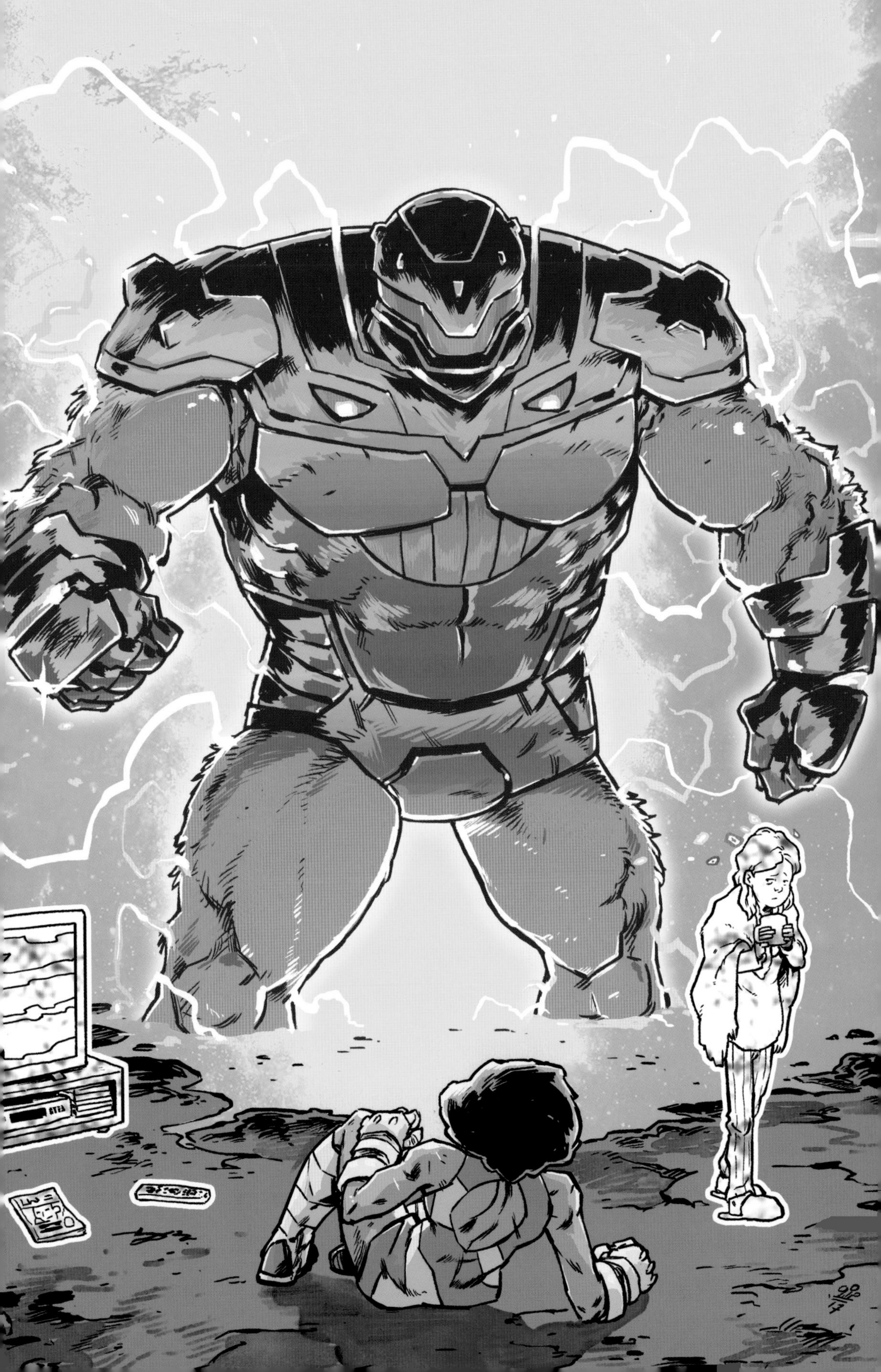

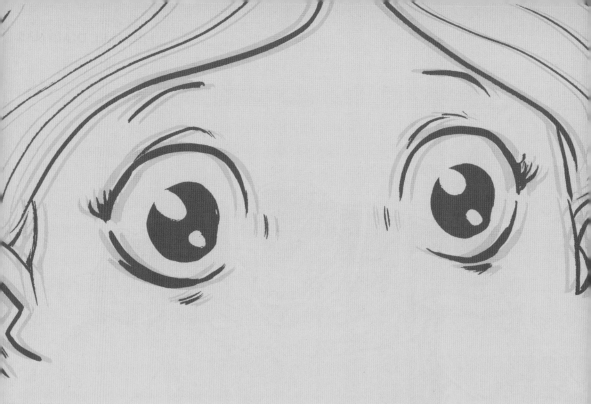

CHAPTER
FIVE

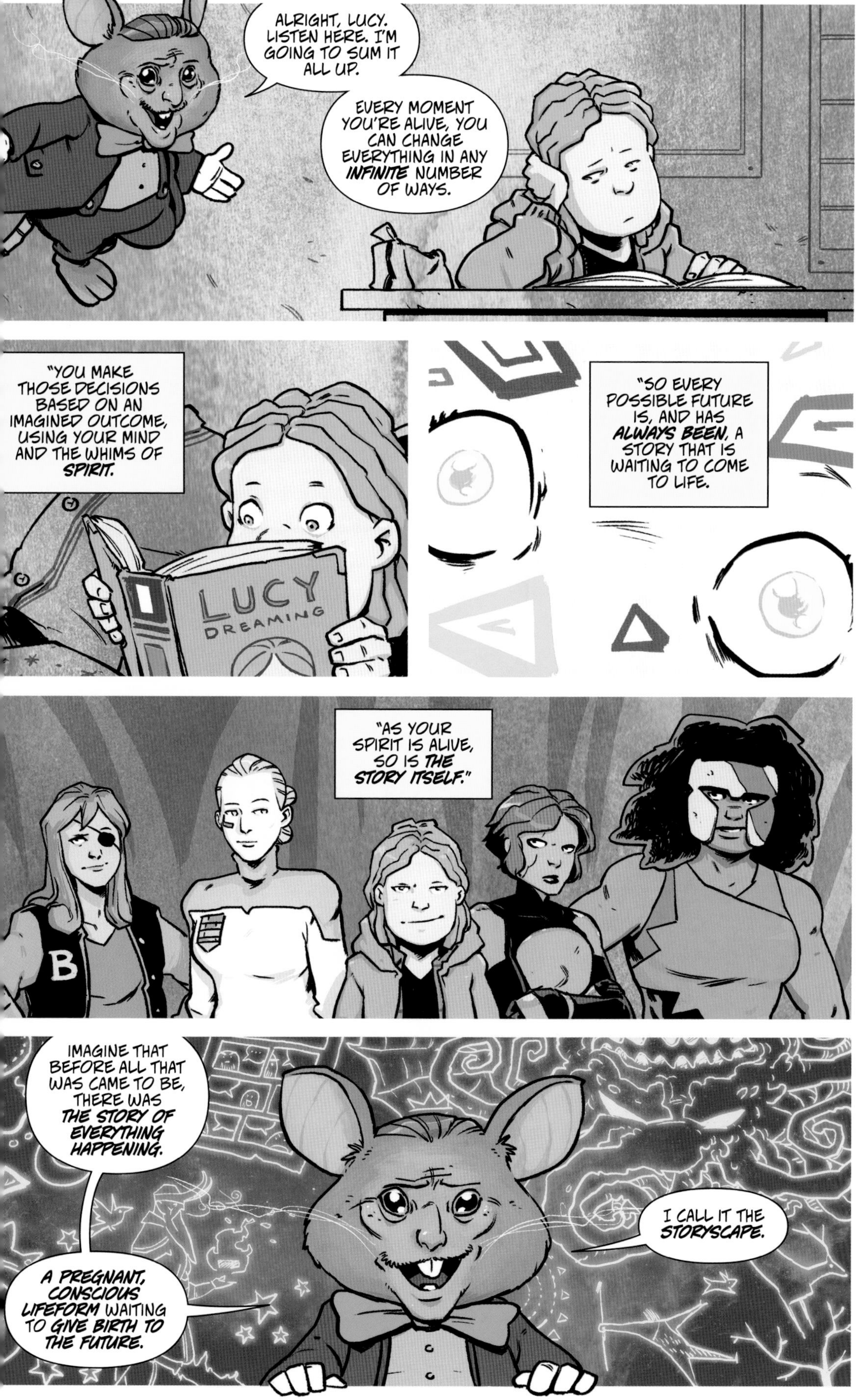
ALRIGHT, LUCY. LISTEN HERE. I'M GOING TO SUM IT ALL UP.
EVERY MOMENT YOU'RE ALIVE, YOU CAN CHANGE EVERYTHING IN ANY INFINITE NUMBER OF WAYS.
"YOU MAKE THOSE DECISIONS BASED ON AN IMAGINED OUTCOME, USING YOUR MIND AND THE WHIMS OF SPIRIT.
LUCY DREAMING
"SO EVERY POSSIBLE FUTURE IS, AND HAS ALWAYS BEEN, A STORY THAT IS WAITING TO COME TO LIFE.
"AS YOUR SPIRIT IS ALIVE, SO IS THE STORY ITSELF."
B
IMAGINE THAT BEFORE ALL THAT WAS CAME TO BE, THERE WAS THE STORY OF EVERYTHING HAPPENING.
A PREGNANT, CONSCIOUS LIFEFORM WAITING TO GIVE BIRTH TO THE FUTURE.
I CALL IT THE STORYSCAPE.

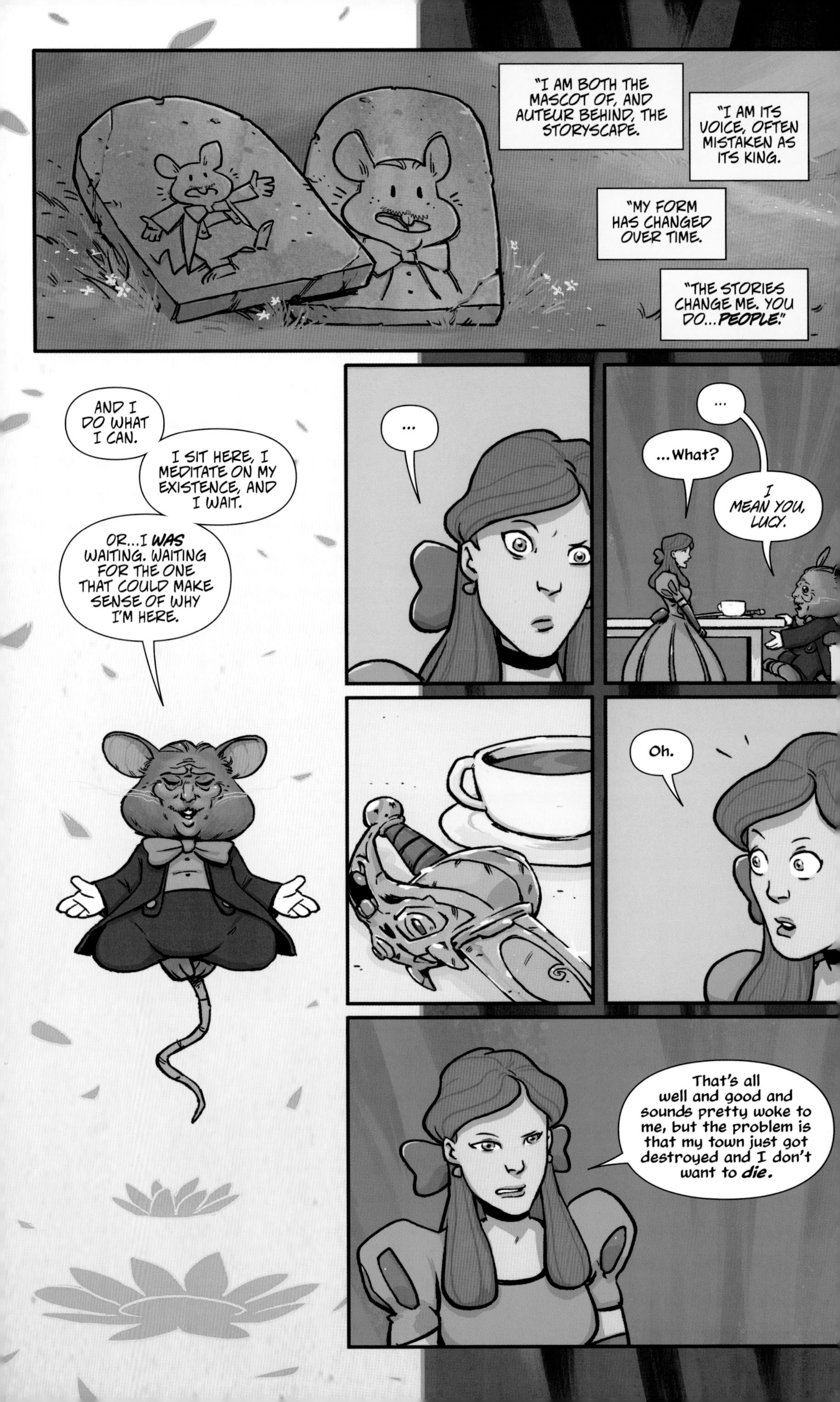
"I AM BOTH THE MASCOT OF, AND AUTEUR BEHIND, THE STORYSCAPE.
"I AM ITS VOICE, OFTEN MISTAKEN AS ITS KING.
"MY FORM HAS CHANGED OVER TIME.
"THE STORIES CHANGE ME. YOU DO... ***PEOPLE.***"
AND I DO WHAT I CAN.
I SIT HERE, I MEDITATE ON MY EXISTENCE, AND I WAIT.
OR...I ***WAS*** WAITING. WAITING FOR THE ONE THAT COULD MAKE SENSE OF WHY I'M HERE.
...
...
...What?
I MEAN YOU, LUCY.
Oh.
That's all well and good and sounds pretty woke to me, but the problem is that my town just got destroyed and I don't want to ***die.***

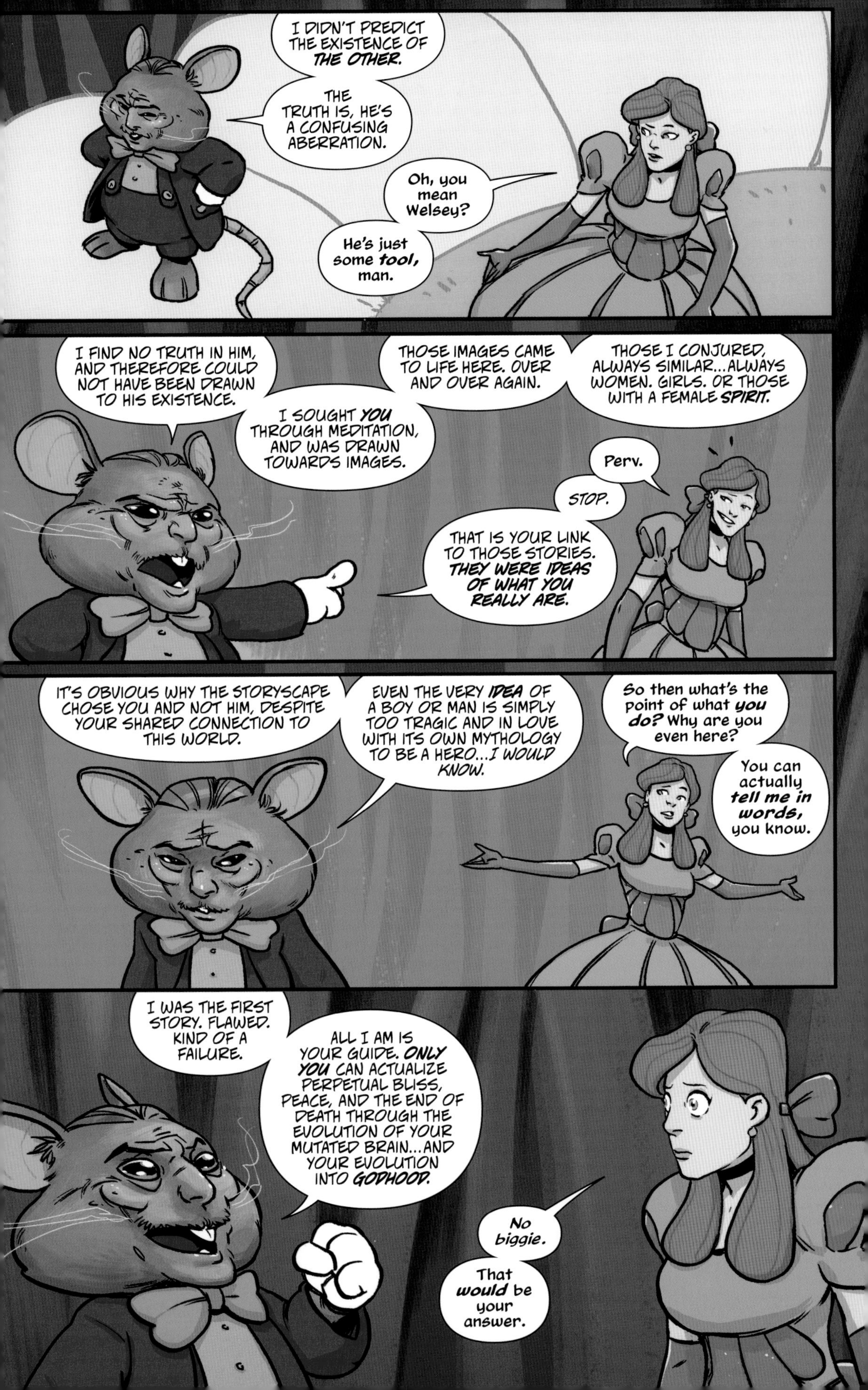
I DIDN'T PREDICT THE EXISTENCE OF THE OTHER.
THE TRUTH IS, HE'S A CONFUSING ABERRATION.
Oh, you mean Welsey?
He's just some tool, man.
I FIND NO TRUTH IN HIM, AND THEREFORE COULD NOT HAVE BEEN DRAWN TO HIS EXISTENCE.
I SOUGHT YOU THROUGH MEDITATION, AND WAS DRAWN TOWARDS IMAGES.
THOSE IMAGES CAME TO LIFE HERE. OVER AND OVER AGAIN.
THOSE I CONJURED, ALWAYS SIMILAR...ALWAYS WOMEN. GIRLS. OR THOSE WITH A FEMALE SPIRIT.
Perv.
STOP.
THAT IS YOUR LINK TO THOSE STORIES. THEY WERE IDEAS OF WHAT YOU REALLY ARE.
IT'S OBVIOUS WHY THE STORYSCAPE CHOSE YOU AND NOT HIM, DESPITE YOUR SHARED CONNECTION TO THIS WORLD.
EVEN THE VERY IDEA OF A BOY OR MAN IS SIMPLY TOO TRAGIC AND IN LOVE WITH ITS OWN MYTHOLOGY TO BE A HERO...I WOULD KNOW.
So then what's the point of what you do? Why are you even here?
You can actually tell me in words, you know.
I WAS THE FIRST STORY. FLAWED. KIND OF A FAILURE.
ALL I AM IS YOUR GUIDE. ONLY YOU CAN ACTUALIZE PERPETUAL BLISS, PEACE, AND THE END OF DEATH THROUGH THE EVOLUTION OF YOUR MUTATED BRAIN...AND YOUR EVOLUTION INTO GODHOOD.
No biggie.
That would be your answer.

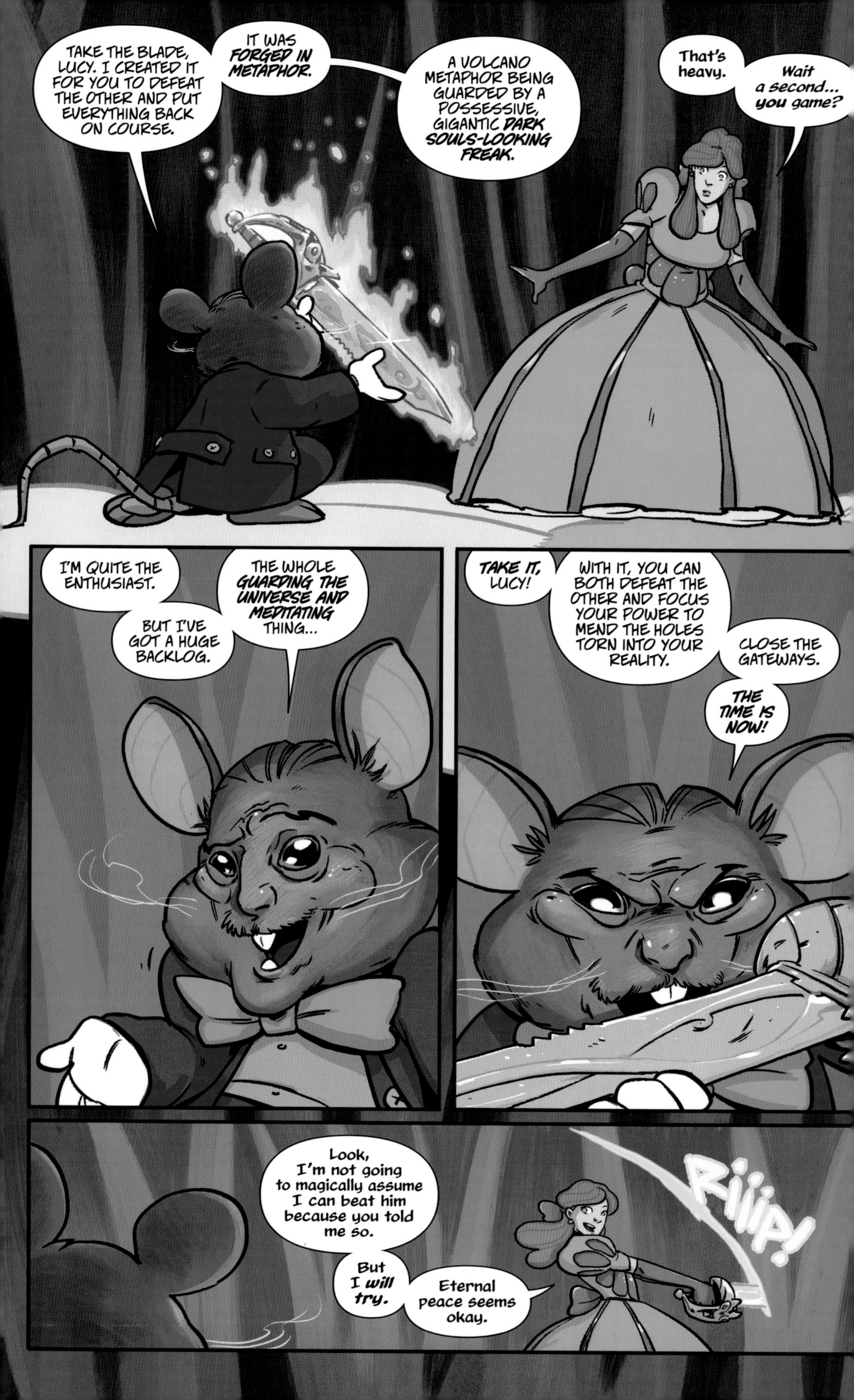
TAKE THE BLADE, LUCY. I CREATED IT FOR YOU TO DEFEAT THE OTHER AND PUT EVERYTHING BACK ON COURSE.
IT WAS **FORGED IN METAPHOR.**
A VOLCANO METAPHOR BEING GUARDED BY A POSSESSIVE, GIGANTIC ***DARK SOULS*-LOOKING FREAK.**
That's heavy.
Wait a second... **you** game?
I'M QUITE THE ENTHUSIAST.
BUT I'VE GOT A HUGE BACKLOG.
THE WHOLE ***GUARDING THE UNIVERSE AND MEDITATING*** THING...
TAKE IT, LUCY!
WITH IT, YOU CAN BOTH DEFEAT THE OTHER AND FOCUS YOUR POWER TO MEND THE HOLES TORN INTO YOUR REALITY.
CLOSE THE GATEWAYS.
THE TIME IS NOW!
Look, I'm not going to magically assume I can beat him because you told me so.
But I ***will try.***
Eternal peace seems okay.
RIIIP!

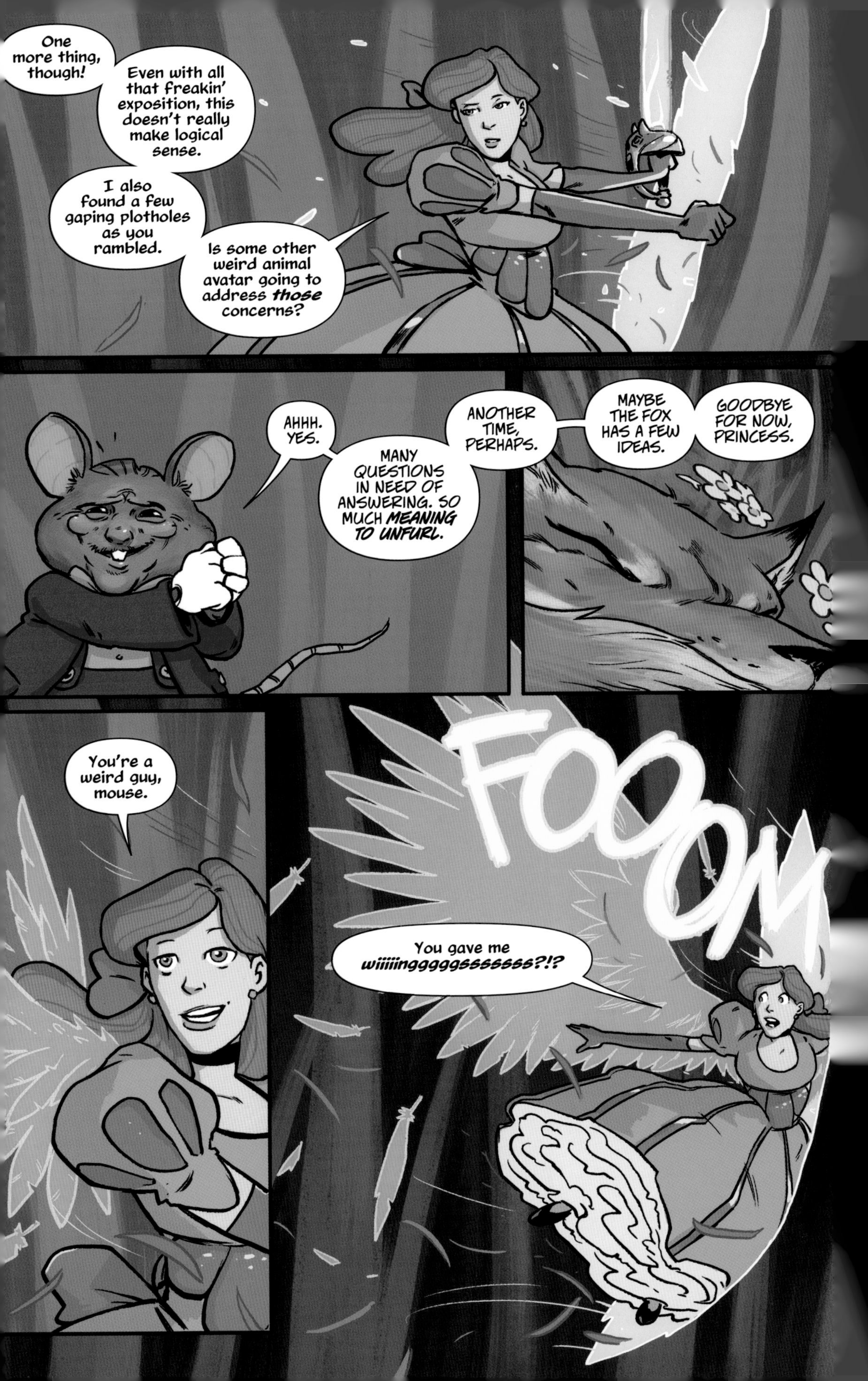

One more thing, though!
Even with all that freakin' exposition, this doesn't really make logical sense.
I also found a few gaping plotholes as you rambled.
Is some other weird animal avatar going to address *those* concerns?
AHHH. YES.
MANY QUESTIONS IN NEED OF ANSWERING. SO MUCH *MEANING TO UNFURL.*
ANOTHER TIME, PERHAPS.
MAYBE THE FOX HAS A FEW IDEAS.
GOODBYE FOR NOW, PRINCESS.
You're a weird guy, mouse.
FOOOOM
You gave me *wiiiiingggggsssssss?!?*

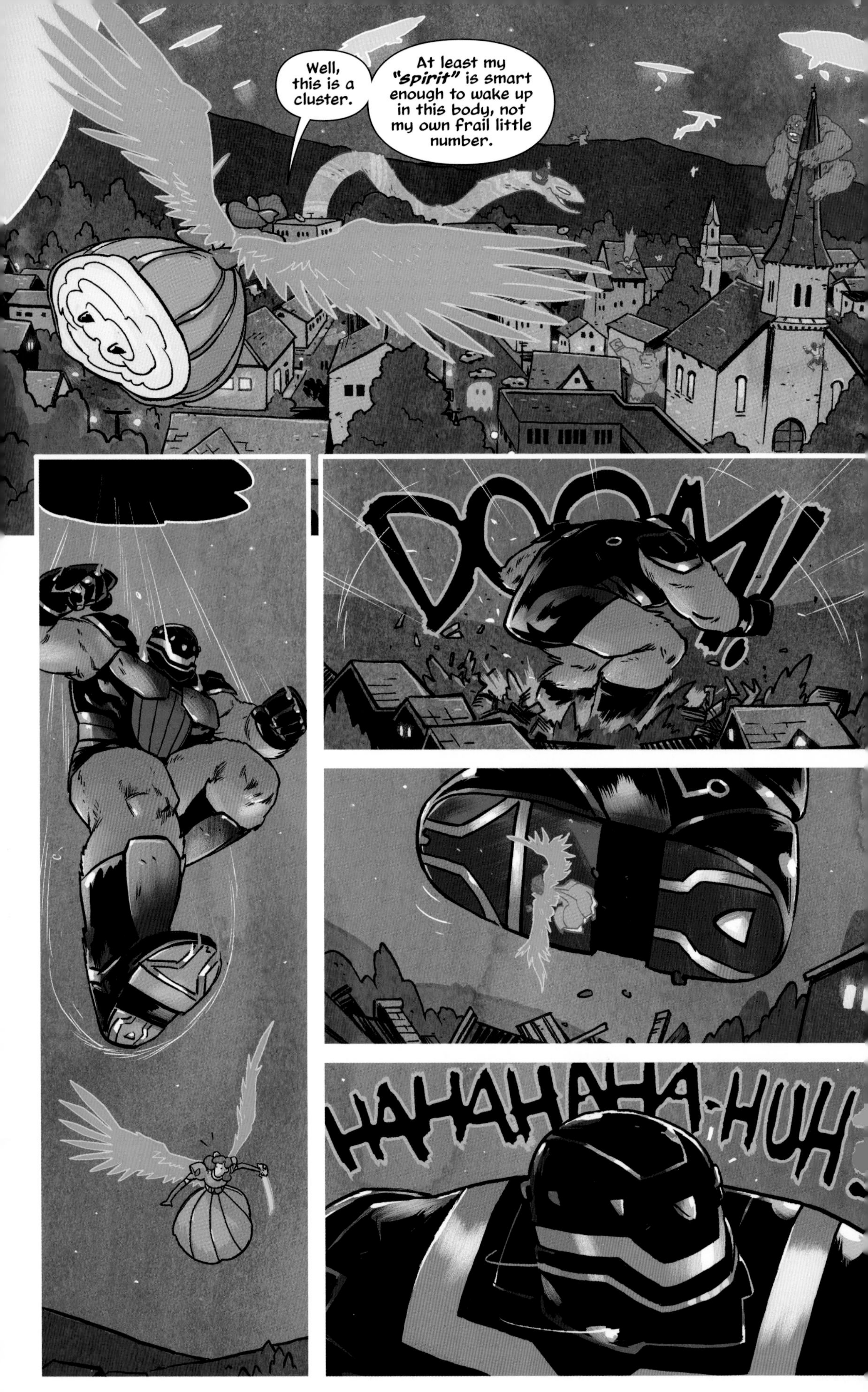

Well, this is a cluster.
At least my "spirit" is smart enough to wake up in this body, not my own frail little number.
DOOM!
HAHAHAHA-HUH?

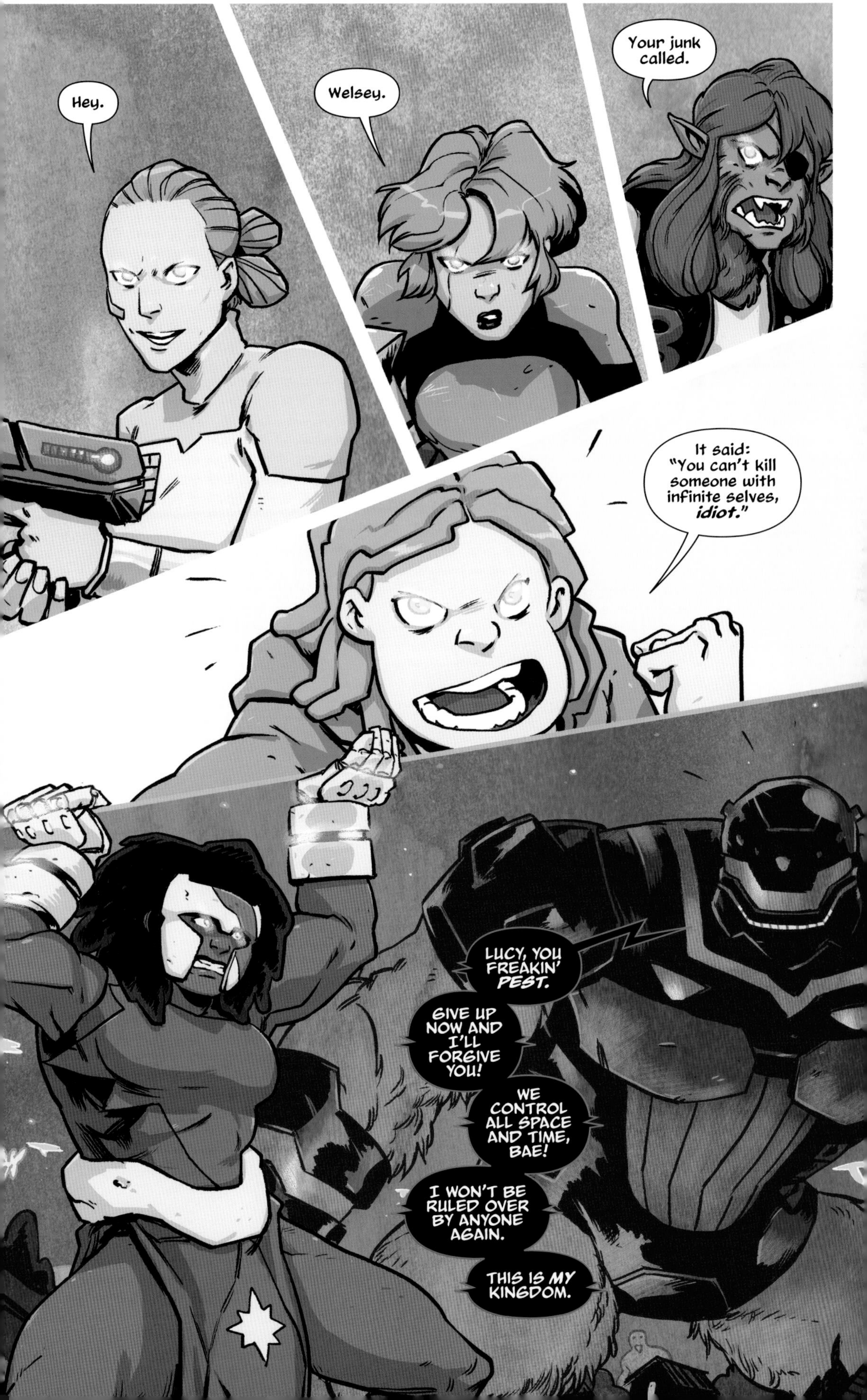
Hey.
Welsey.
Your junk called.
It said: "You can't kill someone with infinite selves, *idiot.*"
LUCY, YOU FREAKIN' *PEST.*
GIVE UP NOW AND I'LL FORGIVE YOU!
WE CONTROL ALL SPACE AND TIME, BAE!
I WON'T BE RULED OVER BY ANYONE AGAIN.
THIS IS *MY* KINGDOM.

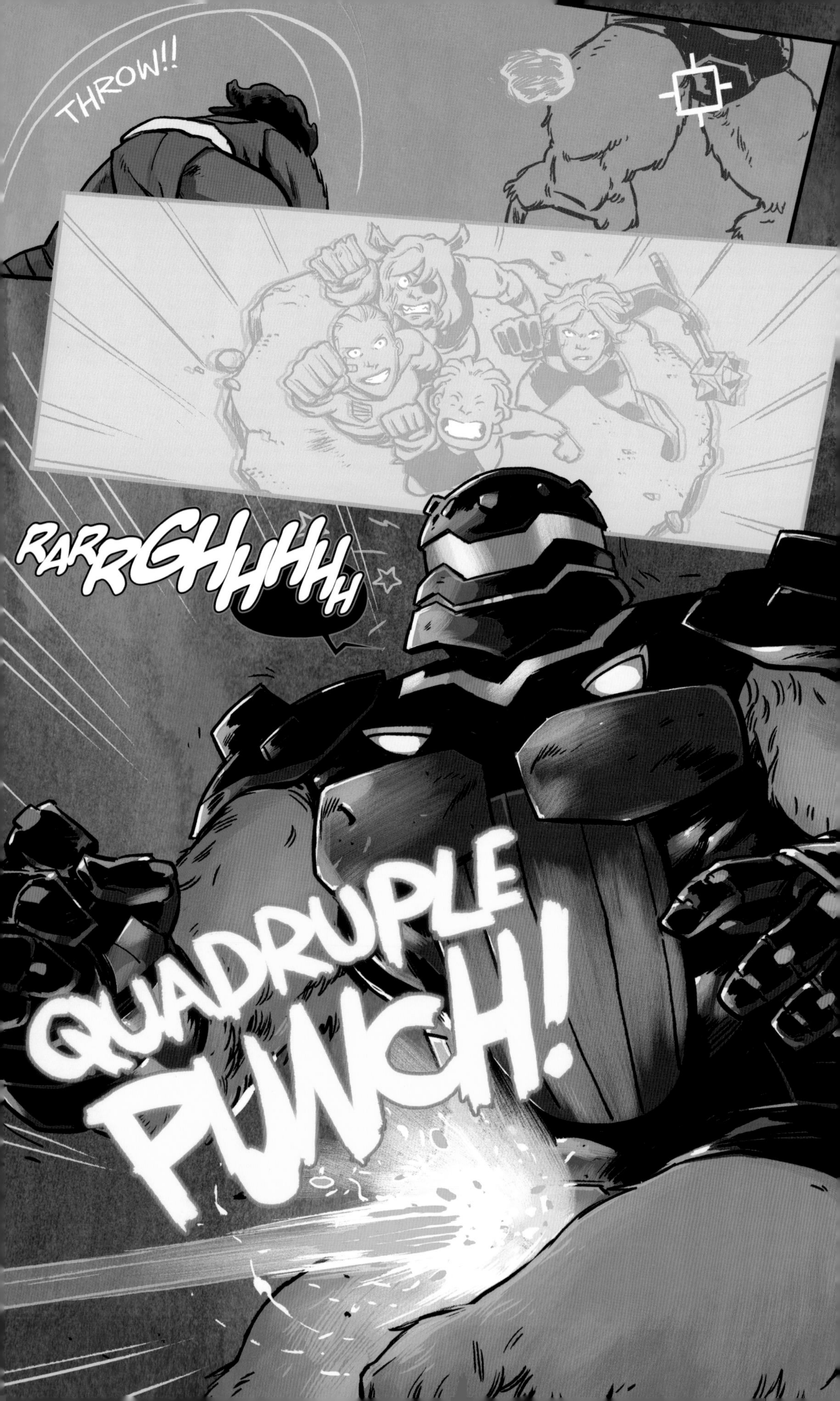
THROW!!
RARRRGHHHHH
QUADRUPLE PUNCH!

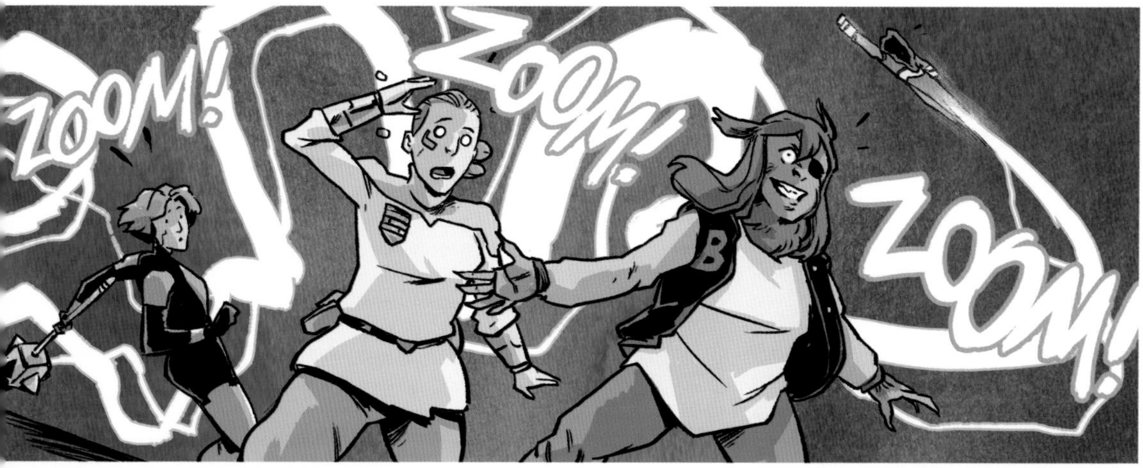
ZOOM!
ZOOM!
ZOOM!
ZOOM!

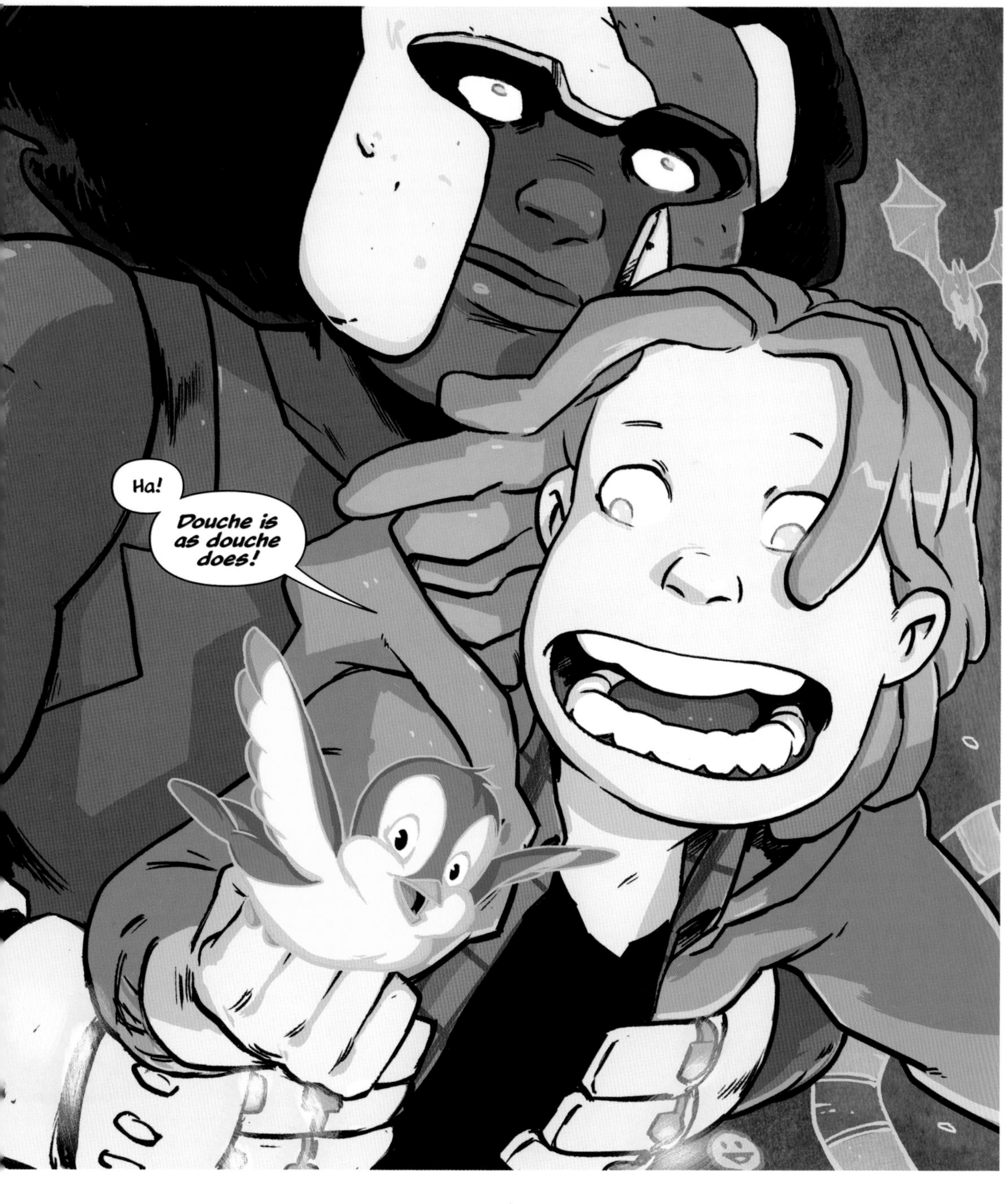
Ha!
Douche is as douche does!

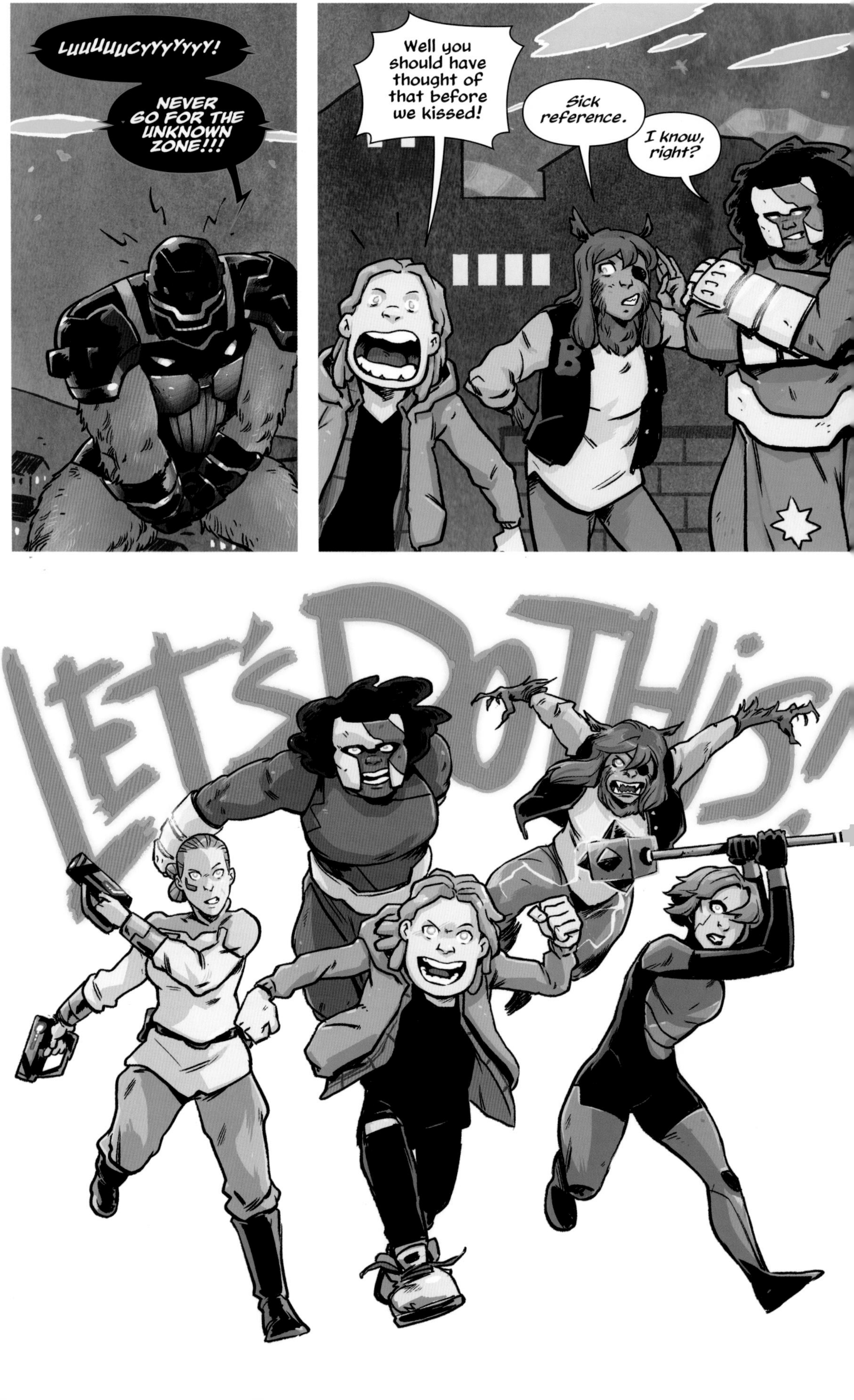
LUUUUUCYYYYYYY!
NEVER GO FOR THE UNKNOWN ZONE!!!
Well you should have thought of that before we kissed!
Sick reference.
I know, right?
LET'S DO THIS!

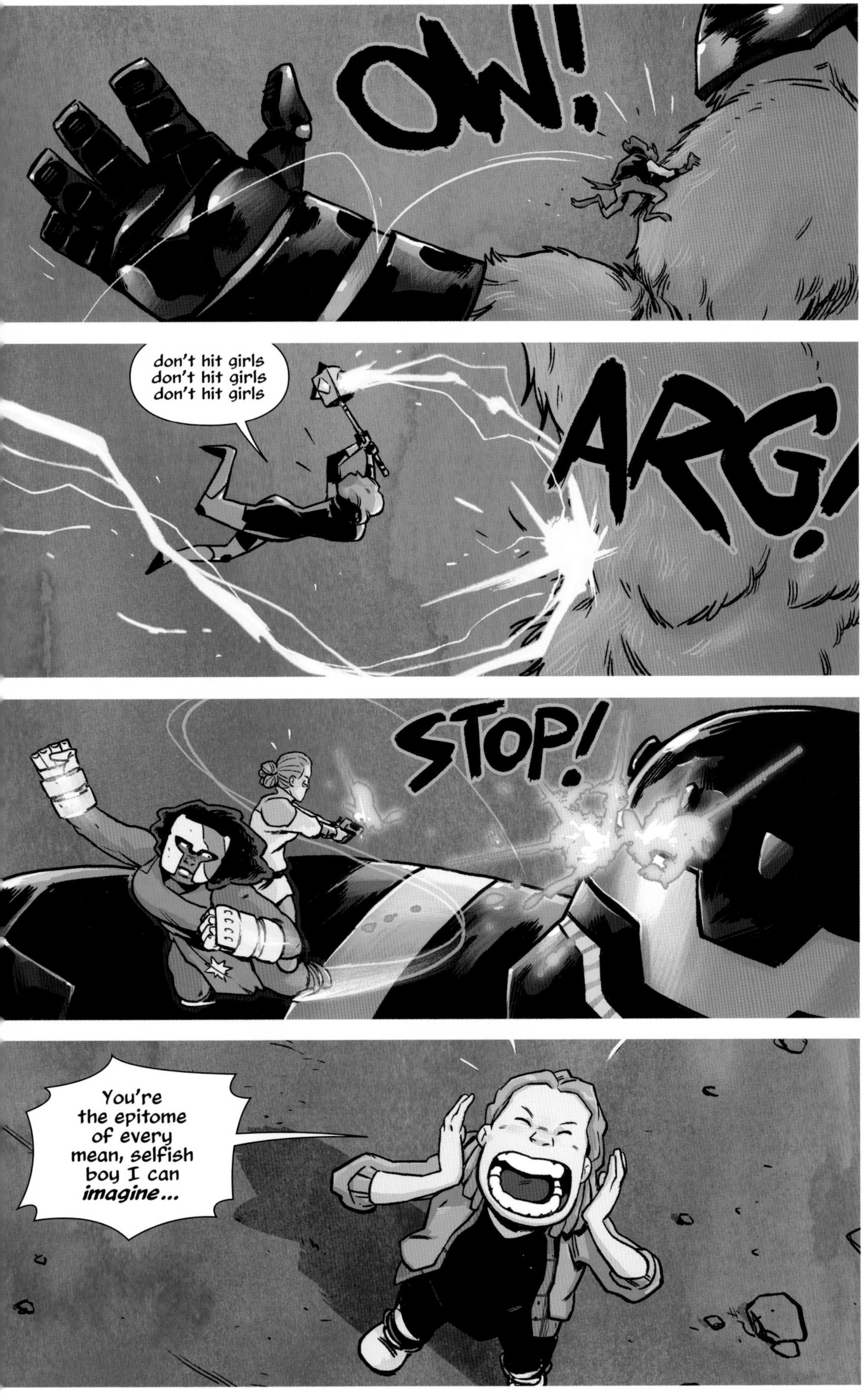
OW!
don't hit girls
don't hit girls
don't hit girls
ARG!
STOP!
You're the epitome of every mean, selfish boy I can *imagine*...

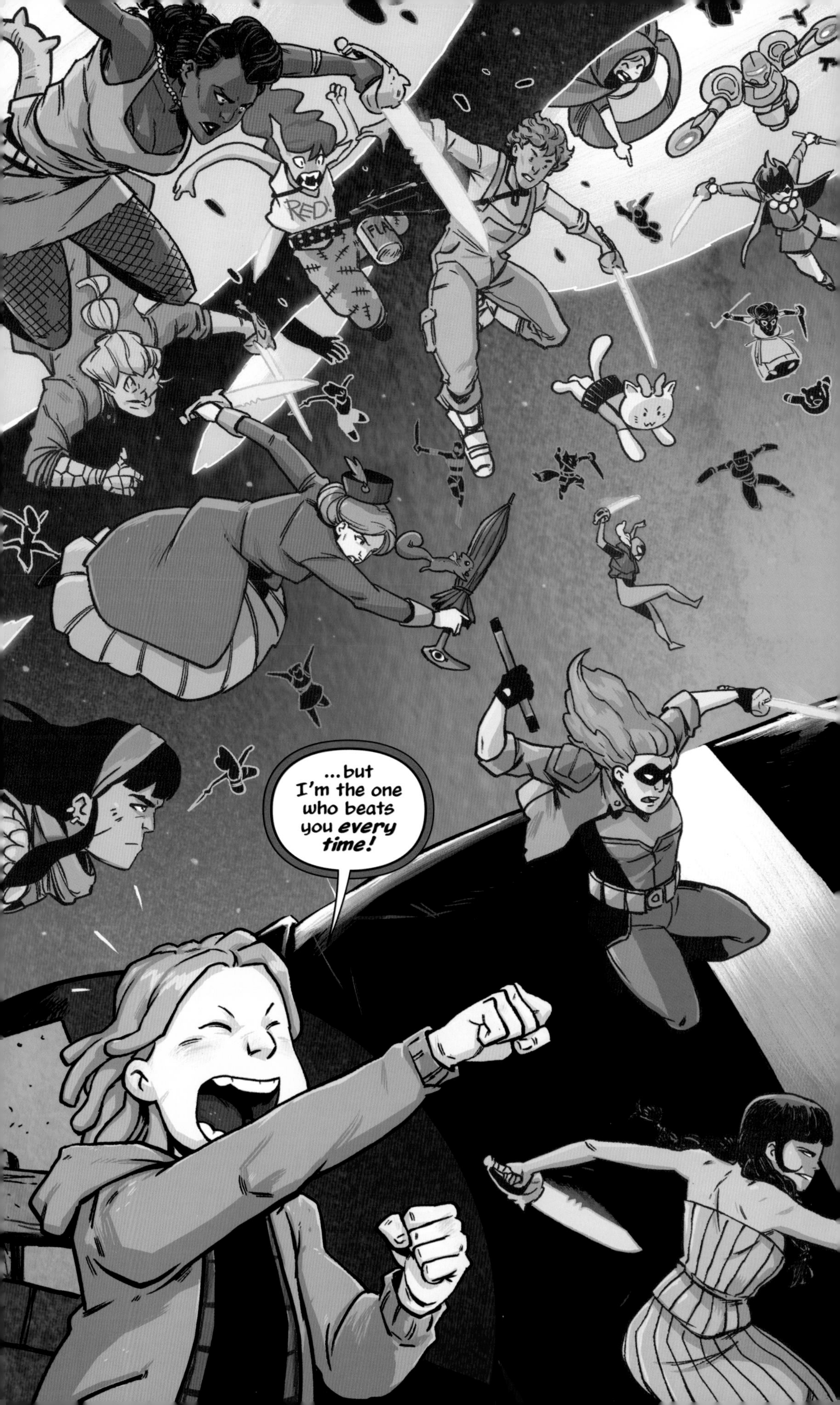

RED!
FLA
...but I'm the one who beats you *every time!*

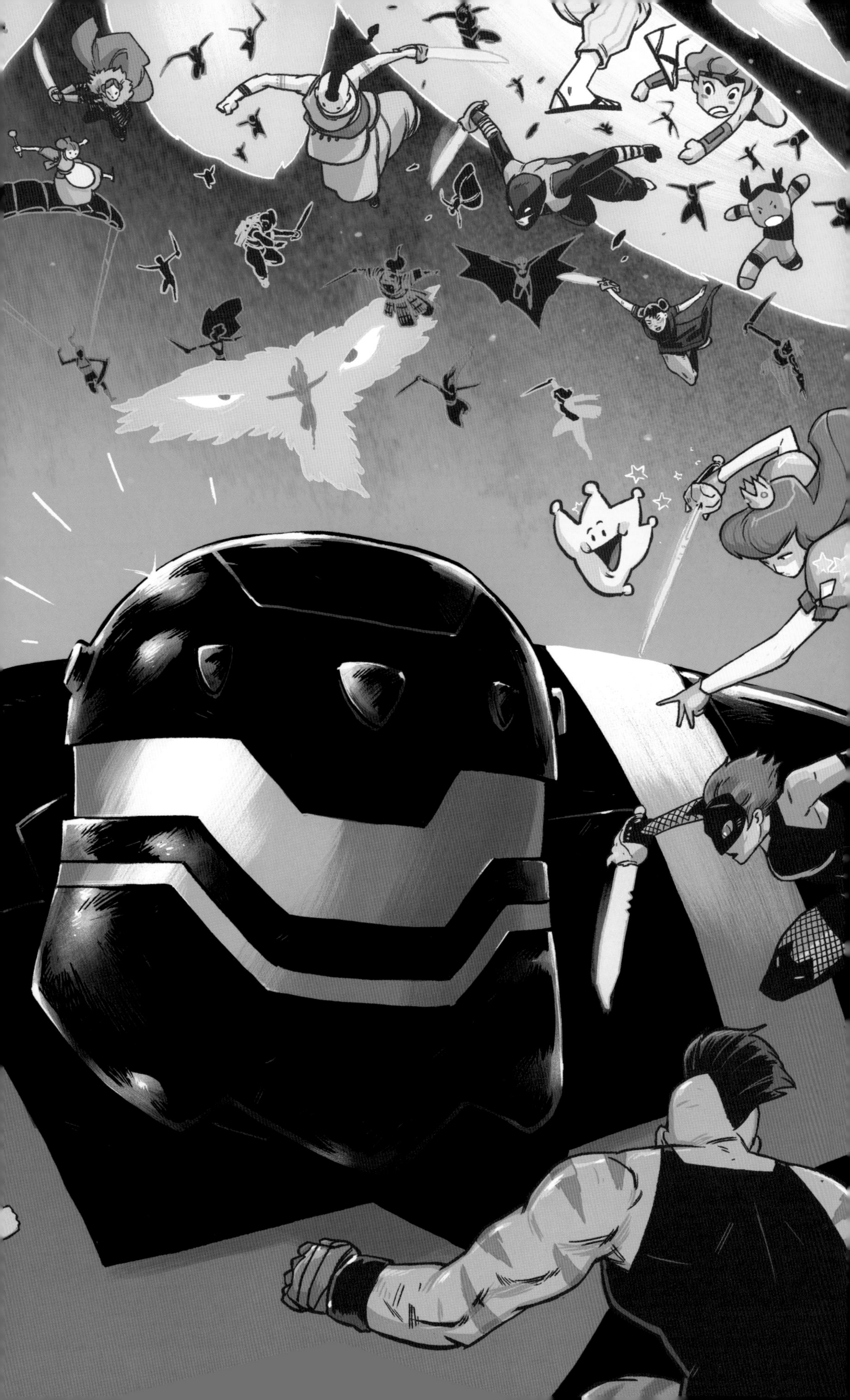

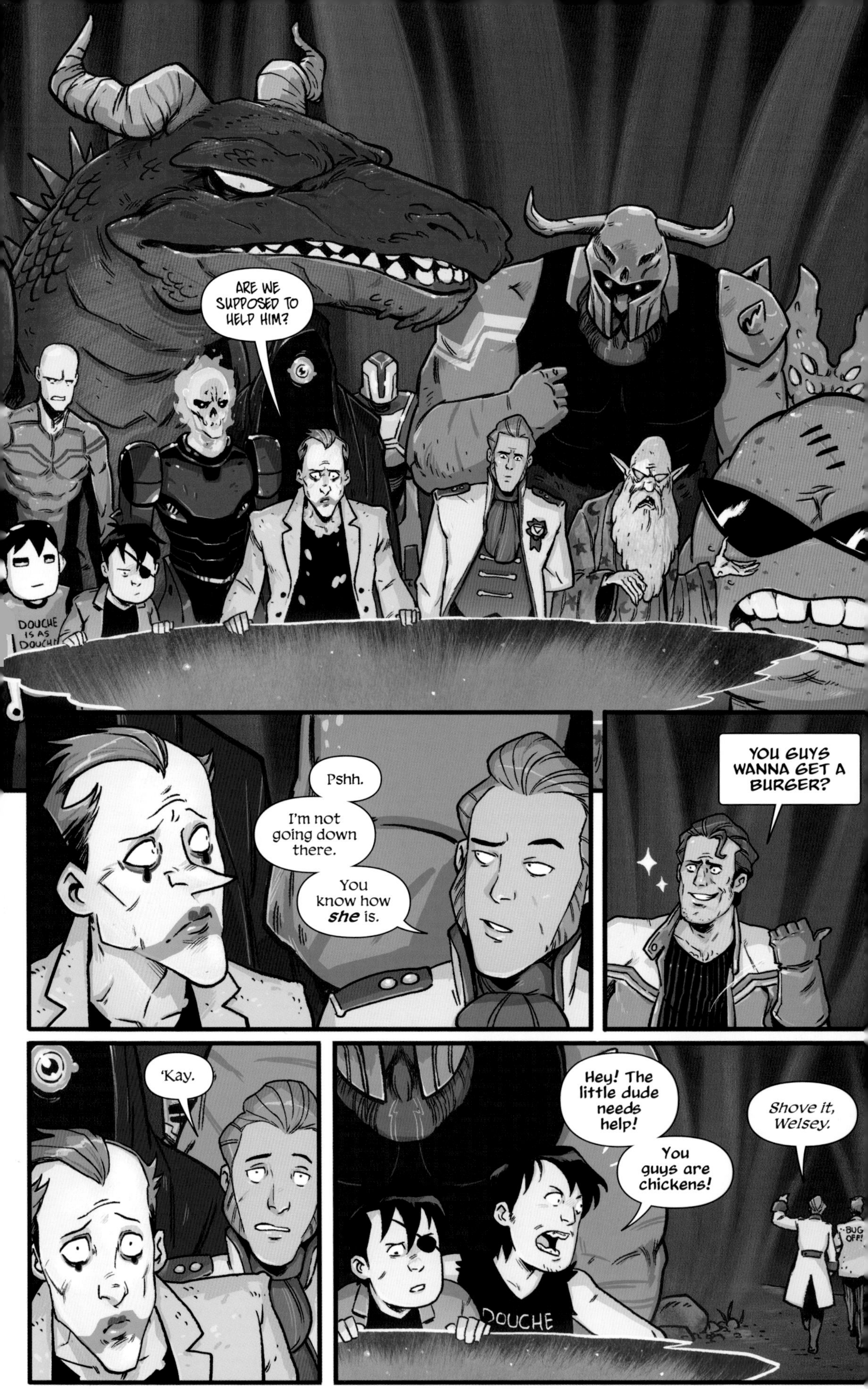

ARE WE SUPPOSED TO HELP HIM?
DOUCHE IS AS DOUCH
Pshh.
I'm not going down there.
You know how *she* is.
YOU GUYS WANNA GET A BURGER?
'Kay.
Hey! The little dude needs help!
You guys are chickens!
Shove it, Welsey.
BUG OFF!
DOUCHE

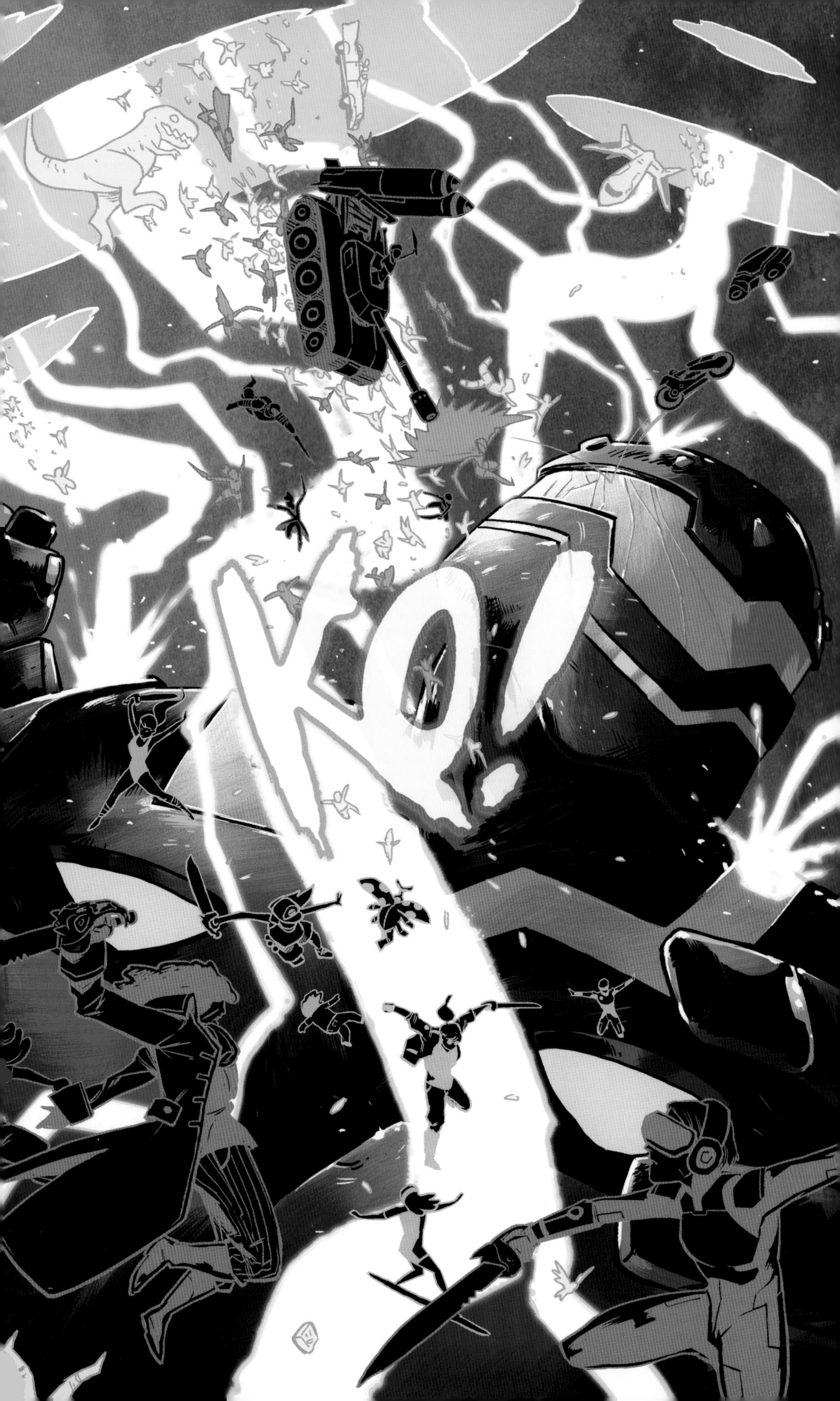
KO!

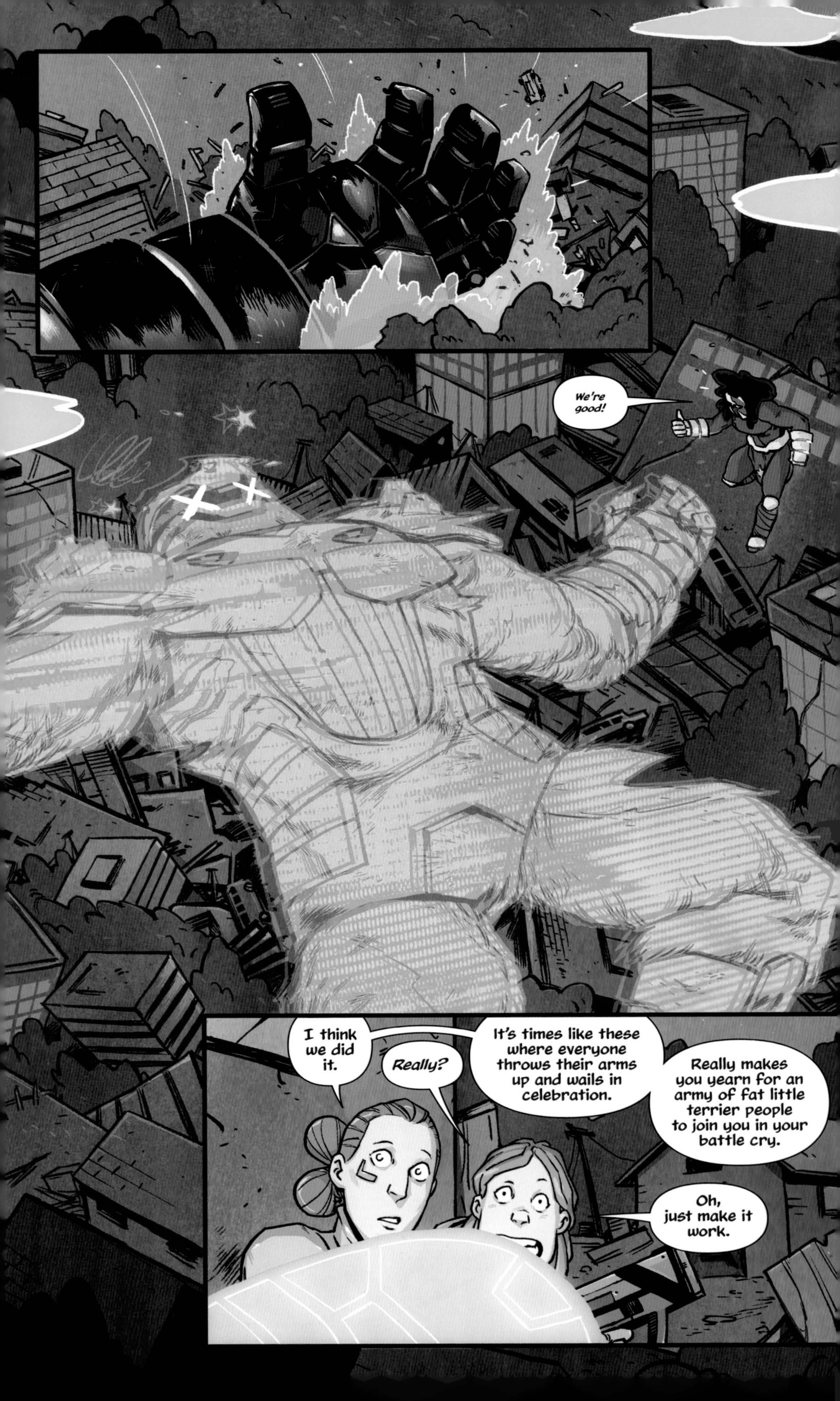

We're good!
I think we did it.
Really?
It's times like these where everyone throws their arms up and wails in celebration.
Really makes you yearn for an army of fat little terrier people to join you in your battle cry.
Oh, just make it work.

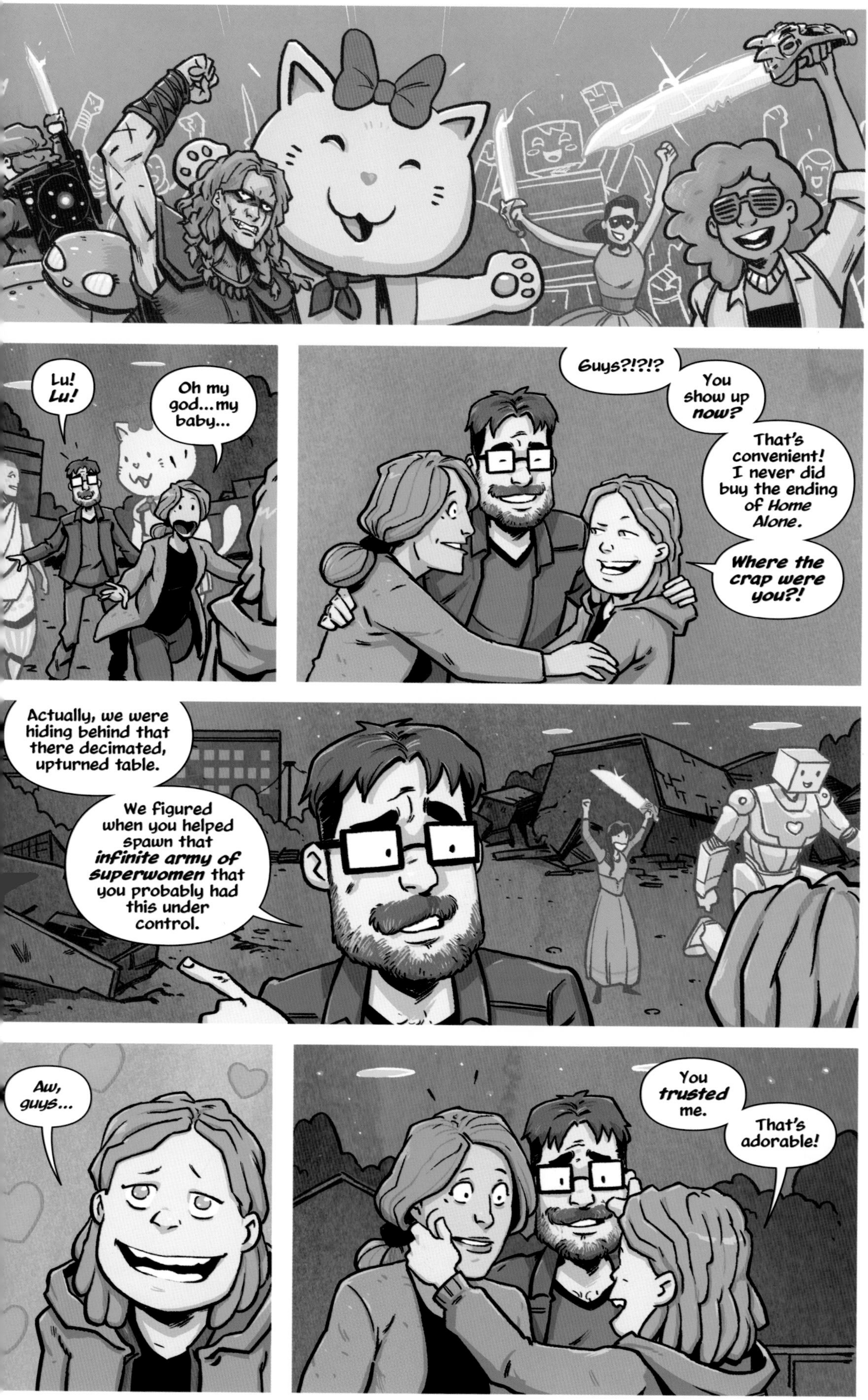
Lu! Lu!
Oh my god...my baby...
Guys?!?!?
You show up now?
That's convenient! I never did buy the ending of Home Alone.
Where the crap were you?!
Actually, we were hiding behind that there decimated, upturned table.
We figured when you helped spawn that infinite army of superwomen that you probably had this under control.
Aw, guys...
You trusted me.
That's adorable!

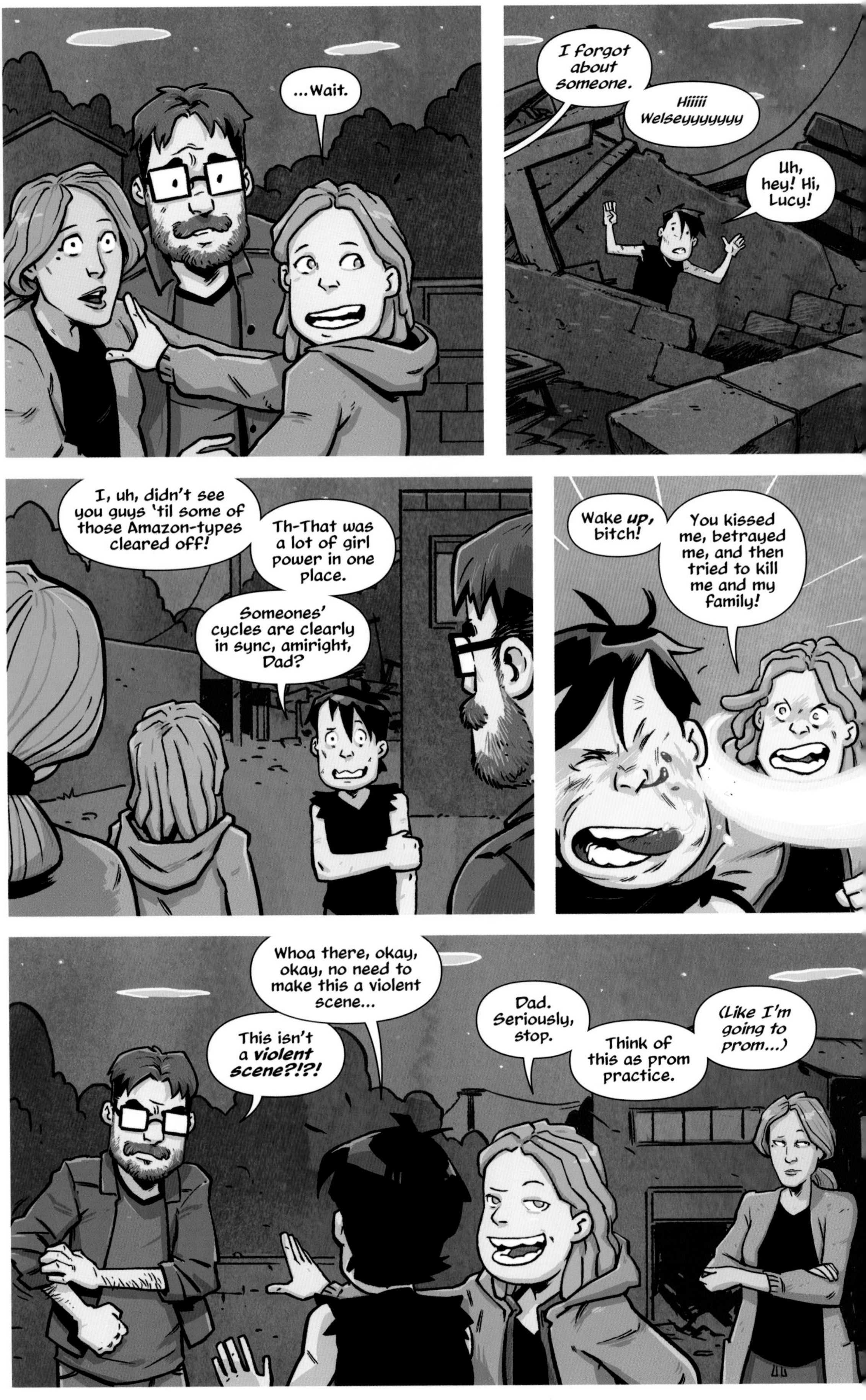
...Wait.
I forgot about someone.
Hiiiii Welseyyyyyyy
Uh, hey! Hi, Lucy!
I, uh, didn't see you guys 'til some of those Amazon-types cleared off!
Th-That was a lot of girl power in one place.
Someones' cycles are clearly in sync, amiright, Dad?
Wake up, bitch!
You kissed me, betrayed me, and then tried to kill me and my family!
Whoa there, okay, okay, no need to make this a violent scene...
This isn't a violent scene?!?!
Dad. Seriously, stop.
Think of this as prom practice.
(Like I'm going to prom...)

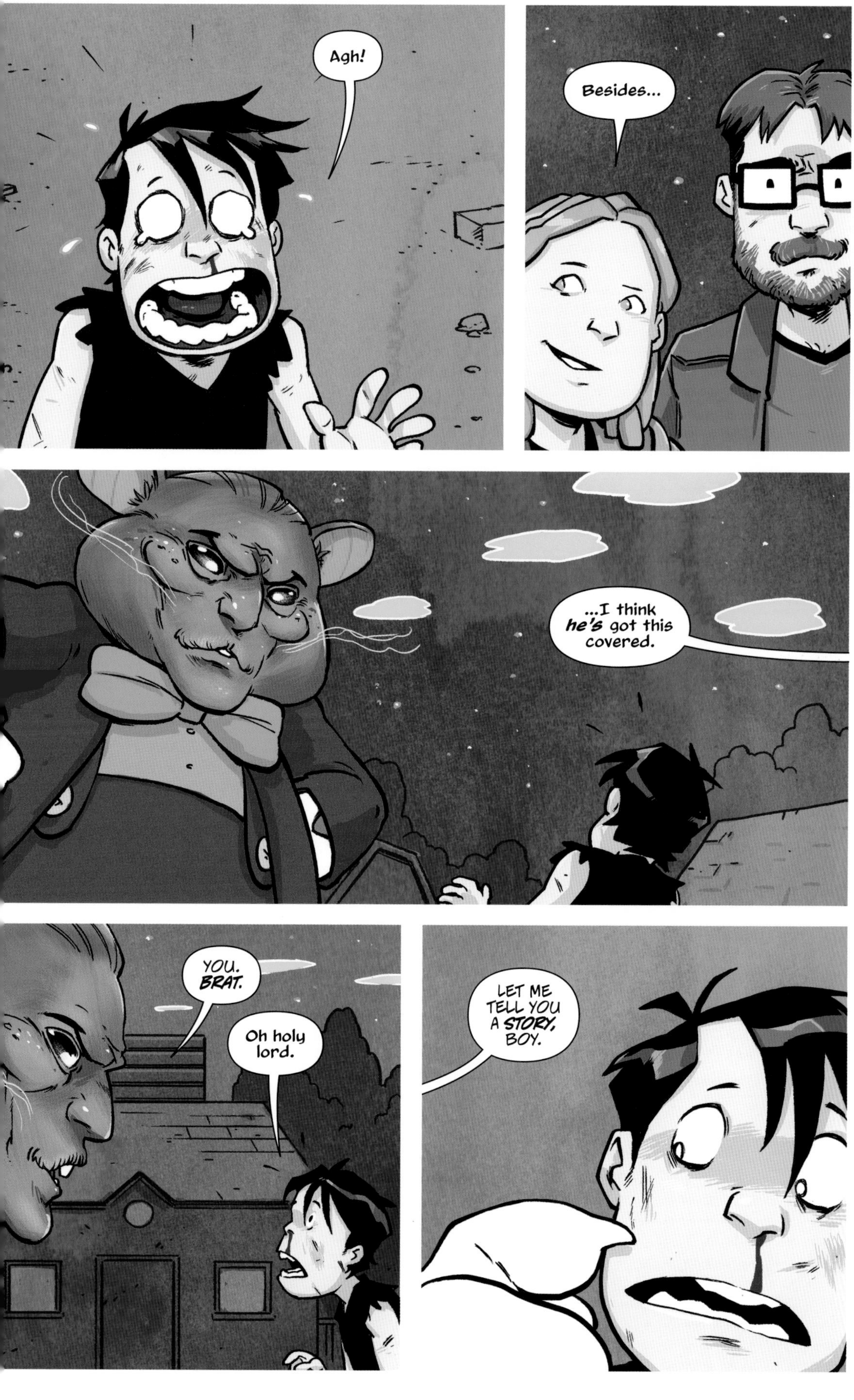
Agh!
Besides...
...I think *he's* got this covered.
YOU. *BRAT.*
Oh holy lord.
LET ME TELL YOU A *STORY,* BOY.

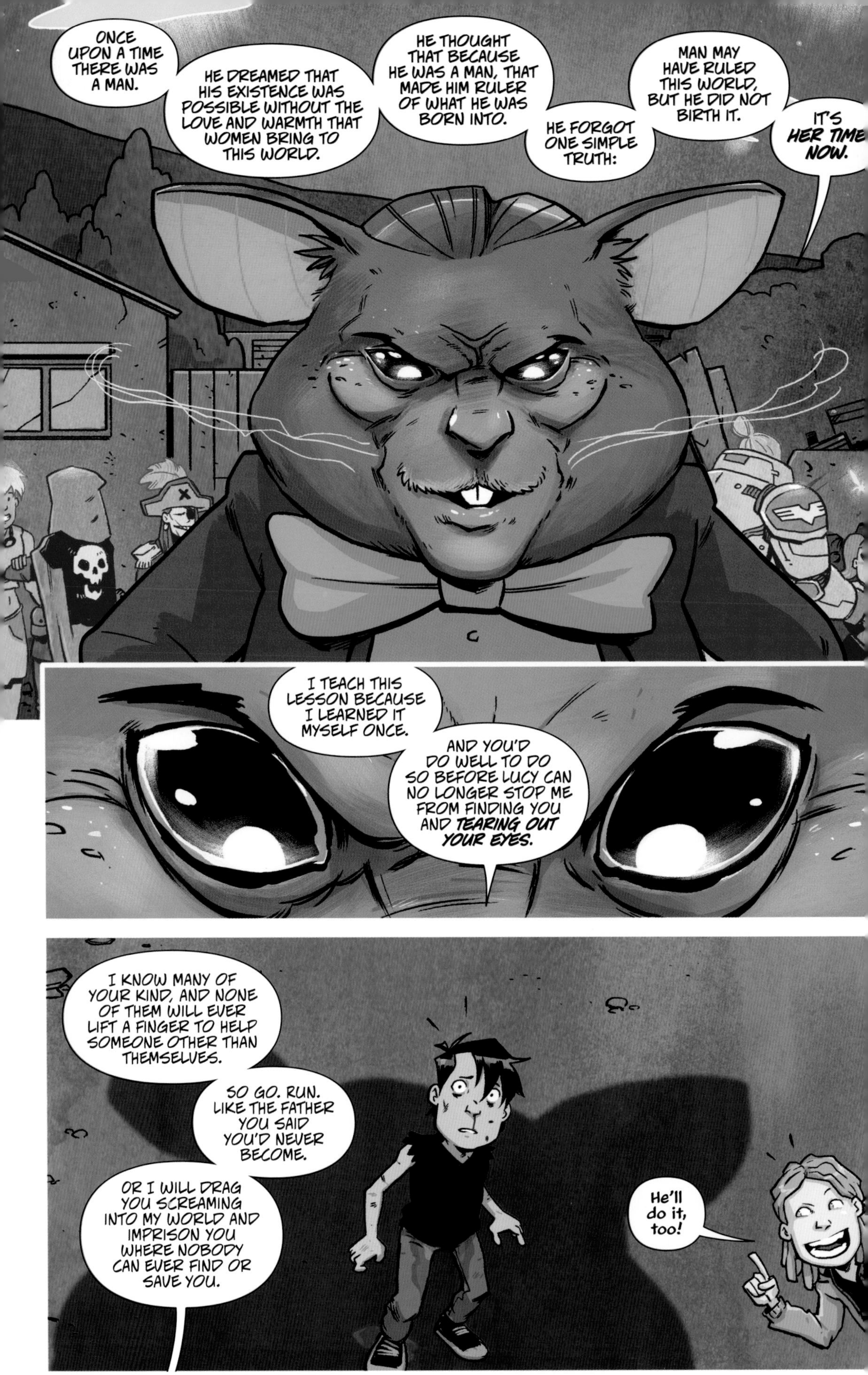
ONCE UPON A TIME THERE WAS A MAN.
HE DREAMED THAT HIS EXISTENCE WAS POSSIBLE WITHOUT THE LOVE AND WARMTH THAT WOMEN BRING TO THIS WORLD.
HE THOUGHT THAT BECAUSE HE WAS A MAN, THAT MADE HIM RULER OF WHAT HE WAS BORN INTO.
HE FORGOT ONE SIMPLE TRUTH:
MAN MAY HAVE RULED THIS WORLD, BUT HE DID NOT BIRTH IT.
IT'S ***HER TIME NOW.***
I TEACH THIS LESSON BECAUSE I LEARNED IT MYSELF ONCE.
AND YOU'D DO WELL TO DO SO BEFORE LUCY CAN NO LONGER STOP ME FROM FINDING YOU AND ***TEARING OUT YOUR EYES.***
I KNOW MANY OF YOUR KIND, AND NONE OF THEM WILL EVER LIFT A FINGER TO HELP SOMEONE OTHER THAN THEMSELVES.
SO GO. RUN. LIKE THE FATHER YOU SAID YOU'D NEVER BECOME.
OR I WILL DRAG YOU SCREAMING INTO MY WORLD AND IMPRISON YOU WHERE NOBODY CAN EVER FIND OR SAVE YOU.
He'll do it, too!

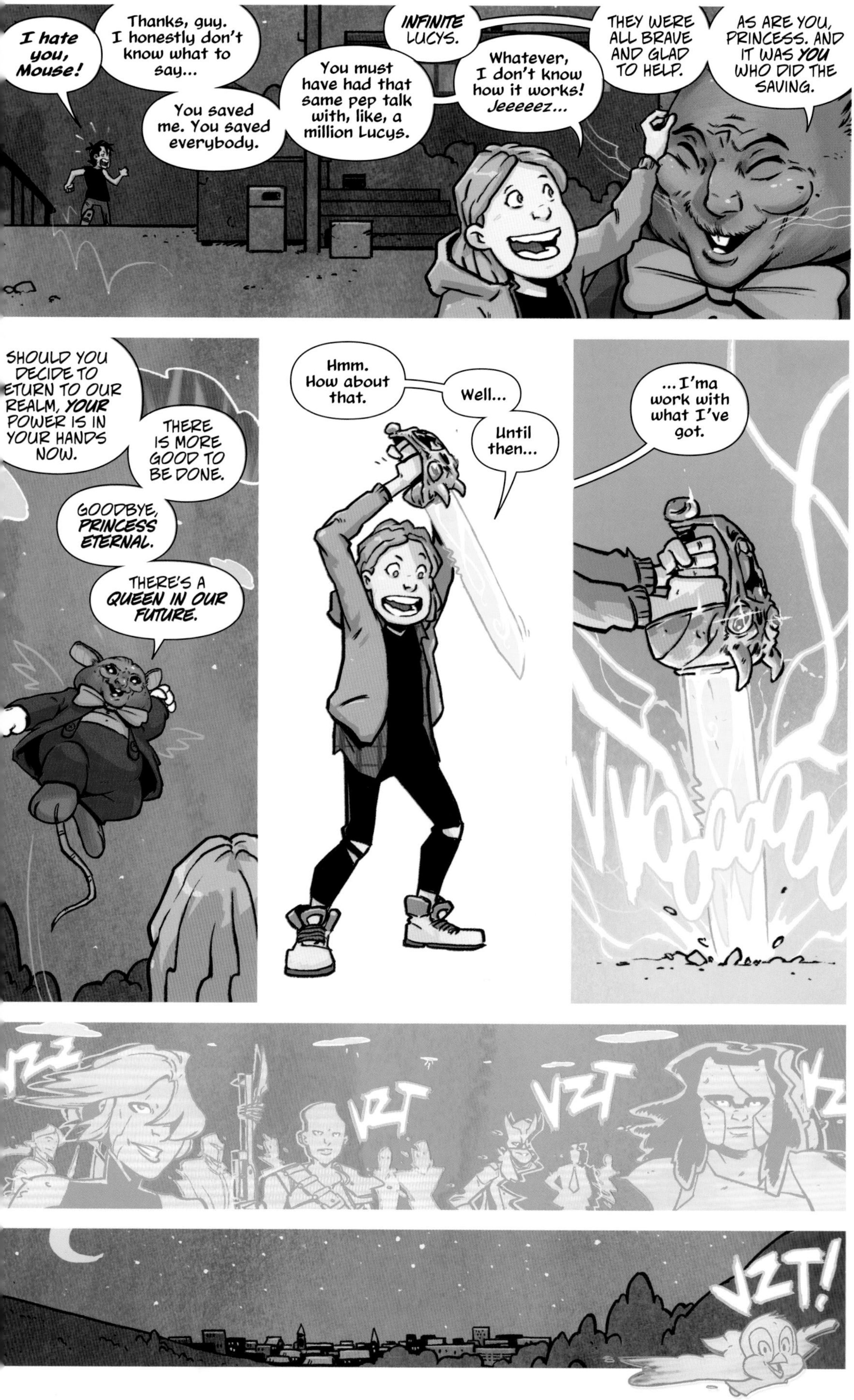

I hate you, Mouse!
Thanks, guy. I honestly don't know what to say...
You saved me. You saved everybody.
You must have had that same pep talk with, like, a million Lucys.
INFINITE LUCYS.
Whatever, I don't know how it works! Jeeeeez...
THEY WERE ALL BRAVE AND GLAD TO HELP.
AS ARE YOU, PRINCESS. AND IT WAS YOU WHO DID THE SAVING.
SHOULD YOU DECIDE TO ETURN TO OUR REALM, YOUR POWER IS IN YOUR HANDS NOW.
THERE IS MORE GOOD TO BE DONE.
GOODBYE, PRINCESS ETERNAL.
THERE'S A QUEEN IN OUR FUTURE.
Hmm. How about that.
Well...
Until then...
...I'ma work with what I've got.
VZT
VZT
VZT
VZT!

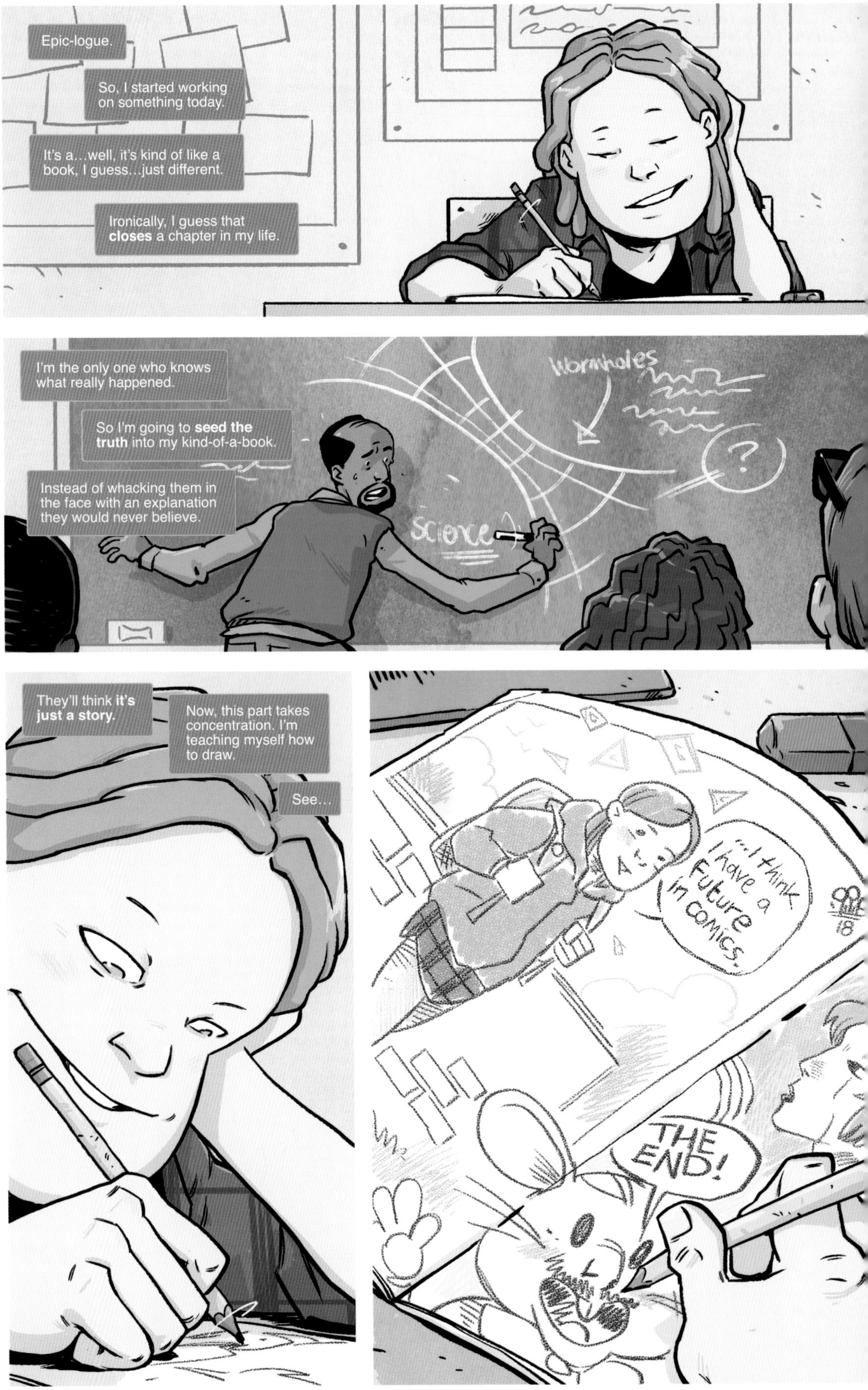
Epic-logue.
So, I started working on something today.
It's a…well, it's kind of like a book, I guess…just different.
Ironically, I guess that **closes** a chapter in my life.
I'm the only one who knows what really happened.
So I'm going to **seed the truth** into my kind-of-a-book.
Instead of whacking them in the face with an explanation they would never believe.
Wormholes
?
science
They'll think **it's just a story.**
Now, this part takes concentration. I'm teaching myself how to draw.
See…
…I think I have a future in comics.
'18
THE END!

ISSUE FIVE COVER BY
MICHAEL DIALYNAS

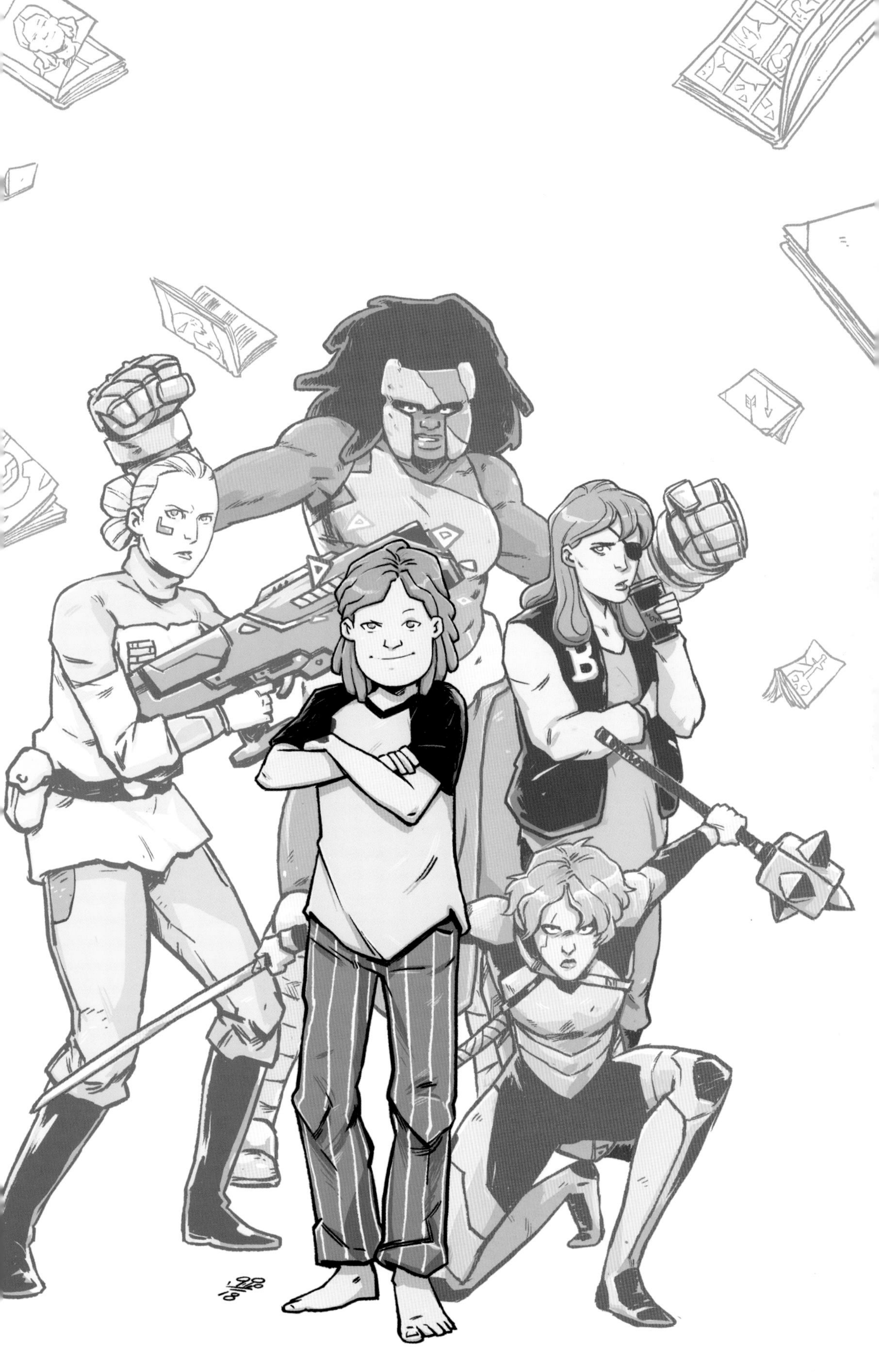

ISSUE ONE C2E2 RETAILER SUMMIT VARIANT COVER BY
JONAS GOONFACE

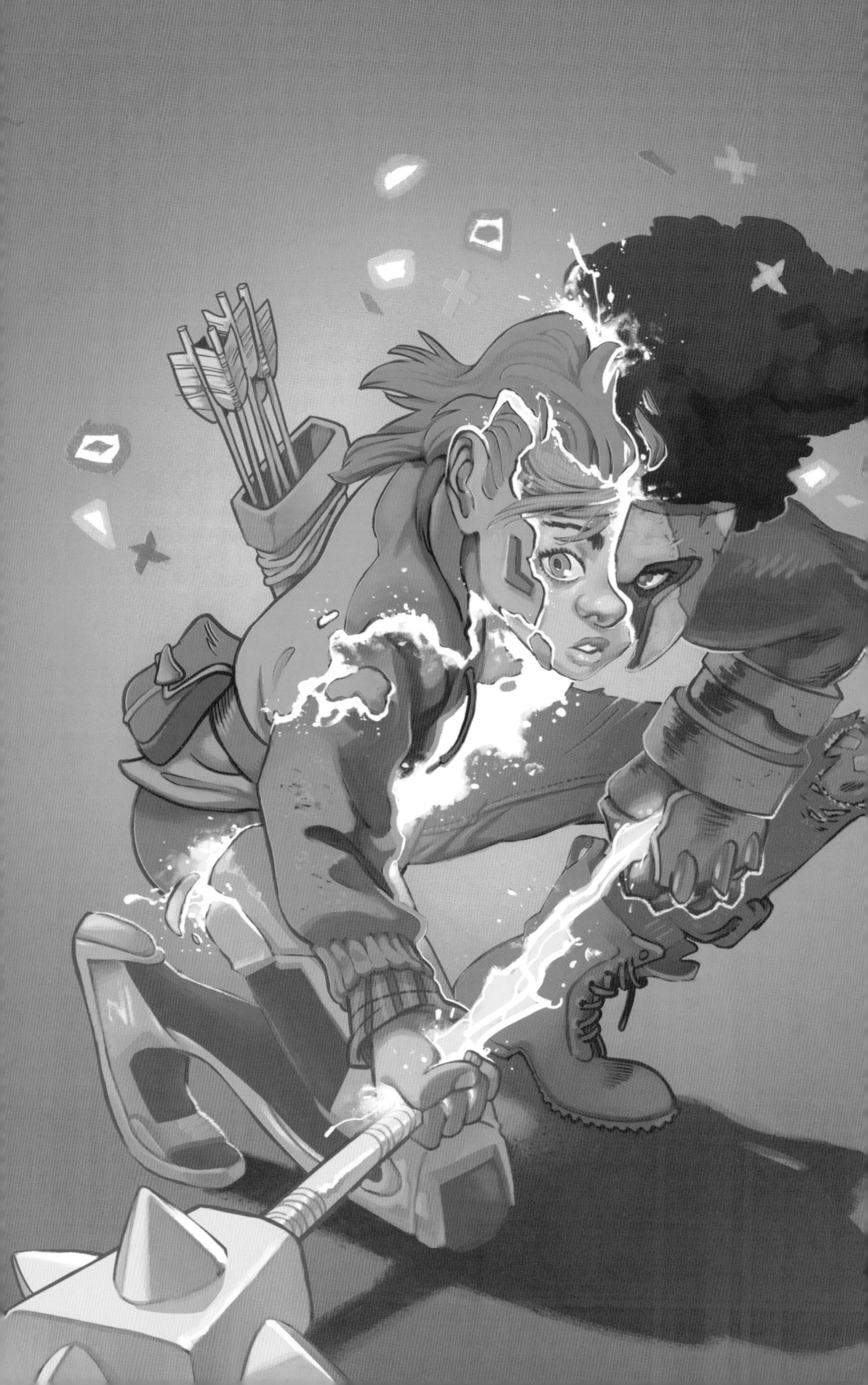

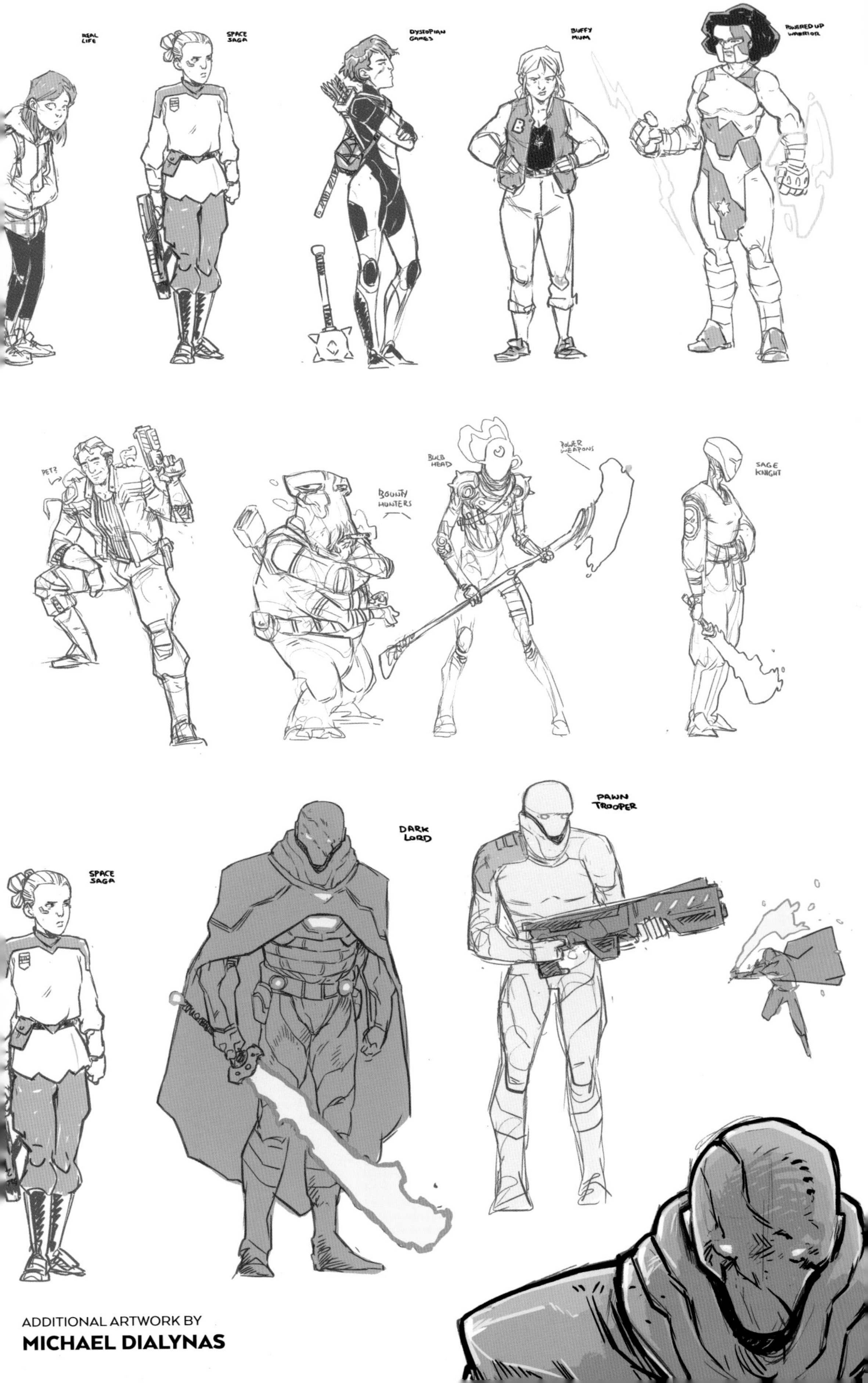

REAL LIFE
SPACE SAGA
DYSTOPIAN GAMES
BUFFY MUM
POWERED UP WARRIOR
PET?
BOUNTY HUNTERS
BULB HEAD
POWER WEAPONS
SAGE KNIGHT
SPACE SAGA
DARK LORD
PAWN TROOPER

ADDITIONAL ARTWORK BY
MICHAEL DIALYNAS

DISCOVER
VISIONARY CREATORS

THE WOODS
JAMES TYNION IV • MICHAEL DIALYNAS
VOL. 1
THE ARROW

"The Spire is fantastic! My kind of genre free-for-all." —BRIAN K. VAUGHAN (Saga)
THE SPIRE
SIMON SPURRIER
JEFF STOKELY
ANDRÉ MAY

MARK WAID • PETER KRAUSE
IRREDEEMABLE
AFTERWORD BY GRANT MORRISON

J.G. JONES
MARK WAID
STRANGE FRUIT
Foreword by ELVIS MITCHELL

MICHAEL ALAN NELSON
DAN MORA
GABRIEL CASSATA
HEXED
THE HARLOT & THE THIEF VOLUME ONE

ABNETT & CULBARD
WILD'S END
FIRST LIGHT
"IT'S REALLY GREAT!" JEFF LEMIRE

BOOM! STUDIOS

AVAILABLE AT YOUR LOCAL COMICS SHOP AND BOOKSTORE
WWW.**BOOM-STUDIOS**.COM

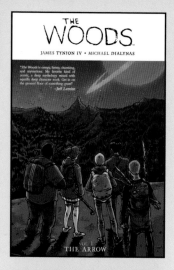

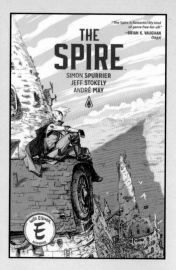

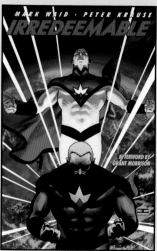

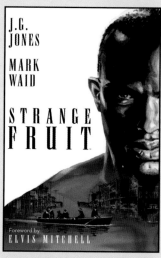

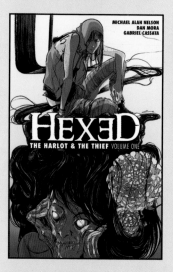

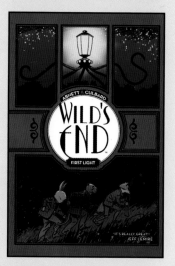

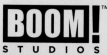

James Tynion IV

The Woods
Volume 1
ISBN: 978-1-60886-454-6 | $9.99 US
Volume 2
ISBN: 978-1-60886-495-9 | $14.99 US
Volume 3
ISBN: 978-1-60886-773-8 | $14.99 US

The Backstagers
Volume 1
ISBN: 978-1-60886-993-0 | $14.99 US

Simon Spurrier

Six-Gun Gorilla
ISBN: 978-1-60886-390-7 | $19.99 US

The Spire
ISBN: 978-1-60886-913-8 | $29.99 US

Weavers
ISBN: 978-1-60886-963-3 | $19.99 US

Mark Waid

Irredeemable
Volume 1
ISBN: 978-1-93450-690-5 | $16.99 US
Volume 2
ISBN: 978-1-60886-000-5 | $16.99 US

Incorruptible
Volume 1
ISBN: 978-1-60886-015-9 | $16.99 US
Volume 2
ISBN: 978-1-60886-028-9 | $16.99 US

Strange Fruit
ISBN: 978-1-60886-872-8 | $24.99 US

Michael Alan Nelson

Hexed The Harlot & The Thief
Volume 1
ISBN: 978-1-60886-718-9 | $14.99 US
Volume 2
ISBN: 978-1-60886-816-2 | $14.99 US

Day Men
Volume 1
ISBN: 978-1-60886-393-8 | $9.99 US
Volume 2
ISBN: 978-1-60886-852-0 | $9.99 US

Dan Abnett

Wild's End
Volume 1: First Light
ISBN: 978-1-60886-735-6 | $19.99 US
Volume 2: The Enemy Within
ISBN: 978-1-60886-877-3 | $19.99 US

Hypernaturals
Volume 1
ISBN: 978-1-60886-298-6 | $16.99 US
Volume 2
ISBN: 978-1-60886-319-8 | $19.99 US